Wa

2015

THE BEST OF
COUNTRY COOKING

Taste *of* Home

For other *Taste of Home* books and products,
visit ShopTasteofHome.com.

SAVOR THE VERY BEST OF COUNTRY COMFORT

It doesn't get any better than sharing a hearty meal while creating memories with loved ones, and *The Best of Country Cooking* will help you do both! Whether you're searching for enticing appetizers, family-friendly main dishes, go-to slow cooker options or sweet treats, you'll find what you need for any occasion right here. All the recipes come from home cooks just like you, meaning they've passed the "This is delicious!" test time and again.

Dig into the following features (and many more):

Contest-Winning Favorites

When you see the blue ribbon icon next to a recipe, you know it's a good one because it placed in a *Taste of Home* contest! Serve one of these stunners at your next gathering to a chorus of accolades.

Cooking for Two

No need to do math when you're expecting a smaller crowd—our special chapter has scaled-down recipes perfect for small households. From breakfast to main dishes to sides, you won't have to worry about leftovers when making these recipes.

Dazzling Desserts

There's nothing more welcoming and comforting than homemade desserts. You'll be ready for any bridal shower, bake sale or birthday party after looking through this chapter. You'll soon be spreading joy by the dozen!

Bring everyone together for some home-cooked love. You can't go wrong when you turn to *The Best of Country Cooking* for your mealtime inspiration.

■ **EDITORIAL**
Editor-in-Chief **Catherine Cassidy**
Creative Director **Howard Greenberg**
Editorial Operations Director **Kerri Balliet**

Managing Editor/Print & Digital Books **Mark Hagen**
Associate Creative Director **Edwin Robles Jr.**
Associate Editor **Molly Jasinski**
Art Director **Catherine Fletcher**
Editorial Production Manager **Dena Ahlers**
Copy Chief **Deb Warlaumont Mulvey**
Copy Editors **Kaitlin Stainbrook, Joanne Weintraub**
Chief Food Editor **Karen Berner**
Food Editors **James Schend; Peggy Woodward, RD**
Recipe Editors **Mary King; Jenni Sharp, RD; Irene Yeh**
Content Operations Manager **Colleen King**
Content Operations Assistant **Shannon Stroud**
Executive Assistant **Marie Brannon**

Test Kitchen & Food Styling Manager **Sarah Thompson**
Test Cooks **Nicholas Iverson (lead), Matthew Hass, Lauren Knoelke**
Food Stylists **Kathryn Conrad (senior), Shannon Roum, Leah Rekau**
Prep Cooks **Megumi Garcia, Melissa Hansen, Bethany Van Jacobson, Sara Wirtz**

Photography Director **Stephanie Marchese**
Photographers **Dan Roberts, Jim Wieland**
Photographer/Set Stylist **Grace Natoli Sheldon**
Set Stylists **Stacey Genaw, Melissa Haberman, Dee Dee Jacq**
Photo Studio Assistant **Ester Robards**

Editorial Business Manager **Kristy Martin**
Editorial Business Associate **Samantha Lea Stoeger**

■ **BUSINESS**
Vice President, Chief Sales Officer **Mark S. Josephson**
General Manager, Taste of Home Cooking School **Erin Puariea**

■ **THE READER'S DIGEST ASSOCIATION, INC.**
President and Chief Executive Officer **Bonnie Kintzer**
Chief Financial Officer **Colette Chestnut**
Vice President, Chief Operating Officer, North America **Howard Halligan**
Vice President, Enthusiast Brands, Books & Retail **Harold Clarke**
Chief Marketing Officer **Leslie Dukker Doty**
Vice President, North American Human Resources **Phyllis E. Gebhardt, SPHR**
Vice President, Brand Marketing **Beth Gorry**
Vice President, Global Communications **Susan Russ**
Vice President, Chief Technology Officer **Aneel Tejwaney**
Vice President, Consumer Marketing Planning **Jim Woods**

© 2015 RDA Enthusiast Brands, LLC
1610 N. 2nd St., Suite 102
Milwaukee, WI 53212-3906

All Rights Reserved.

Taste of Home is a registered trademark of The Reader's Digest Association, Inc.

International Standard Book Number: 978-1-61765-397-1

Printed In China

International Standard Serial Number: 1097-8321

1 3 5 7 9 10 8 6 4 2

Component Number: 117000043H00

PICTURED ON THE FRONT COVER Hearty Butternut Squash Soup (p. 53), Deviled Eggs Extraordinaire (p. 6), Blueberry Sour Cream Coffee Cake (p. 115) and Easy Cheddar Chicken Potpie (p. 63).

PICTURED ON THE BACK COVER Black Forest Icebox Cookies (p. 154), Watermelon Cooler for Two (p. 139) and Grilled Goat Cheese & Arugula Sandwiches (p. 56).

Contents

Snacks & Beverages

No matter the occasion, start your gathering on a delicious note. With these tasty sippers and tempting appetizers on the menu, you might have to remind guests to save room for the main meal!

ASPARAGUS WITH HORSERADISH DIP

Serve the asparagus on a decorative platter with lemon wedges on the side for garnish. If you want, switch up the recipe by using chopped garlic in place of the horseradish.

—MILDRED LYNN CARUSO BRIGHTON, TN

START TO FINISH: 15 MIN. • **MAKES:** 16 APPETIZERS

- 32 **fresh asparagus spears (about 2 pounds), trimmed**
- 1 **cup reduced-fat mayonnaise**
- ¼ **cup grated Parmesan cheese**
- 1 **tablespoon prepared horseradish**
- ½ **teaspoon Worcestershire sauce**

1. Place asparagus in a steamer basket; place in a large saucepan over 1 in. of water. Bring to a boil; cover and steam for 2-4 minutes or until crisp-tender. Drain and immediately place in ice water. Drain and pat dry.
2. In a small bowl, combine the remaining ingredients. Serve with asparagus.

DEVILED EGGS EXTRAORDINAIRE

These creamy, mild deviled eggs boast a pleasant mustard flavor. They're perfect for summertime picnics but could also work for formal occasions.

—CAROL ROSS ANCHORAGE, AK

PREP: 40 MIN. • **MAKES:** 4 DOZEN

- 24 **hard-cooked eggs, peeled**
- 4 **ounces cream cheese, softened**
- ½ **cup mayonnaise**
- 2 **tablespoons prepared mustard**
- 1 **teaspoon cider vinegar**
- ¼ **teaspoon salt**
- ¼ **teaspoon onion powder**

Cut eggs in half lengthwise. Remove yolks; set whites aside. In a small bowl, mash yolks. Add cream cheese, mayonnaise, mustard, vinegar, salt and onion powder; mix well. Stuff or pipe into egg whites. Refrigerate until serving.

PRETTY DEVILED EGGS PRESENTATION
I put deviled eggs inside paper cupcakes liners and set them in muffin tins to serve. The eggs will stay upright and won't slide around on plates.
—SALLY T. LAS CRUCES, NM

STRAWBERRY LEMONADE SMOOTHIE

We love the blend of sweet and citrus in this refreshing smoothie. It's such a cinch to throw together, I often find myself making one for breakfast or a midday snack.

—**JAMIE KING** DULUTH, MN

START TO FINISH: 5 MIN. • **MAKES:** 4 SERVINGS

- 2 **cups lemonade**
- ¾ **cup (6 ounces) lemon yogurt**
- ½ **teaspoon vanilla extract**
- 2 **cups frozen unsweetened strawberries**

Place all ingredients in a blender; cover and process 15 seconds or until blended. Serve immediately.

FRIED CLAMS

The clams' crunchy golden coating will truly melt in your mouth. At first taste, you'll understand why these are considered to be such a delicacy!

—**TIM CONNOLLY** FREEPORT, ME

START TO FINISH: 30 MIN. • **MAKES:** 1 DOZEN

- 1½ **cups yellow cornmeal, divided**
- ½ **cup cake flour, divided**
- ⅔ **cup water**
- 12 **fresh cherrystone clams, shucked**
  Oil for deep-fat frying
- ½ **teaspoon salt**
  Tartar sauce or seafood cocktail sauce, optional

1. In a shallow bowl, combine ¾ cup cornmeal and ¼ cup flour with the water, forming a batter. In another bowl, combine the remaining cornmeal and flour.
2. Dip clams in batter; shake off excess. Coat with the cornmeal mixture.
3. In an electric skillet or deep-fat fryer, heat oil to 375°. Fry clams, a few at a time, for 4-5 minutes or until golden brown. Drain on paper towels; sprinkle with salt.
4. Serve immediately with sauce if desired.

RAINBOW SPRITZER

Follow the rainbow to this fizzy treasure. Kids will love sipping their way through pretty layers of colorful fruit.
—**WENDY HERR** O'FALLON, MO

START TO FINISH: 20 MIN. • **MAKES:** 4 SERVINGS

- ½ **cup fresh blueberries**
- ½ **cup chopped peeled kiwifruit**
- ½ **cup chopped fresh pineapple**
- ½ **cup sliced fresh strawberries or fresh raspberries**
- 1 **cup chilled ginger ale**
- ½ **cup chilled unsweetened pineapple juice**
- ½ **cup chilled lemonade**

In four tall glasses, layer blueberries, kiwi, pineapple and strawberries. In a 2-cup glass measure or small pitcher, mix remaining ingredients; pour over fruit. Serve immediately.

SWEET POTATO CROSTINI

For party time, I turn this sweet potato side dish into an appetizer by serving it on slices of a French baguette.
—**STEVE WESTPHAL** WIND LAKE, WI

START TO FINISH: 30 MIN. • **MAKES:** 2 DOZEN

- 24 **slices French bread baguette (¼ inch thick)**
- ¼ **cup butter, melted**
- 2 **tablespoons sugar**
- ½ **teaspoon ground cinnamon**

TOPPING
- 2 **cups mashed sweet potatoes**
- ¼ **cup chopped pecans**
- 3 **tablespoons packed brown sugar**
- 2 **tablespoons butter, melted**
- 1¼ **cups miniature marshmallows, halved**
  Minced fresh rosemary, optional

1. Place bread in a single layer on ungreased baking sheets; brush with butter. In a small bowl, mix sugar and cinnamon; sprinkle over tops. Bake at 400° for 2-3 minutes or until lightly browned.

2. Meanwhile, in another bowl, mix the sweet potatoes, pecans, brown sugar and butter. Spoon onto toasts; top with marshmallows, pressing lightly to adhere. Broil 3-4 in. from the heat for 1-2 minutes or until marshmallows are lightly browned. Sprinkle with rosemary if desired.

HERB & ROASTED PEPPER CHEESECAKE

Roasted red peppers and a medley of fresh herbs add a slight touch of sweetness while a surprising peppery finish completes this savory cheesecake. Just before serving, add a drizzle of oil, garnish with minced chives and more peppers, and pass out the pita chips for scooping.

—LAURA JULIAN AMANDA, OH

PREP: 20 MIN. • **BAKE:** 35 MIN. + CHILLING • **MAKES:** 24 SERVINGS

- 3 packages (8 ounces each) cream cheese, softened
- ¾ cup whole-milk ricotta cheese
- 1½ teaspoons salt
- ¾ teaspoon pepper
- 3 eggs, lightly beaten
- 1½ cups roasted sweet red peppers, drained and finely chopped
- ¾ cup minced fresh basil
- ⅓ cup minced fresh chives
- 3 tablespoons minced fresh thyme
- 3 tablespoons crumbled cooked bacon
- 3 garlic cloves, minced
- 1 tablespoon olive oil
  Roasted sweet red pepper strips and additional minced chives, optional
  Baked pita chips

1. Preheat oven to 350°. Place a greased 9-in. springform pan on a double thickness of heavy-duty foil (about 18 in. square). Securely wrap foil around pan.
2. Place cream cheese, ricotta cheese, salt and pepper in a food processor; cover and process until smooth. Add eggs; pulse just until combined. Add red peppers, herbs, bacon and garlic; cover and pulse just until blended. Pour filling into prepared pan. Place springform pan in a large baking pan; add 1 in. of boiling water to larger pan.
3. Bake 35-45 minutes or until center is just set and top appears dull. Remove springform pan from water bath; remove foil. Cool cheesecake on a wire rack 10 minutes; loosen edges from pan with a knife. Cool 1 hour longer. Refrigerate overnight.
4. Remove rim from pan. Just before serving, drizzle cheesecake with oil; top with red pepper strips and chives if desired. Serve with pita chips.

BBQ CHICKEN WAFFLE FRIES

Trust me, barbecue chicken leftovers are fantastic with fries. My family likes this snack with lettuce, tomato and pickle, but you can add almost any toppings.

—JANET TELLEEN RUSSELL, IA

PREP: 10 MIN. • **BAKE:** 25 MIN. • **MAKES:** 8 SERVINGS

- 1 package (22 ounces) frozen waffle-cut fries
- 12 ounces refrigerated shredded barbecued chicken (1½ cups)
- 1 cup (4 ounces) shredded Colby-Monterey Jack cheese
- ¼ cup chopped red onion
- ½ cup shredded lettuce
- 1 medium tomato, chopped
- ¼ cup chopped dill pickle
  Pickled banana peppers

Bake fries according to package directions. Transfer to a 10-in. ovenproof skillet. Top with chicken, cheese and onion. Bake 5 minutes longer or until cheese is melted. Top with lettuce, tomato and pickle; serve with peppers.

HAM AND BROCCOLI PUFFS

These starters look complex, but they're easy to make. Your guests will be impressed with their simple elegance.

—LYNDA MCCULLOCH SAN ANTONIO, TX

PREP: 30 MIN. • **BAKE:** 15 MIN./BATCH • **MAKES:** 32 APPETIZERS

- 4 cups frozen broccoli florets, thawed and finely chopped
- 1 carton (8 ounces) spreadable chive and onion cream cheese
- 1 cup (4 ounces) shredded Swiss cheese
- ¼ pound thinly sliced deli ham, finely chopped
- ½ cup finely chopped fresh mushrooms
- ¼ teaspoon salt
- 1 package (17.3 ounces) frozen puff pastry, thawed
- 2 eggs, beaten

1. In a large bowl, combine the first six ingredients. On a lightly floured surface, unfold puff pastry. Roll each sheet into a 12-in. square. Cut each into 16 squares.

2. Place a heaping tablespoonful of broccoli mixture in the center of each square. Brush edges of pastry with eggs. Bring opposite corners over filling; pinch seams to seal.

3. Place on ungreased baking sheets. Bake at 425° for 12-15 minutes or until golden brown. Serve warm.

QUICK MUSHROOM CLEANING

Gently remove dirt from fresh mushrooms by rubbing them with a mushroom brush or wiping them down with a damp paper towel. You can also rinse them under cold water, drain and pat dry.

ICED LEMON TEA

Stir in lemonade drink mix to traditional iced tea for a cool and refreshing twist.

—DAWN E. LOWENSTEIN HATBORO, PA

PREP: 15 MIN. • **COOK:** 10 MIN. + COOLING
MAKES: 12 SERVINGS (1 CUP EACH)

- 3½ teaspoons Crystal Light lemonade drink mix
- 4 cups cold water
- 8 cups water
- 8 individual decaffinated tea bags
- 1 mint-flavored black tea bag
  Ice cubes
  Fresh mint leaves and lemon slices, optional

1. In a 3-qt. pitcher, combine lemonade mix and cold water. Refrigerate until chilled.

2. Meanwhile, in a large saucepan, bring water to a boil. Remove from the heat; add tea bags. Cover and steep for 3-5 minutes. Discard tea bags. Cool; stir into lemonade mixture. Serve over ice with mint and lemon if desired.

MAPLE CRUNCH POPCORN

For a snack that's sure to bring smiles, try this medley of popcorn and pecans covered in a buttery coating.

—ELMIRA TROMBETTI PADUCAH, KY

START TO FINISH: 25 MIN. • **MAKES:** 3½ QUARTS

- 10 cups popped popcorn
- 1½ cups pecan halves, toasted
- 1⅓ cups sugar
- 1 cup butter, cubed
- ¼ cup maple syrup
- ¼ cup corn syrup
- ½ teaspoon salt
- 1 teaspoon maple flavoring

1. Place popcorn and pecans in a large bowl; set aside. In a large heavy saucepan, combine the sugar, butter, maple syrup, corn syrup and salt. Cook and stir over medium heat until a candy thermometer reads 300° (hard-crack stage). Remove from the heat; stir in maple flavoring. Quickly pour over popcorn mixture and mix well.

2. Transfer to baking sheets lined with waxed paper to cool. Break into clusters. Store in airtight containers.

NOTE *We recommend that you test your candy thermometer before each use by bringing water to a boil; the thermometer should read 212°. Adjust your recipe temperature up or down based on your test.*

PEA SOUP SHOOTERS

Appetizers really don't get any more perfect than this. These shooters can be made ahead, they're colorful, and they won't weigh you down. Top with a dollop of yogurt for a little more tang.
—**JACYN SIEBERT** WALNUT CREEK, CA

PREP: 20 MIN. + CHILLING • **MAKES:** 2 DOZEN

- 1 package (16 ounces) frozen peas, thawed
- 1 cup reduced-sodium chicken broth
- ¼ cup minced fresh mint
- 1 tablespoon lime juice
- 1 teaspoon ground cumin
- ¼ teaspoon salt
- 1½ cups plain yogurt
  Fresh mint leaves

1. Place the first six ingredients in a blender; cover and process until smooth. Add yogurt; process until blended. Transfer to a pitcher; refrigerate 1 hour to allow flavors to blend.
2. To serve, pour soup into shot glasses; top with fresh mint leaves.

SPINACH DIP PULL-APARTS

Even picky eaters who don't normally like to eat spinach will dig into these tasty little bites.
—**KELLY WILLIAMS** FORKED RIVER, NJ

PREP: 35 MIN. • **BAKE:** 45 MIN. + COOLING • **MAKES:** 15 SERVINGS

- 1 package (8 ounces) cream cheese, softened
- 2 garlic cloves, minced
- ¼ teaspoon pepper
- 1 package (10 ounces) frozen chopped spinach, thawed and squeezed dry
- ½ cup shredded part-skim mozzarella cheese
- ¼ cup grated Parmesan cheese
- ¼ cup mayonnaise
- 2 tubes (one 6 ounces, one 12 ounces) refrigerated buttermilk biscuits
  Marinara sauce, warmed, optional

1. Preheat oven to 350°. In a small bowl, beat cream cheese, garlic and pepper until blended. Stir in spinach, cheeses and mayonnaise.
2. Separate biscuit dough. Using a serrated knife, cut each biscuit horizontally in half. Wrap each half around 1 tablespoon spinach mixture, pinching to seal and forming a ball.
3. Layer in a greased 10-in. fluted tube pan. Bake 45-50 minutes or until golden brown. Cool in pan 10 minutes before inverting onto a serving plate. Serve warm with marinara sauce if desired.

CHEDDAR & ONION BEEF SLIDERS

My girlfriend and I threw an outdoor party for a bunch of friends and these sliders were an instant hit. We also like to make them for a quick meal.

—**KIRK BROOKS** TUCSON, AZ

PREP: 1¼ HOURS • **COOK:** 10 MIN. • **MAKES:** 8 SERVINGS

- ¼ cup butter, cubed
- 1 medium red onion, halved and thinly sliced
- 2¼ teaspoons Montreal steak seasoning, divided
- 1 cup dry red wine
- 1 pound ground beef
- 2 slices cheddar cheese, quartered
- 8 dinner rolls, split

1. In a large skillet, heat butter over medium heat. Add onion and ¼ teaspoon steak seasoning; cook and stir 6-8 minutes or until onion is softened. Reduce heat to medium-low; cook 40-45 minutes or until deep golden brown, stirring occasionally. Stir in wine. Bring to a boil; cook 10-12 minutes or until liquid is almost evaporated.
2. In a bowl, combine the beef and remaining steak seasoning, mixing lightly but thoroughly. Shape into eight ½-in.-thick patties.
3. In a large nonstick skillet, cook burgers over medium heat 3-4 minutes on each side or until a thermometer reads 160°; top with cheese during the last 1-2 minutes of cooking. Serve on rolls; top with onion.

ARTICHOKE MUSHROOM CAPS

These crumb-topped appetizers never last long at our get-togethers. The rich filling of cream cheese, artichoke hearts, Parmesan cheese and green onion is irresistible.

—**RUTH LEWIS** WEST NEWTON, PA

PREP: 30 MIN. • **GRILL:** 10 MIN. • **MAKES:** ABOUT 2 DOZEN

- 1 package (3 ounces) cream cheese, softened
- ¼ cup mayonnaise
- 1 jar (6½ ounces) marinated artichoke hearts, drained and finely chopped
- ¼ cup grated Parmesan cheese
- 2 tablespoons finely chopped green onion
- 20 to 25 large fresh mushrooms, stems removed
- ¼ cup seasoned bread crumbs
- 2 teaspoons olive oil

1. In a large bowl, beat cream cheese and mayonnaise until smooth. Beat in the artichokes, Parmesan cheese and onion.
2. Lightly spray tops of mushrooms with cooking spray. Spoon cheese mixture into mushroom caps. Combine bread crumbs and oil; sprinkle over mushrooms.
3. Grill, covered, over indirect medium heat for 8-10 minutes or until mushrooms are tender.

BAKED REUBEN DIP

I love a Reuben sandwich, and this recipe combines all of its flavors into a great party dip.

—**JEFFREY METZLER** CHILLICOTHE, OH

PREP: 10 MIN. • **BAKE:** 25 MIN. • **MAKES:** 8 CUPS

- 1 jar (32 ounces) sauerkraut, rinsed and well drained
- 10 ounces sliced deli corned beef, chopped
- 2 cups (8 ounces) shredded sharp cheddar cheese
- 2 cups (8 ounces) shredded Swiss cheese
- 1 cup mayonnaise
- ¼ cup Russian salad dressing
- 1 teaspoon caraway seeds, optional
  Rye crackers

In a large bowl, mix the first six ingredients; stir in caraway seeds, if desired. Transfer to a greased 13x9-in. baking dish. Bake at 350° for 25-30 minutes or until bubbly. Serve with rye crackers.

SHRIMP SALSA

For a salsa with lots of texture, color and mouthwatering taste, look no further! A medley of chopped shrimp, avocado, tomato, cucumber, onion and cilantro are tossed in lime juice and perked up with a blend of mild spices.

—**ELIZA NOVOA-GONZALEZ** HENDERSON, NV

START TO FINISH: 30 MIN. • **MAKES:** 8 CUPS

- 1 pound peeled and deveined cooked medium shrimp, chopped
- 5 medium tomatoes, seeded and chopped
- 2 medium ripe avocados, peeled and chopped
- 1 medium cucumber, peeled and chopped
- 1 cup minced fresh cilantro
- ⅓ cup chopped sweet onion
- ⅓ cup orange juice
- ¼ cup Key lime juice
- 2 tablespoons lime juice
- 1 teaspoon salt
- 1 teaspoon garlic powder
- 1 teaspoon garlic salt
- 1 teaspoon coarsely ground pepper
  Tostones or tortilla chips

In a large bowl, combine the first 13 ingredients. Serve immediately with tostones.

CHILLY COFFEE PUNCH

For a twist on the usual fruit punch, try a flavored coffee with ice cream. Put it together just before serving.

—**JUDY WILSON** SUN CITY WEST, AZ

PREP: 10 MIN. + CHILLING • **MAKES:** 24 SERVINGS

- 6 **cups hot strong brewed coffee**
- ¼ **cup sugar**
- ½ **cup coffee liqueur**
- 1 **carton (1½ quarts) vanilla ice cream, softened**
- 1 **carton (1½ quarts) chocolate ice cream, softened**
  Optional toppings: whipped cream, chocolate syrup and chocolate shavings

1. In a pitcher, combine coffee and sugar, stirring to dissolve sugar. Refrigerate, covered, until cold, about 45 minutes.

2. Stir liqueur into coffee. Just before serving, spoon ice cream into a punch bowl. Stir in coffee mixture. If desired, serve with toppings.

RUSTIC TOMATO CHEESE TART

My fresh tomato tart is wonderful when you want a taste of summer, no matter the time of year. The crust stays nice and crisp.

—**MOJI DABNEY** EGG HARBOR TOWNSHIP, NJ

PREP: 30 MIN. • **BAKE:** 30 MIN. • **MAKES:** 12 SERVINGS

- 7 **sheets phyllo dough (14 inches x 9 inches)**
- ⅓ **cup olive oil**
- 7 **tablespoons crumbled goat cheese**
- 1 **cup thinly sliced sweet onion**
- 1 **cup (4 ounces) shredded fontina cheese**
- 4 **plum tomatoes, thinly sliced**
- 2 **tablespoons minced chives**
- 1 **tablespoon minced fresh basil or 1 teaspoon dried basil**
- ¼ **teaspoon salt**
- ¼ **teaspoon pepper**

1. Place one sheet of phyllo dough on a parchment-lined baking sheet. Brush with oil and sprinkle with 1 tablespoon goat cheese. (Keep remaining phyllo covered with plastic wrap and a damp towel to prevent it from drying out.) Repeat layers, brushing oil all the way to edges.

2. Sprinkle onion over top to within 1 in. of edges; sprinkle with fontina cheese. Arrange tomato slices in a slightly overlapping pattern over fontina cheese. Sprinkle with chives, basil, salt and pepper. Bring up the edges of the tart over filling.

3. Bake at 375° for 30-35 minutes or until the crust is golden brown.

Game Day Go-To's

Ready, set, eat! When your favorite team is playing, invite your home crowd over for a day of cheering and delicious bites. No matter the final score, you'll come away with a win when serving these recipes.

BUFFALO WING BITES

The chicken wing fans in my family were more than happy to taste test when I invented these snacks. We love them anytime, but they're especially popular during football games.

—**JASEY McBURNETT** ROCK SPRINGS, WY

PREP: 25 MIN. • **BAKE:** 15 MIN.
MAKES: 2 DOZEN (2 CUPS DRESSING)

- 2 **tablespoons grated Parmesan cheese**
- 1 **envelope ranch salad dressing mix, divided**
- 1 **cup mayonnaise**
- 1 **cup 2% milk**
- ¼ **cup crumbled blue cheese, optional**
- 1¼ **cups finely chopped cooked chicken breast**
- 1¼ **cups (5 ounces) shredded cheddar-Monterey Jack cheese**
- ¼ **cup Buffalo wing sauce**
- 1 **tube (13.8 ounces) refrigerated pizza crust**
- 2 **tablespoons butter, melted**

1. Preheat the oven to 400°. In a small bowl, combine Parmesan cheese and 1 teaspoon dressing mix. In another bowl, mix mayonnaise, milk and remaining dressing mix. If desired, stir in blue cheese. Refrigerate until serving.
2. In a large bowl, mix chicken, cheddar-Monterey Jack cheese and wing sauce. On a lightly floured surface, unroll pizza crust dough and pat into a 14x12-in. rectangle. Cut into 24 squares.
3. Place 1 rounded tablespoon chicken mixture on the center of each square. Pull corners together to enclose filling; pinch to seal. Place 1 in. apart on greased baking sheets, seam side down. Brush tops with butter; sprinkle with Parmesan cheese mixture.
4. Bake 15-17 minutes or until golden brown. Serve with dressing.

LUSCIOUS LIME SLUSH

Adults love this sweet-tart sipper anytime of year. For a kids' version, simply leave out the alcohol.

—**BONNIE JOST** MANITOWOC, WI

PREP: 20 MIN. + FREEZING • **MAKES:** 28 SERVINGS (¾ CUP EACH)

- 9 **cups water**
- 4 **individual green tea bags**
- 2 **cans (12 ounces each) frozen limeade concentrate, thawed**
- 2 **cups sugar**
- 2 **cups lemon rum or rum**
- 7 **cups lemon-lime soda, chilled**

1. In a Dutch oven, bring water to a boil. Remove from the heat; add tea bags. Cover and steep for 3-5 minutes. Discard tea bags. Stir in the limeade concentrate, sugar and rum.
2. Transfer to a 4-qt. freezer container; cool. Cover and freeze for 6 hours or overnight.
TO USE FROZEN LIMEADE MIXTURE *Combine the limeade mixture and soda in a 4-qt. pitcher. Or for one serving, combine ½ cup limeade mixture and ¼ cup soda in a glass. Serve immediately.*

¾ teaspoon grated orange peel
¾ teaspoon ground ancho chili pepper
½ cup 60% cacao bittersweet chocolate baking chips

1. Preheat oven to 275°. In a large bowl, beat egg white and water until frothy. Add nuts; stir gently to coat. Combine the sugar, pie spice, orange peel and chili pepper; add to nut mixture and gently stir to coat.

2. Spread into an ungreased 15x10x1-in. baking pan. Bake 35-40 minutes or until lightly browned, stirring once. Sprinkle with chips. Cool completely. Break into pieces. Store in an airtight container.

WHITE PIZZA DIP

I first served this dip during a Super Bowl party, and boy, did it disappear fast. It's a great addition to a snack table because it can be made ahead of time and refrigerated until you're ready to pop it in the oven.

—**MOLLY SEIDEL** EDGEWOOD, NM

PREP: 10 MIN. • **BAKE:** 35 MIN. • **MAKES:** 12 SERVINGS (¼ CUP EACH)

2 cups (16 ounces) sour cream
1 cup whole-milk ricotta cheese
1 cup (4 ounces) shredded part-skim mozzarella cheese, divided
¼ cup chopped pepperoni
1 envelope Lipton savory herb with garlic soup mix
French bread baguette slices, toasted

1. Preheat oven to 350°. In a small bowl, mix sour cream, ricotta cheese, ¾ cup mozzarella cheese, pepperoni and soup mix until blended. Spread into a greased 9-in. pie plate. Sprinkle with remaining mozzarella cheese.

2. Bake, uncovered, 35-40 minutes or until bubbly. Serve with baguette slices.

BLACKBERRY BEER COCKTAIL

This refreshing hard lemonade has a mild alcohol flavor; the beer adds just enough fizz to dance on your tongue as you sip. Sorry, adults only!

—**GINGER SULLIVAN** CUTLER BAY, FL

START TO FINISH: 10 MIN. • **MAKES:** 10 SERVINGS

4 bottles (12 ounces each) beer, chilled
1 can (12 ounces) frozen raspberry lemonade concentrate, thawed
¾ cup fresh or frozen blackberries, thawed
½ cup vodka
Ice cubes
Lemon slices

In a large pitcher, combine the beer, lemonade concentrate, blackberries and vodka. Serve over ice and garnish with lemon slices.

ORANGE-ANCHO SPICED NUTS

Prepare your taste buds for an adventure. These nuts offer an enticing combination of orange, ancho chili pepper and chocolate. The pepper adds a smoky taste.

—**LEIGH DOUTT** PUEBLO WEST, CO

PREP: 15 MIN. • **BAKE:** 35 MIN. + COOLING • **MAKES:** 4 CUPS

1 egg white
1 tablespoon water
1 package (10 ounces) deluxe mixed nuts
½ cup sugar
1 teaspoon pumpkin pie spice

FRUIT SALSA WITH CINNAMON TORTILLA CHIPS

If you're wanting to get in your fruit servings, this is a fun way to do it! The bright red fruit salsa is addictive. I recommend eating it a day after it's prepared.

—**NANCY LEAVITT** LOGANDALE, NV

PREP: 20 MIN. + CHILLING • **COOK:** 5 MIN./BATCH
MAKES: 6 CUPS SALSA AND 16 DOZEN TORTILLA STRIPS

- 1 **pound fresh strawberries, finely chopped**
- 2 **medium apples, peeled and finely chopped**
- 1 **package (12 ounces) frozen unsweetened raspberries, thawed and well drained**
- 2 **medium kiwifruit, peeled and finely chopped**
- 3 **tablespoons peach or apricot preserves**
- 2 **tablespoons sugar**
- 1 **tablespoon brown sugar**

CINNAMON TORTILLA CHIPS
- **Oil for deep-fat frying**
- 10 **flour tortillas (10 inches)**
- ½ **cup sugar**
- 2 **teaspoons ground cinnamon**

In a large bowl, combine the first seven ingredients; cover and chill for 20 minutes or until serving. In an electric skillet or deep-fat fryer, heat oil to 375°. Cut each tortilla in half; cut each half into 10 strips. Fry strips, a few at a time, until light golden brown on both sides. Drain on paper towels. Combine sugar and cinnamon; sprinkle over strips and toss to coat. Serve with salsa.

CREAMY JALAPENO POPPER DIP

This recipe will remind you of a jalapeno popper without all the mess. If my husband had his way, we'd have this dip every weekend. This versatile dip can be also be served with whole-wheat crackers or pita chips.

—**DEBORAH PEIRCE** VIRGINIA BEACH, VA

PREP: 15 MIN. • **BAKE:** 30 MIN. • **MAKES:** 2 CUPS

- 4 **bacon strips, chopped**
- 1 **package (8 ounces) cream cheese, softened**
- 2 **cups (8 ounces) shredded cheddar cheese**
- ½ **cup sour cream**
- ¼ **cup 2% milk**
- 3 **jalapeno peppers, seeded and chopped**
- 1 **teaspoon white wine vinegar**
- ⅓ **cup panko (Japanese) bread crumbs**
- 2 **tablespoons butter**
  Tortilla chips

1. Preheat oven to 350°. In a small skillet, cook bacon over medium heat until crisp, stirring occasionally. Remove with a slotted spoon; drain on paper towels. Discard drippings, reserving 1 tablespoon.
2. In a large bowl, mix cream cheese, cheddar cheese, sour cream, milk, jalapenos, vinegar, cooked bacon and reserved drippings. Transfer to a greased 8-in.-square baking dish. Sprinkle with bread crumbs; dot with butter.
3. Bake 30-35 minutes or until bubbly and topping is golden brown. Serve with chips.

NOTE *Wear disposable gloves when cutting hot peppers; the oils can burn skin. Avoid touching your face.*

HERBED CHEESE STICKS

We love the breadsticks we get at our local pizza parlor when they're hot from the oven. Now I make that same wonderful goodness at home.
—**HEATHER BATES** ATHENS, ME

START TO FINISH: 30 MIN. • **MAKES:** 16 CHEESE STICKS

- 1 package (6½ ounces) pizza crust mix
- 1½ teaspoons garlic powder
- 1 tablespoon olive oil
- 1 cup (4 ounces) shredded part-skim mozzarella cheese
- ¼ cup shredded Parmesan cheese
- 1 teaspoon Italian seasoning
  Pizza sauce

1. Preheat oven to 450°. Mix pizza dough according to package directions, adding garlic powder to dry mix. Cover; let rest 5 minutes.
2. Knead dough 4-5 times or until easy to handle. On a greased baking sheet, press dough into an 8-in. square. Brush top with oil; sprinkle with cheeses and Italian seasoning.
3. Bake 6-8 minutes or until cheese is lightly browned. Cut in half; cut each half crosswise into eight strips. Serve with pizza sauce.

BACON-WRAPPED TATER TOTS

Indulge in just one of these scrumptious bacon-wrapped goodies and you'll taste why they're always a hit. They'll go fast, so you may want to double the recipe!
—**JONI HILTON** ROCKLIN, CA

START TO FINISH: 25 MIN. • **MAKES:** 32 APPETIZERS

- 16 bacon strips, cut in half
- ½ cup maple syrup
- 1 teaspoon crushed red pepper flakes
- 32 frozen Tater Tots

1. Cook bacon in a large skillet over medium heat until partially cooked but not crisp. Remove to paper towels to drain; keep warm.
2. Combine syrup and pepper flakes. Dip each bacon piece in syrup mixture, then wrap around a Tater Tot. Secure with toothpicks.

HOW LONG DOES BACON LAST?
Once a package of bacon is opened, it should be used within a week. For long-term storage, freeze bacon for up to 1 month.

Side Dishes & Condiments

Every main dish needs a side dish or two for company. Whether it's roasted veggies, a comforting casserole or a homemade dressing for a green salad, let this chapter be your guide for rounding out a down-home meal.

SPICY CRAN-APPLE SAUCE

Looking for a delicious way to get extra vitamin C and fiber in your diet? Give this versatile sauce a try. It's great as a condiment or side dish to turkey, pork, fish or chicken. It also makes a terrific dessert or snack mixed with a serving of vanilla ice cream, yogurt or as a topping on your favorite cheesecake. The possibilities are truly endless.

—KYE FEASEL CANAL WINCHESTER, OH

PREP: 15 MIN. • **COOK:** 20 MIN. • **MAKES:** ABOUT 5 CUPS

- 1 can (20 ounces) unsweetened pineapple tidbits, undrained
- 1 package (12 ounces) fresh or frozen cranberries
- 2 medium apples, peeled and cut into ½-inch pieces
- ½ cup sugar
- ¼ cup pitted dried plums, chopped
- 1 teaspoon ground cinnamon
- ¼ teaspoon ground cloves
- ¼ teaspoon ground nutmeg

1. In a large saucepan, combine all ingredients. Cook over medium heat until berries pop and apples are tender, about 20 minutes. Remove from the heat; mash if desired.
2. Transfer to a large bowl; chill until serving.

CRUNCHY COOL COLESLAW

I love the Honey Roasted Peanut Slaw at Lucille's Smokehouse BBQ, a popular chain in California. This recipe is my version of it. I think it's a pretty close match!

—ELAINE HOFFMANN SANTA ANA, CA

START TO FINISH: 30 MIN. • **MAKES:** 16 SERVINGS

- 2 packages (16 ounces each) coleslaw mix
- 2 medium Honeycrisp apples, julienned
- 1 large carrot, shredded
- ¾ cup chopped red onion
- ½ cup chopped green pepper
- ½ cup cider vinegar
- ⅓ cup canola oil
- 1½ teaspoons sugar
- ½ teaspoon celery seed
- ½ teaspoon salt
- ½ cup coarsely chopped dry roasted peanuts or cashews

1. In a large bowl, combine the first five ingredients. In a small bowl, whisk the vinegar, oil, sugar, celery seed and salt.
2. Just before serving, pour dressing over salad; toss to coat. Sprinkle with peanuts.

ROASTED BRUSSELS SPROUTS & CAULIFLOWER

My grandkids aren't huge fans of cauliflower, but the bacon transformed this dish into one they love. They like it even more with golden cauliflower instead of white.

—**PATRICIA HUDSON** RIVERVIEW, FL

PREP: 25 MIN. • **COOK:** 20 MIN.
MAKES: 12 SERVINGS (½ CUP EACH)

- 8 **bacon strips, chopped**
- 6 **garlic cloves, minced**
- 1 **tablespoon olive oil**
- 1 **tablespoon butter, melted**
- ¼ **teaspoon kosher salt**
- ¼ **teaspoon coarsely ground pepper**
- 4 **cups Brussels sprouts, halved**
- 4 **cups fresh cauliflowerets**
- ¼ **cup grated Parmesan cheese**
  Additional grated Parmesan cheese, optional

1. In a large skillet, cook bacon over medium heat until crisp, stirring occasionally. Remove with a slotted spoon; drain on paper towels. Discard drippings, reserving 1 tablespoon.

2. In a large bowl, mix the garlic, oil, butter, salt, pepper and reserved drippings. Add Brussels sprouts and cauliflowerets; toss to coat. Transfer to two greased 15x10x1-in. baking pans.

3. Bake at 350° for 15 minutes. Sprinkle each pan with 2 tablespoons cheese. Bake 3-5 minutes longer or until vegetables are tender. Sprinkle with bacon and, if desired, additional cheese.

GOUDA MIXED POTATO MASH

Everything's better with cheese, right? This two-potato mash is no exception. If you cube the cheese, you'll discover pockets of melted cheese throughout the dish.

—**SHELBY GODDARD** BATON ROUGE, LA

PREP: 20 MIN. • **COOK:** 15 MIN.
MAKES: 12 SERVINGS (⅔ CUP EACH)

- 6 **medium Yukon Gold potatoes, peeled and cubed**
- 2 **medium sweet potatoes, peeled and cubed**
- ½ **cup 2% milk**
- 1 **cup (4 ounces) shredded Gouda cheese**
- 1 **teaspoon paprika**
- ½ **teaspoon salt**
- ½ **teaspoon pepper**

1. Place Yukon Gold and sweet potatoes in a Dutch oven; add water to cover. Bring to a boil. Reduce heat; cook, uncovered, 10-15 minutes or until tender. Drain; return to the pan.

2. Mash potatoes, gradually adding milk. Stir in cheese, paprika, salt and pepper.

GARDEN POTATO PANCAKES

My family eats these all the time, and you'd never guess the pancakes are full of fresh veggies. We especially like them with the cheese mixed in.

—**PEGGY ROOS** MINNEAPOLIS, MN

PREP: 20 MIN. • **COOK:** 5 MIN./BATCH • **MAKES:** 12 PANCAKES

- 2 **medium zucchini, grated**
- 2 **eggs**
- ¼ **cup whole wheat flour**
- ½ **teaspoon salt**
- ¼ **teaspoon pepper**
- ¼ **teaspoon dried basil**
- 1 **large onion, finely chopped**
- 1 **medium potato, grated**
- 1 **medium carrot, grated**
- ⅓ **cup frozen corn, thawed**
- ¼ **cup shredded sharp white cheddar cheese**
  Oil for frying
  Cracked black pepper and sour cream, optional

1. In a strainer or colander, drain zucchini, squeezing to remove excess liquid. Pat dry. In a large bowl, whisk eggs, flour, salt, pepper and basil until blended. Stir in onion, potato, carrot, corn, cheese and zucchini.
2. In an electric skillet, heat ¼ in. of oil to 375°. Working in batches, drop vegetable mixture by ⅓ cupfuls into oil; press to flatten slightly. Fry 2-3 minutes on each side or until golden brown. Drain on paper towels. If desired, sprinkle with cracked pepper and serve with sour cream.

BACON COLLARD GREENS

Collard greens are a staple vegetable of Southern cuisine. This side dish is often made with smoked or salt-cured meats, such as ham hocks, pork or fatback, so you can swap out the bacon if you'd like.

—**MARSHA ANKENEY** NICEVILLE, FL

PREP: 25 MIN. • **COOK:** 55 MIN. • **MAKES:** 9 SERVINGS

- 2 **pounds collard greens**
- 4 **thick-sliced bacon strips, chopped**
- 1 **cup chopped sweet onion**
- 5 **cups reduced-sodium chicken broth**
- 1 **cup sun-dried tomatoes (not packed in oil), chopped**
- ½ **teaspoon garlic powder**
- ¼ **teaspoon salt**
- ¼ **teaspoon crushed red pepper flakes**

1. Trim thick stems from collard greens; coarsely chop leaves. In a Dutch oven, saute bacon for 3 minutes. Add onion; cook 8-9 minutes longer or until onion is tender and bacon is crisp. Add greens; cook just until wilted.
2. Stir in remaining ingredients. Bring to a boil. Reduce heat; cover and simmer for 45-50 minutes or until greens are tender.

HERB ROASTED ROOT VEGETABLES

Here's a simple-to-fix side to serve at a festive dinner. It looks beautiful with any entree. Roasting brings out the vegetables' natural sweetness.

—DEIRDRE COX KANSAS CITY, MO

PREP: 30 MIN. • **BAKE:** 20 MIN. • **MAKES:** 10 SERVINGS

- 1 large potato, peeled and cut into 1-inch cubes
- 1 medium sweet potato, peeled and cut into 1-inch cubes
- 2 medium carrots, halved lengthwise and cut into 2-inch pieces
- 1 medium parsnip, peeled, halved lengthwise and cut into 2-inch pieces
- 1 small turnip, peeled and cut into 1-inch cubes
- ½ pound kohlrabi, peeled and cut into 1-inch cubes
- 6 large shallots, halved
- 3 tablespoons olive oil
- 2 teaspoons coarsely ground pepper
- 1 teaspoon salt
- 6 fresh thyme sprigs
- 6 fresh rosemary sprigs

1. Preheat oven to 425°. Place first seven ingredients in a Dutch oven and cover with water. Bring to a boil. Cover and cook for 6-8 minutes or until crisp-tender; drain.

2. Transfer vegetables to a large bowl. Combine oil, pepper and salt; drizzle over vegetables and toss to coat. Divide mixture between two greased 15x10x1-in. baking pans; arrange herb sprigs over vegetables.

3. Bake, uncovered, for 20-25 minutes or until tender, stirring occasionally.

VEGGIE-TOPPED POLENTA SLICES

Even though we didn't have too many ingredients in the kitchen at the time, this amazing side came from a stroke of genius I had.
—JENNIFER TIDWELL FAIR OAKS, CA

PREP: 20 MIN. • **COOK:** 20 MIN. • **MAKES:** 4 SERVINGS

- 1 tube (1 pound) polenta, cut into 12 slices
- 2 tablespoons olive oil, divided
- 1 medium zucchini, chopped
- 2 shallots, minced
- 2 garlic cloves, minced
- 3 tablespoons reduced-sodium chicken broth
- ½ teaspoon pepper
- ⅛ teaspoon salt
- 4 plum tomatoes, seeded and chopped
- 2 tablespoons minced fresh basil or 2 teaspoons dried basil
- 1 tablespoon minced fresh parsley
- ½ cup shredded part-skim mozzarella cheese

1. In a large nonstick skillet, cook polenta in 1 tablespoon oil over medium heat for 9-11 minutes on each side or until golden brown.

2. Meanwhile, in another large skillet, saute zucchini in remaining oil until tender. Add shallots and garlic; cook 1 minute longer. Add the broth, pepper and salt. Bring to a boil; cook until liquid is almost evaporated.

3. Stir in the tomatoes, basil and parsley; heat through. Serve with polenta; sprinkle with cheese.

GRILLED CORN MEDLEY

Who knew a store-bought dressing could add so much pizzazz to a recipe? Highlight garden-fresh veggies when you make this medley. Feel free to sub in your favorites!
—TASTE OF HOME TEST KITCHEN

START TO FINISH: 20 MIN. • **MAKES:** 8 SERVINGS

- 3 medium ears sweet corn, cut into 2-inch pieces
- 1 medium sweet red pepper, cut into 1-inch pieces
- 1 medium zucchini, sliced
- 20 small fresh mushrooms
- ¼ cup creamy Caesar salad dressing
- ¼ teaspoon salt
- ¼ teaspoon pepper

In a large bowl, combine all ingredients; toss to coat. Transfer to a disposable foil pan. Grill, covered, over medium-hot heat for 5 minutes; stir. Grill 3-5 minutes longer or until vegetables are tender.

VEGGIES IN A JAR

I'll cut sweet red peppers, green peppers and onions separately ahead of time, then place them in glass jars to keep in the refrigerator.
—CHARLEY G. TUCSON, AZ

PECAN STUFFED BUTTERNUT SQUASH

I love autumn, when butternut squash is at its peak. The squash in this side is tender, and the creamy pecan filling is fabulous.
—**SHERRY LITTLE** SHERWOOD, AR

PREP: 10 MIN. • **BAKE:** 1¼ HOURS • **MAKES:** 8 SERVINGS

- 2 medium butternut squash (about 3 pounds each)
- ¾ teaspoon salt
  Pepper, optional
- 4 ounces cream cheese, softened
- ¼ cup butter, softened
- 3 tablespoons brown sugar
- ½ cup chopped pecans

1. Cut each squash in half lengthwise; discard seeds. Place squash cut side down in two 13x9-in. baking dishes; add ½-in. water. Bake, uncovered, at 350° for 1 hour.
2. Turn squash over; sprinkle with salt and pepper if desired. In a small bowl, beat the cream cheese, butter and brown sugar until light and fluffy; stir in pecans. Spoon into squash cavities.
3. Bake 15-20 minutes longer or until filling is lightly browned and squash is tender.

SIMPLE TURKEY GRAVY

Everyone needs a classic from-scratch gravy recipe. Consider this one yours! Switch up the herbs to fit your preferences, or simply use what you have on hand.
—*TASTE OF HOME* TEST KITCHEN

START TO FINISH: 20 MIN. • **MAKES:** 16 SERVINGS (¼ CUP EACH)

  Turkey drippings
- 3 to 3½ cups chicken broth, divided
- ½ cup all-purpose flour
- ½ teaspoon dried thyme
- ½ teaspoon rubbed sage
- ½ teaspoon pepper

1. Pour turkey drippings and loosened browned bits from roasting pan into a 4-cup measuring cup. Skim fat, reserving 2 tablespoons. Add enough broth to the drippings to measure 3 cups.
2. In a large saucepan, whisk the flour, ¾ cup broth and reserved fat until smooth. Add thyme, sage and pepper; gradually whisk in the drippings mixture. Bring to a boil, stirring constantly; cook and stir for 2-3 minutes or until thickened.

PEAR APPLESAUCE

Here's a light way to satisfy your sweet tooth. You can enjoy a serving for only 120 calories.
—**JENNY COHEN** BALTIMORE, MD

START TO FINISH: 30 MIN. • **MAKES:** ABOUT 2 CUPS

- 3 medium apples, peeled and coarsely chopped
- 2 medium pears, peeled and coarsely chopped
- ¾ cup water
- 2 tablespoons sugar
- ¼ teaspoon ground cinnamon
- ⅛ teaspoon ground nutmeg

In a large saucepan, combine all ingredients. Bring to a boil. Reduce heat; cover and simmer for 15-20 minutes or until tender, stirring occasionally. Mash until sauce is desired consistency. Serve warm or cold.

Yes, You Can!

There's something so satisfying about that "pop" when opening a homemade condiment, letting you know your canning was a success. Whether it's pickles, marmalade or jelly, soon you'll be a canning pro.

WATERMELON RIND PICKLES

Waste not, want not has always been smart advice, especially when it produces results that are as sweet and refreshing as these watermelon rind pickles.
—*TASTE OF HOME* TEST KITCHEN

PREP: 45 MIN. + CHILLING • **PROCESS:** 10 MIN. • **MAKES:** 4 PINTS

- 8 **cups sliced peeled watermelon rind (2x1-in. pieces)**
- 6 **cups water**
- 1 **cup canning salt**
- 4 **cups sugar**
- 2 **cups white vinegar**
- 6 **cinnamon sticks (3 inches), divided**
- 1 **teaspoon whole cloves**
- 1 **teaspoon whole peppercorns**

1. Place rind in a large nonreactive bowl; stir in water and salt. Refrigerate for several hours or overnight. Rinse and drain well.

2. In a Dutch oven, mix sugar, vinegar, 2 cinnamon sticks, cloves and peppercorns. Bring to a boil. Add rinds; return to a boil. Reduce heat; simmer, uncovered, 10 minutes or until tender. Discard cinnamon sticks.

3. Carefully ladle the hot mixture into four hot 1-pint jars, leaving ½-in. headspace. Add a remaining cinnamon stick to each jar. Remove air bubbles and adjust the headspace, if necessary, by adding hot mixture. Wipe rims. Center lids on jars; screw on bands until fingertip tight.

4. Place jars into canner with simmering water, ensuring that they are completely covered with water. Bring to a boil; process for 10 minutes. Remove jars and cool.

NOTES *To prepare watermelon rind, remove dark green peel from watermelon rind and discard. The processing time listed is for altitudes of 1,000 feet or less. For altitudes up to 3,000 feet, add 5 minutes; 6,000 feet, add 10 minutes; 8,000 feet, add 15 minutes; 10,000 feet, add 20 minutes.*

RHUBARB-ORANGE MARMALADE

Rhubarb and orange belong together in this versatile marmalade. It's an ideal glaze for meat or poultry, but you can't go wrong with spreading some on toast.
—**JOAN MARKYTAN** ELYSIAN, MN

PREP: 2 HOURS + CHILLING • **PROCESS:** 10 MIN.
MAKES: 7 HALF-PINTS

- 6 **cups diced fresh or frozen rhubarb**
- 6 **cups sugar, divided**
- 2 **medium oranges**
- 1 **cup coarsely chopped walnuts**
- 1 **cup raisins**

1. In a large bowl, combine rhubarb and 4 cups sugar; cover and refrigerate overnight.

2. Peel rind from oranges; cut into very thin strips, about 1 in. long. Place strips in a small bowl; cover with boiling water. Let stand 30 minutes; drain. Trim white pith from oranges; discard pith. Cut oranges into ½-in. chunks, reserving juices. Discard membranes and seeds.

3. In a Dutch oven, combine rhubarb mixture, orange peel, orange chunks with juices, walnuts, raisins and remaining sugar. Bring to a boil. Reduce heat; simmer, uncovered, 1 to 1½ hours or until thickened.

4. Remove from heat; skim off foam. Carefully ladle hot mixture into seven hot sterilized half-pint jars, leaving ¼-in. headspace. Remove air bubbles and adjust headspace, if necessary, by adding hot mixture. Wipe rims. Center lids on jars; screw on bands until fingertip tight.

5. Place jars into canner with simmering water, ensuring that they are completely covered with water. Bring to a boil; process for 10 minutes. Remove jars and cool.

APPLE PEAR & WALNUT CONSERVE

Fruit and walnuts pair wonderfully in this spread. It's great on bread, pound cake or scoops of vanilla ice cream.

—**GINNY BEADLE** SPOKANE, WA

PREP: 30 MIN. • **PROCESS:** 10 MIN. • **MAKES:** 8 HALF-PINTS

- 4 cups finely chopped peeled tart apples
- 4 cups finely chopped peeled ripe pears
- 3 clementines, peeled and chopped
- ½ cup lemon juice
- 2 packages (1¾ ounces each) powdered fruit pectin
- 6 cups sugar
- ½ teaspoon ground cinnamon
- 1 cup chopped walnuts, toasted

1. In a Dutch oven over medium-high heat, bring the apples, pears, clementines and lemon juice to a boil, stirring constantly. Reduce heat; simmer, uncovered, 10 minutes or until fruit is tender, stirring occasionally.

2. Stir in pectin. Bring to a full rolling boil over high heat, stirring constantly. Stir in sugar and cinnamon; return to bring to a full rolling boil. Boil and stir 1 minute.

3. Remove from heat; skim off foam. Stir in walnuts. Ladle the hot mixture into eight hot half-pint jars, leaving ¼-in. headspace. Remove air bubbles and adjust headspace, if necessary, by adding hot mixture. Wipe rims. Center lids on jars; screw on bands until fingertip tight.

4. Place jars into canner with simmering water, ensuring that they are completely covered with water. Bring to a boil; process 10 minutes. Remove jars and cool.

NOTE *The processing time listed is for altitudes of 1,000 feet or less. Add 1 minute to the processing time for each 1,000 feet of additional altitude.*

HONEY LEMON JELLY

I love both honey and lemon, so I combined them into a doubly delightful jelly. Spread it on toast, bagels, English muffins or scones for a tangy breakfast treat. For extra fun, decorate the jars to make a sweet gift for loved ones.

—**RAMONA WYSONG** BARLOW, KY

PREP: 50 MIN. • **PROCESS:** 5 MIN. • **MAKES:** 3 HALF-PINTS

- 2½ cups honey
- ¾ cup lemon juice
- 6 tablespoons grated lemon peel
- 1 pouch (3 ounces) liquid fruit pectin

1. In a Dutch oven, combine honey, lemon juice and peel. Bring to a full rolling boil over high heat, stirring constantly. Stir in pectin. Continue to boil 1 minute, stirring constantly.

2. Remove from heat; skim off foam. Ladle hot mixture into three hot sterilized half-pint jars, leaving ¼-in. headspace. Wipe rims. Center the lids on jars; screw on bands until fingertip tight.

3. Place jars into canner with simmering water, ensuring that they are completely covered with water. Bring to a boil; process for 5 minutes. Remove jars and cool.

NOTE *The processing time listed is for altitudes of 1,000 feet or less. Add 1 minute to the processing time for each 1,000 feet of additional altitude.*

BLUE CHEESE BREAD PUDDING

You can play with the flavor of this recipe by changing the type of blue cheese you use, from sharp Stilton to saltier Gorgonzola.

—CRYSTAL BRUNS ILIFF, CO

PREP: 30 MIN. + STANDING • **BAKE:** 40 MIN. + STANDING
MAKES: 12 SERVINGS

- ¼ cup butter, cubed
- 1 medium onion, chopped
- 3 garlic cloves, minced
- 2 French bread baguettes (10½ ounces each), cut into 1-inch cubes
- 4 cups (16 ounces) crumbled blue cheese
- 5 eggs
- 5 egg yolks
- 3 cups heavy whipping cream
- 1 teaspoon salt
- ½ teaspoon pepper

1. In a small skillet over medium heat, melt butter. Add onion; cook and stir until softened. Reduce heat to medium-low; cook, stirring occasionally, for 20 minutes or until onion is golden brown. Add garlic; cook 2 minutes longer.
2. Place half of the bread in a greased 13x9-in. baking dish. Layer with onion mixture and half of blue cheese. Top with remaining bread and blue cheese.
3. In a large bowl, whisk the eggs, egg yolks, cream, salt and pepper. Pour over bread; let stand for 15 minutes or until bread is softened.
4. Bake, uncovered, at 375° for 40-45 minutes or until a knife inserted near the center comes out clean. Let stand 10 minutes before serving. Serve warm.

BASIL CORN & TOMATO BAKE

When sweet Jersey corn is in season, I turn to this casserole. Combined with tomatoes, zucchini and basil, you can serve this corn bake for brunch, lunch or dinner.

—ERIN CHILCOAT CENTRAL ISLIP, NY

PREP: 30 MIN. • **BAKE:** 45 MIN. + STANDING • **MAKES:** 10 SERVINGS

- 2 teaspoons olive oil
- 1 medium onion, chopped
- 2 eggs
- 1 can (10¾ ounces) reduced-fat reduced-sodium condensed cream of celery soup, undiluted
- 4 cups fresh or frozen corn
- 1 small zucchini, chopped
- 1 medium tomato, seeded and chopped
- ¾ cup soft whole wheat bread crumbs
- ⅓ cup minced fresh basil
- ½ teaspoon salt
- ½ cup shredded part-skim mozzarella cheese
  Additional minced fresh basil, optional

1. Preheat oven to 350°. In a small skillet, heat oil over medium heat. Add onion; cook and stir until tender. In a large bowl, whisk eggs and condensed soup until blended. Stir in vegetables, bread crumbs, basil, salt and onion. Transfer mixture to an 11x7-in. baking dish coated with cooking spray.
2. Bake, uncovered, 40-45 minutes or until bubbly. Sprinkle with cheese. Bake 5-10 minutes longer or until cheese is melted. Let stand 10 minutes before serving. If desired, sprinkle with additional basil.
NOTE *To make soft bread crumbs, tear bread into pieces and place in a food processor or blender. Cover and pulse until crumbs form. One slice of bread yields ½ to ¾ cup crumbs.*

HERBED NOODLES WITH EDAMAME

Serve this recipe and you'll give your meal a lot of flavor and color. All the fresh herbs make it taste extra special.

—MARIE RIZZIO INTERLOCHEN, MI

START TO FINISH: 30 MIN. • **MAKES:** 4 SERVINGS

- 3½ cups uncooked egg noodles
- 2 tablespoons butter
- 1 green onion, sliced
- 1 tablespoon finely chopped sweet red pepper
- ½ cup frozen shelled edamame, thawed
- ¼ cup reduced-sodium chicken broth
- 1 tablespoon minced fresh parsley
- 1½ teaspoons minced fresh marjoram
- 1½ teaspoons minced fresh chives
- 1 tablespoon olive oil
- ¼ cup grated Romano cheese

1. Cook noodles according to package directions. Meanwhile, in a large skillet, heat butter over medium-high heat. Add onion and red pepper; cook and stir until tender. Stir in edamame and broth; heat through. Add herbs.

2. Drain noodles and add to skillet; toss to combine. Transfer to a serving plate. Drizzle with oil and sprinkle with cheese.

DR PEPPER BBQ SAUCE

My family is stationed in Italy with my husband, Lieutenant William Robert Blackman. William grew up in Memphis, and I'm from Texas, so the dish that spells "home" for us is a good ol' barbecue. I have my own recipe for barbecue sauce that we like to pour all over sliced brisket.

—TINA BLACKMAN NAPLES, AE

PREP: 5 MIN. • **COOK:** 35 MIN. • **MAKES:** 1 CUP

- 1 can (12 ounces) Dr Pepper
- 1 cup crushed tomatoes
- ¼ cup packed brown sugar
- 2 tablespoons spicy brown mustard
- 1 tablespoon orange juice
- 1 tablespoon Worcestershire sauce
- 1 garlic clove, minced
- ¼ teaspoon salt
- ⅛ teaspoon pepper

In a small saucepan, combine all ingredients; bring to a boil. Reduce heat; simmer, uncovered, for 30-35 minutes or until slightly thickened, stirring occasionally. Refrigerate leftovers.

SPICED GARLIC CARROTS

Serve this popular Moroccan side dish hot or as a cold salad. The natural sweetness of the carrots tempers the garlic and balances the sizzle of the pepper flakes.

—**DAVID FEDER** BUFFALO GROVE, IL

START TO FINISH: 30 MIN. • **MAKES:** 6 SERVINGS

- 2 **pounds medium carrots, cut diagonally into ¼-inch slices**
- 2 **cinnamon sticks (3 inches)**
- 1 **teaspoon cumin seeds**
- ¼ **cup olive oil**
- 12 **garlic cloves, peeled and slightly crushed**
- ½ **teaspoon crushed red pepper flakes**
- ¼ **teaspoon salt**

1. Place carrots in a large saucepan and cover with water. Bring to a boil. Cover and cook for 5-8 minutes or until tender; drain.
2. In a large dry skillet, toast cinnamon sticks and cumin seeds over medium heat until aromatic, stirring occasionally. Add oil; heat over medium-high heat. Add the carrots, crushed garlic, pepper flakes and salt; cook and stir for 3-5 minutes or until carrots and garlic are lightly browned. Remove cinnamon sticks.

POTATO AND MUSHROOM GRATIN

Inspired by some of my favorite ingredients, I created this yummy recipe. It's a perfect take-along for potlucks or open houses.

—**LAURIE LACLAIR** NORTH RICHLAND HILLS, TX

PREP: 20 MIN. • **BAKE:** 55 MIN. • **MAKES:** 8 SERVINGS

- 2 **jars (4½ ounces each) sliced mushrooms, drained**
- 3 **shallots, finely chopped**
- 1 **tablespoon olive oil**
- 2 **tablespoons Marsala wine**
- 3 **large potatoes (about 1½ pounds), peeled and thinly sliced**
- 1 **cup (4 ounces) shredded Swiss cheese**
- ½ **cup shredded Parmesan cheese**
- 2 **tablespoons minced fresh basil or 2 teaspoons dried basil**
- 1½ **cups heavy whipping cream**
- 1 **tablespoon butter, cubed**
- ⅛ **teaspoon salt**
- ⅛ **teaspoon pepper**

1. In a large skillet, saute mushrooms and shallots in oil until tender. Add wine; cook and stir for 2 minutes.
2. Arrange a third of the potatoes in a greased 10-in. round shallow baking dish. Layer with half of the mushroom mixture, cheeses, basil and another third of potatoes. Repeat layers. Pour cream over top. Dot with butter; sprinkle with salt and pepper.
3. Bake, uncovered, at 350° for 55-65 minutes or until potatoes are tender.

SMOKY CAULIFLOWER

The smoked Spanish paprika gives the roasted cauliflower extra depth. This is definitely a favorite for me.

—**JULIETTE MULHOLLAND** CORVALLIS, OR

START TO FINISH: 30 MIN. • **MAKES:** 8 SERVINGS

- 1 large head cauliflower, broken into 1-inch florets (about 9 cups)
- 2 tablespoons olive oil
- 1 teaspoon smoked paprika
- ¾ teaspoon salt
- 2 garlic cloves, minced
- 2 tablespoons minced fresh parsley

1. Place cauliflower in a large bowl. Combine the oil, paprika and salt. Drizzle over cauliflower; toss to coat. Transfer to a 15x10x1-in. baking pan. Bake, uncovered, at 450° for 10 minutes.

2. Stir in garlic. Bake 10-15 minutes longer or until cauliflower is tender and lightly browned, stirring occasionally. Sprinkle with parsley.

BROILED PARMESAN TOMATOES

Planning to serve steak or tenderloin? These cheesy tomatoes make the ideal accompaniment.

—**MARY PRICE** YOUNGSTOWN, OH

START TO FINISH: 10 MIN. • **MAKES:** 4 SERVINGS

- 2 medium tomatoes, halved
- 2 tablespoons plus ¼ cup butter, divided
- 4 green onions, chopped
- 3 tablespoons dry bread crumbs
- 1 tablespoon grated Parmesan cheese
- ⅛ teaspoon salt
- ⅛ teaspoon garlic powder
- ¼ cup shredded Swiss cheese

1. Place tomatoes, cut side up, in an ungreased 15x10x1-in. baking pan; dot with 2 tablespoons butter. Broil 4 in. from heat 4-6 minutes or until butter is melted.

2. Meanwhile, in a small microwave-safe bowl, combine remaining butter and onions. Microwave, uncovered, on high 2-3 minutes or until onions are tender. Stir in bread crumbs, Parmesan cheese, salt and garlic powder; spoon over tomatoes. Sprinkle with Swiss cheese. Broil for 1-2 minutes or until cheese is melted.

BROILED ITALIAN TOMATOES *Substitute shredded mozzarella for the Swiss cheese. Stir in 1 tablespoon chopped fresh basil to the crumb mixture.*

SPINACH-BASIL PESTO

Toss this garlicky, rich pesto with pasta or use as a spread. It also freezes well for later use.

—JAYE BEELER GRAND RAPIDS, MI

START TO FINISH: 10 MIN. • **MAKES:** 1¾ CUPS

- 6 garlic cloves, halved
- 3 cups fresh baby spinach
- 1½ cups loosely packed basil leaves
- ¾ cup chopped walnuts or pine nuts, toasted
- 1 cup grated Parmesan cheese
- ½ teaspoon salt
  Dash pepper
- ¾ cup olive oil

Place garlic in a food processor; pulse until finely chopped. Add spinach, basil and walnuts. Pulse until chopped. Add cheese, salt and pepper. Continue processing while gradually adding oil in a steady stream.

FREEZE OPTION *Freeze pesto in freezer containers. To use, thaw in refrigerator.*

POMEGRANATE GLAZED BEETS

A ruby red pomegranate glaze lends a tart, slightly sweet taste to the beets. They'd be the perfect addition to any festive table.

—TASTE OF HOME TEST KITCHEN

PREP: 20 MIN. • **BAKE:** 35 MIN. • **MAKES:** 6 SERVINGS

- 2 pounds fresh beets, trimmed and peeled
- 2 tablespoons olive oil
- ¾ teaspoon salt, divided
- 1 cup pomegranate juice
- ¼ cup sugar
- 1 tablespoon brown sugar
- 1 cinnamon stick (3 inches)
- 1½ teaspoons grated orange peel
- ⅛ teaspoon pepper

1. Cut each beet into six wedges; place in a large bowl. Add oil and ½ teaspoon salt; toss to coat.

2. Place a piece of heavy-duty foil (about 24 in. long) in a 15x10-in. baking pan. Arrange beets on foil; fold foil around beets and seal tightly. Bake at 400° for 35-40 minutes or until beets are tender. Open foil carefully to allow steam to escape.

3. Meanwhile, in a large saucepan, combine pomegranate juice, sugar, brown sugar, cinnamon stick, orange peel, pepper and remaining salt. Bring to a boil. Reduce heat; simmer, uncovered, until mixture is syrupy and reduced to ⅓ cup. Carefully remove beets from foil; add to syrup and toss gently to coat.

ORZO WITH PEPPERS & SPINACH

Sweet bell peppers are a good source of vitamin C, which helps the body fight infection and absorb folate and iron.

—TAMMI KETTENBACH JERSEYVILLE, IL

START TO FINISH: 30 MIN. • **MAKES:** 5 SERVINGS

- 1 cup uncooked orzo pasta
- 1 each medium sweet orange, red and yellow pepper, chopped
- 1 cup sliced fresh mushrooms
- 1 tablespoon olive oil
- 3 garlic cloves, minced
- 2 cups fresh baby spinach
- ½ teaspoon Italian seasoning
- ¼ teaspoon each salt and pepper
- ½ cup grated Parmesan cheese

1. Cook pasta according to package directions. Meanwhile, in a large skillet, cook the peppers and mushrooms in oil over medium heat until tender. Add garlic; cook 1 minute longer. Add the spinach, Italian seasoning, salt and pepper; cook and stir 1-2 minutes longer or just until spinach is wilted.

2. Drain pasta. Add with cheese to skillet; heat through.

ORZO WITH MUSHROOMS *Omit peppers, spinach and cheese. Use ½ pound thinly sliced assorted fresh mushrooms, such as portobello, button and/or shiitake. With the mushrooms, saute ¾ pound fresh snow peas. Sprinkle dish with ½ cup toasted pine nuts.*

HEAVENLY BAKED SWEET POTATOES

These luscious baked sweet potatoes taste a little bit like a pumpkin pie. They also feature fruits and nuts for added crunch. If you like, toss some mini marshmallows on top to make it extra indulgent.

—**CYNTHIA PETERSON** ROSWELL, NM

PREP: 30 MIN. • **BAKE:** 55 MIN. • **MAKES:** 10 SERVINGS

- 1 **can (8 ounces) unsweetened pineapple chunks**
- ½ **cup packed brown sugar**
- ¼ **cup apple cider or unsweetened apple juice**
- ¼ **cup maple syrup**
- ¼ **cup butter, cubed**
- ¾ **teaspoon ground cinnamon**
- ⅛ **teaspoon ground cloves**
- 3 **large sweet potatoes, peeled and cut into ¼-inch slices**
- 3 **medium apples, peeled and cut into ¼-inch slices**
- ¾ **teaspoon salt**
- ⅓ **cup chopped pecans**

1. Drain pineapple, reserving juice; set pineapple aside. In a small saucepan, combine brown sugar, apple cider, maple syrup, butter and reserved pineapple juice. Bring to a boil; cook until liquid is reduced to ¾ cup and syrupy, about 20 minutes. Stir in the cinnamon and cloves; set aside and keep warm.
2. Preheat oven to 400°. Layer half the potatoes, apples and pineapple in a 13x9-in. baking dish coated with cooking spray. Repeat layers. Sprinkle with salt. Pour reduced liquid over top. Cover and bake 40 minutes or just until tender.
3. Sprinkle with pecans. Bake, uncovered, 13-18 minutes longer or until potatoes and apples are tender.

DIJON ROASTED ASPARAGUS

Asparagus is a natural side dish to serve at Easter. In this mouthwatering recipe, Dijon mustard, cayenne pepper and Asiago cheese provide big, bold flavor.

—**JAMIE BROWN-MILLER** NAPA, CA

START TO FINISH: 30 MIN. • **MAKES:** 4 SERVINGS

- ¼ **cup Dijon mustard**
- ¼ **cup olive oil**
- 4 **garlic cloves, minced**
- ¼ **teaspoon cayenne pepper**
- 1 **slice Brioche bread (½ inch thick), toasted**
- 1 **pound fresh asparagus, trimmed**
- ½ **cup shredded Asiago cheese**

1. In a small bowl, combine the mustard, oil, garlic and cayenne. Place bread in a food processor; cover and process until fine crumbs form. In a small bowl, combine bread crumbs and 1 tablespoon mustard mixture.
2. Place asparagus in an ungreased 13x9-in. baking dish; drizzle with remaining mustard mixture. Sprinkle with bread crumb mixture and cheese. Bake, uncovered, at 425° for 14-18 minutes or until golden brown.

QUICK & EASY HONEY MUSTARD

Since this easy mustard is made with rice vinegar and honey, it seems to have more flavor than any other honey mustard dressing I have ever tried.

—**SHARON REHM** NEW BLAINE, AR

START TO FINISH: 5 MIN. • **MAKES:** 1 CUP

- ½ **cup stone-ground mustard**
- ¼ **cup honey**
- ¼ **cup rice vinegar**

In a small bowl, whisk all the ingredients. Refrigerate until serving.

MAKE-AHEAD CORN BREAD DRESSING

My family has always been big veggie eaters. I wanted to share a little taste of my childhood with my in-laws, so I created this dish. You don't have to let it sit overnight, but it's a nice make-ahead option and the flavors mesh more that way. Your family will love it.
—**PATRICIA BROUSSARD** LAFAYETTE, LA

PREP: 1½ HOURS + CHILLING • **BAKE:** 55 MIN.
MAKES: 14 SERVINGS (¾ CUP EACH)

- 1 **medium spaghetti squash (about 4 pounds)**
- 1 **package (8½ ounces) corn bread/muffin mix**
- 1 **medium onion, finely chopped**
- 2 **celery ribs, thinly sliced**
- ½ **cup butter, cubed**
- 2 **garlic cloves, minced**
- ½ **pound bulk pork sausage, cooked and drained**
- 1 **cup frozen corn**
- 2 **tablespoons poultry seasoning**
- ¾ **teaspoon salt**
- ¼ **teaspoon pepper**
- 1 **cup chopped walnuts, toasted**
- 1 **cup chicken broth**
- ¼ **cup grated Parmesan cheese**

1. Cut squash lengthwise in half; remove and discard seeds. Place squash in a roasting pan, cut side down; add ½ in. of hot water. Bake, uncovered, at 375° for 45 minutes. Drain water from pan; turn squash cut side up. Bake 5 minutes longer or until squash is tender.

2. Prepare and bake corn bread mix according to package directions, using an 8-in. square baking dish. Cool to room temperature; crumble bread. Place in an ungreased 13x9-in. baking pan. Bake at 350° for 8-13 minutes or until lightly browned, stirring twice.

3. In a large skillet, cook onion and celery in butter over medium heat for 4 minutes. Add garlic; cook 2 minutes longer. Stir in the sausage, corn, poultry seasoning, salt and pepper; heat through.

4. When squash is cool enough to handle, use a fork to separate strands. In a large bowl, combine the sausage mixture, corn bread, squash and walnuts. Stir in broth.

5. Transfer to a greased 13x9-in. baking dish. Cover and refrigerate for 8 hours or overnight. Remove from the refrigerator 30 minutes before baking. Cover and bake at 350° for 45 minutes. Uncover; sprinkle with cheese; bake 10-15 minutes longer or until heated through.

GREEN BEANS WITH YELLOW-PEPPER BUTTER

Colorful, crunchy and buttery, these beans come together quickly and will be a hit at your table. For variation, sprinkle toasted pine nuts over the top just before serving.

—**JUDIE WHITE** FLORIEN, LA

START TO FINISH: 30 MIN. • **MAKES:** 12 SERVINGS

- 3 **medium sweet yellow peppers, divided**
- 2 **tablespoons plus ½ cup butter, softened, divided**
- ⅓ **cup pine nuts**
- 1 **to 2 tablespoons lemon juice**
- ½ **teaspoon salt**
- ¼ **teaspoon pepper**
- 2¼ **pounds fresh green beans**

1. Finely chop 1½ yellow peppers. In a large skillet, heat 2 tablespoons butter over medium-high heat. Add chopped peppers; cook and stir until tender.
2. Place pine nuts, lemon juice, salt, pepper and remaining butter in a food processor; process until blended. Add cooked peppers; process to blend.
3. Place beans in a Dutch oven and cover with water. Cut remaining 1½ peppers into thin strips; add to beans. Bring to a boil. Cook, covered, 5-7 minutes or until vegetables are crisp-tender; drain well and return to pot. Add butter mixture and toss to coat.

GRANDMA'S POTATO DUMPLINGS

If you happen to make too many mashed potatoes, great! Day-old rolls and leftover spuds are scrumptious the second time around, especially when they're turned into buttery potato dumplings.

—**WENDY STENMAN** GERMANTOWN, WI

START TO FINISH: 25 MIN. • **MAKES:** 4 SERVINGS

- 2 **day-old hard rolls**
- ½ **cup water**
- 2 **teaspoons canola oil**
- ½ **cup leftover mashed potatoes**
- 1 **egg, lightly beaten**
  Dash ground nutmeg
- 1 **to 2 tablespoons all-purpose flour**
- ¼ **cup butter, cubed**

1. Tear rolls into ½-in. pieces; place in a 15x10x1-in. baking pan. Drizzle with water and squeeze dry.
2. In a large skillet, heat oil over medium-high heat. Add torn rolls; cook and stir 1-2 minutes or until lightly toasted.
3. In a small bowl, combine potatoes, egg, nutmeg and bread. Add enough flour to achieve a shaping consistency. With floured hands, shape mixture into 3-in. balls.
4. Fill a Dutch oven two-thirds full with water; bring to a boil. Carefully add dumplings. Reduce heat; simmer, uncovered, 8-10 minutes or until a toothpick inserted in center of dumplings comes out clean. Meanwhile, in a small heavy saucepan, melt butter over medium heat. Heat 4-6 minutes or until golden brown. Serve warm dumplings with butter.

TOMATO PIE

Make sure your tomatoes are firm and not too ripe.
Ripe tomatoes will add too much moisture to the pie.
—**LOIS MORGAN** EDISTO BEACH, SC

PREP: 50 MIN. + CHILLING • **BAKE:** 30 MIN. • **MAKES:** 8 SERVINGS

- 1 cup plus 2 tablespoons all-purpose flour
- ¼ teaspoon salt
- ½ cup cold butter, cubed
- 2 to 3 tablespoons ice water

FILLING

- ¾ cup mayonnaise
- ½ cup shredded cheddar cheese
- ⅓ cup thinly sliced green onions
- 1 tablespoon minced fresh oregano
- ½ teaspoon ground coriander
- ¼ teaspoon salt
- ¼ teaspoon pepper
- 6 medium tomatoes (1¾ pounds), cut into ¼-inch slices
- 4 bacon strips, cooked and crumbled

1. In a large bowl, mix flour and salt; cut in butter until crumbly. Gradually add ice water, tossing with a fork until dough holds together when pressed. Shape into a disk; wrap in plastic wrap. Refrigerate 30 minutes or overnight.
2. Preheat the oven to 350°. On a lightly floured surface, roll dough to a ⅛ in.-thick circle; transfer to a 9-in. pie plate. Trim pastry to ½ in. beyond rim of plate; flute edge. Line unpricked pastry with a double thickness of foil. Fill with pie weights, dried beans or uncooked rice.
3. Bake 20-25 minutes or until bottom is lightly browned. Remove foil and weights; bake 5-10 minutes longer or until light brown. Cool on a wire rack.

4. In a small bowl, mix mayonnaise, cheese, green onions and seasonings. Arrange one-third of the tomatoes in crust; spread with one-third of the mayonnaise mixture. Repeat layers twice. Bake 25 minutes. Top with bacon; bake for 5-10 minutes longer or until filling is bubbly. Let stand for 10 minutes.

CRISPY POTATO PUFFS

Crunchy cornflakes and sesame seeds surround a velvety potato filling in these adorable puffs.
—**EVA TOMLINSON** BRYAN, OH

PREP: 35 MIN. • **BAKE:** 15 MIN.
MAKES: 12 SERVINGS (2 PUFFS EACH)

- 4 pounds cubed peeled potatoes (about 11 cups)
- ½ cup 2% milk
- ¼ cup butter, cubed
- 1½ teaspoons salt
- ½ cup shredded cheddar cheese
- 1½ cups crushed cornflakes
- 6 tablespoons sesame seeds, toasted

1. Place potatoes in a large saucepan; add water to cover. Bring to a boil. Reduce heat; cook, uncovered, 10-15 minutes or until tender. Drain; return to pan.
2. Mash potatoes, gradually adding milk, butter and salt; stir in cheese. Transfer to a large bowl; refrigerate, covered, 2 hours or until firm enough to shape.
3. In a shallow dish, combine cornflakes and sesame seeds. Shape potato mixture into 1½-in. balls; roll in the cornflake mixture.
4. Place on baking sheets; cover and freeze until firm. Transfer to resealable plastic freezer bags. Freeze up to 3 months.
TO SERVE *Preheat oven to 400°. Place frozen potato puffs on greased baking sheets. Bake 15-20 minutes or until golden brown and heated through.*

DILL & CHIVE PEAS

Growing my own vegetables and herbs helps keep things fresh in the kitchen. This side is a breeze to get ready.

—TANNA RICHARD CEDAR RAPIDS, IA

START TO FINISH: 10 MIN. • **MAKES:** 4 SERVINGS

- 1 package (16 ounces) frozen peas
- ¼ cup snipped fresh dill
- 2 tablespoons minced fresh chives
- 1 tablespoon butter
- 1 teaspoon lemon-pepper seasoning
- ¼ teaspoon kosher salt

Cook peas according to package directions. Stir in the remaining ingredients; serve immediately.

DAD'S BAKED BEANS

I always use this recipe when I need to make beans for any occasion; they are the best baked beans I've ever had.

—KIMBERLY WALLACE DENNISON, OH

PREP: 15 MIN. • **BAKE:** 1 HOUR • **MAKES:** 8 SERVINGS

- 3 cans (15½ ounces each) great northern beans, rinsed and drained
- 5 hot dogs, sliced
- 1½ cups ketchup
- ½ cup packed brown sugar
- 2 tablespoons molasses
- 1 medium onion, chopped
- ½ teaspoon ground mustard
- ¼ teaspoon salt
- ¼ teaspoon pepper

In an ungreased 2-qt. baking dish, combine all the ingredients. Cover and bake at 350° for 1-1½ hours or until heated through.

LENTIL WHITE BEAN PILAF

Vegetarians will be happy to see this hearty meatless grain pilaf on the buffet table. I like to make this when I have extra cooked lentils, barley, quinoa and rice on hand.

—JULI MEYERS HINESVILLE, GA

PREP: 35 MIN. • **COOK:** 15 MIN. • **MAKES:** 10 SERVINGS

- 1 cup dried lentils, rinsed
- ½ cup quick-cooking barley
- ½ cup quinoa, rinsed
- ⅓ cup uncooked long grain rice
- ½ pound sliced baby portobello mushrooms
- 3 medium carrots, finely chopped
- 3 celery ribs, finely chopped
- 1 large onion, finely chopped
- ¼ cup butter, cubed
- 3 garlic cloves, minced
- 2 teaspoons minced fresh rosemary or ½ teaspoon dried rosemary, crushed
- ½ cup vegetable broth
- ½ teaspoon salt
- ½ teaspoon pepper
- 2 cups canned white kidney or cannellini beans, rinsed and drained

1. Cook the lentils, barley, quinoa and rice according to package directions; set aside.

2. In a Dutch oven, saute the mushrooms, carrots, celery and onion in butter until tender. Add garlic and rosemary; cook 1 minute longer. Add broth, salt and pepper, stirring to loosen browned bits from pan. Stir in beans and the cooked lentils, barley, quinoa and rice; heat through.

NOTE *Look for quinoa in the cereal, rice or organic food aisle.*

Soups, Salads & Sandwiches

Chase away the chill when you serve a bowl of warm, hearty soup (and don't forget to offer a dunkable sandwich on the side). While you're at it, toss together a leafy salad for a complete meal... without a lot of effort!

ASPARAGUS SOUP WITH LEMON CREME FRAICHE

Pureed asparagus makes for an incredible soup. Serve it warm or chilled, depending on the weather or your personal preference.
—**FERN VITENSE** TIPTON, IA

PREP: 25 MIN. • **COOK:** 25 MIN. • **MAKES:** 6 SERVINGS

- 1 **tablespoon butter**
- 1 **tablespoon olive oil**
- 1 **small onion, chopped**
- 4 **cups cut fresh asparagus (1-inch pieces)**
- 3 **medium red potatoes, peeled and cubed**
- 2 **cans (14½ ounces each) vegetable broth**
- 2 **teaspoons grated lemon peel**
- ½ **teaspoon salt**
- ½ **teaspoon pepper**
- ½ **teaspoon ground coriander**
- ¼ **teaspoon ground ginger**

GARNISH

- ¼ **cup minced chives**
- ¼ **cup creme fraiche or sour cream**
- 1 **tablespoon lemon juice**
- ½ **teaspoon grated lemon peel**

1. In a large saucepan, heat butter and oil over medium-high heat. Add onion; cook and stir until tender. Add the asparagus and potatoes; cook 3 minutes longer. Stir in broth, lemon peel and seasonings. Bring to a boil. Reduce heat; simmer, covered, 15-20 minutes or until potatoes are tender.

2. Cool slightly. Process soup in batches in a blender until smooth. Return all to pan and heat through. Combine garnish ingredients; serve with soup.

CITRUS & ROASTED BEETS SALAD

Glistening oranges, tangerines and grapefruit star in this colorful, tangy salad. It's a refreshing mix of bright flavors. Just add chicken and it's a complete meal.
—**PETER ELDRIDGE** CLERMONT, FL

PREP: 20 MIN. • **BAKE:** 1 HOUR + COOLING • **MAKES:** 6 SERVINGS

- 3 **medium fresh beets (about 1 pound)**
- 8 **cups fresh arugula or baby spinach**
- 1 **can (14 ounces) hearts of palm, drained and sliced**
- 1 **medium grapefruit, peeled and sectioned**
- 1 **medium orange, peeled and sectioned**
- 1 **tangerine, peeled and sectioned**
- 1 **cup crumbled goat cheese**

DRESSING

- 3 **tablespoons balsamic vinegar**
- 4 **teaspoons grated orange peel**
- 2 **teaspoons grated tangerine peel**
- 1 **tablespoon orange juice**
- 2 **teaspoons Dijon mustard**
- 2 **teaspoons honey**
- ¼ **cup olive oil**

1. Scrub beets and trim tops to 1 in. Wrap in foil; place on a baking sheet. Bake at 400° for 1 hour or until tender. Remove foil; allow beets to cool.

2. Peel beets and cut into ½-in. cubes. On six salad plates, arrange the arugula, beets, heart of palm, grapefruit, orange and tangerine; sprinkle with cheese. Whisk the vinegar, orange and tangerine peel, orange juice, mustard and honey; gradually whisk in oil. Drizzle over salads. Serve immediately.

HEIRLOOM TOMATO SOUP

During the late summer months I make this soup about once a week. Even my son, who normally does not like tomatoes, enjoys this one.

—**KIMBERLY DANEK PINKSON** SAN ANSELMO, CA

PREP: 30 MIN. • **COOK:** 20 MIN. • **MAKES:** 20 SERVINGS (5 QUARTS)

- 1 large sweet onion, halved and thinly sliced
- ¼ cup extra virgin olive oil
- 6 garlic cloves, minced
- 12 medium heirloom tomatoes, quartered (about 8 pounds)
- 1 large carrot, chopped
- 1 cup fresh corn
- ¼ cup loosely packed basil leaves
- 2 teaspoons sea salt
- 5½ cups reduced-sodium chicken broth
- ⅓ cup heavy whipping cream

1. In a stockpot, saute onion in oil until tender. Add garlic; cook 1 minute longer. Add the tomatoes, carrot, corn, basil and salt. Stir in broth. Bring to a boil. Reduce heat; cover and simmer for 15-20 minutes or until tomatoes are softened, stirring occasionally. Cool slightly.

2. In a food processor, process soup in batches until smooth. Return all to pan and heat through. Ladle into bowls; drizzle each with ¾ teaspoon cream.

MOMMA'S WARM POTATO SALAD

A friend of mine has a mom, known to all as Momma, who makes the absolute best potato salad. It is like a really good egg salad with potatoes in it.

—**PAMELA VITTI KNOWLES** HENDERSONVILLE, NC

START TO FINISH: 25 MIN. • **MAKES:** 6 SERVINGS

- 3 medium Yukon Gold potatoes (about 1½ pounds), peeled and cubed
- 6 hard-cooked eggs, chopped
- 2 celery ribs, chopped
- 1 small onion, chopped
- ½ cup chopped green pepper
- ½ cup mayonnaise
- 2 tablespoons Dijon mustard
- ¾ teaspoon salt
- ½ teaspoon pepper
- ⅛ teaspoon hot pepper sauce

1. Place potatoes in a large saucepan; add water to cover. Bring to a boil. Reduce heat; cook, uncovered, 10-15 minutes or until tender. Drain potatoes and place in a large bowl. Add the eggs, celery, onion and green pepper.

2. In a small bowl, mix the remaining ingredients; add to potato mixture. Toss gently to coat. Serve warm. Cover and refrigerate leftovers.

SALMON BURGERS WITH TANGY SLAW

I thought I'd made salmon every way possible, until now. The tangy slaw, made with fennel and avocado, adds another layer of taste that goes well with other seafood offerings, too. It might become your favorite burger recipe before long.

—**AMBER MASSEY** ARGYLE, TX

PREP: 25 MIN. + CHILLING • **GRILL:** 10 MIN. • **MAKES:** 4 SERVINGS

SLAW
- 3 cups thinly sliced cabbage
- 1½ cups thinly sliced fennel bulb
- 1 cup thinly sliced cucumber
- ½ cup thinly sliced red onion
- ¼ cup minced fresh cilantro
- 1 jalapeno pepper, seeded and finely chopped
- ½ teaspoon salt
- ¼ teaspoon pepper
- 2 medium ripe avocados, peeled and cubed
- ¼ cup lime juice

HONEY MUSTARD
- 1 tablespoon Dijon mustard
- 1 tablespoon honey

SALMON BURGERS
- 1 pound skinless salmon fillets, cut into 1-inch pieces, divided
- 2 tablespoons grated lime peel
- 1 tablespoon Dijon mustard
- 3 tablespoons finely chopped shallot
- 2 tablespoons minced fresh cilantro
- 1 tablespoon reduced-sodium soy sauce
- 1 tablespoon honey
- 3 garlic cloves, minced
- ½ teaspoon salt
- ¼ teaspoon pepper
- 4 hamburger buns, split

1. Place the first eight ingredients in a large bowl; toss to combine. In a small bowl, gently toss avocados with lime juice; add to cabbage mixture. Refrigerate until serving. In a small bowl, mix honey mustard ingredients.

2. For burgers, place a fourth of the salmon in a food processor. Add lime peel and mustard; process until smooth. Transfer to a large bowl.

3. Place remaining salmon in food processor; pulse until coarsely chopped and add to puree. Fold in shallot, cilantro, soy sauce, honey, garlic, salt and pepper. Shape into four ½-in.-thick patties.

4. Moisten a paper towel with cooking oil; using long-handled tongs, rub on grill rack to coat lightly. Grill burgers, covered, over medium heat or broil 4 in. from heat 4-5 minutes on each side or until a thermometer reads 145°.

5. Serve on buns with honey mustard; top each with ½ cup slaw. Serve remaining slaw on the side.

NOTE *Wear disposable gloves when cutting hot peppers; the oils can burn skin. Avoid touching your face.*

MINTED SUGAR SNAP PEA SALAD

You'll catch spring fever with just one bite of this lovely salad. Shallot, honey and mustard add savory elements to crisp mint-flavored peas.

—DARLENE MORRIS FRANKLINTON, LA

START TO FINISH: 25 MIN. • **MAKES:** 4 SERVINGS

- 1½ pounds fresh sugar snap peas, trimmed and strings removed
- ¼ cup crumbled goat cheese

DRESSING

- 3 tablespoons minced fresh mint
- 3 tablespoons olive oil
- 1 small shallot, finely chopped
- 1 tablespoon lemon juice
- 1 teaspoon grated lemon peel
- 1 teaspoon Dijon mustard
- 1 teaspoon honey
- ½ teaspoon salt
- ¼ teaspoon pepper

1. In a large saucepan, bring 2 quarts water to a boil. Add peas; cook, uncovered, 2-3 minutes or just until crisp-tender. Drain and immediately place in ice water. Drain and pat dry. Cut in half crosswise; place in a large bowl. Sprinkle with goat cheese.

2. In a small bowl, whisk dressing ingredients. Pour over pea mixture; toss to coat.

CREAMY TURNIP SOUP

They serve this soup at a nearby fall festival. If you need to, it reheats nicely in a slow cooker.

—LIZ WHEELER WILMINGTON, VT

PREP: 20 MIN. • **COOK:** 20 MIN. • **MAKES:** 9 SERVINGS (2¼ QUARTS)

- 2 tablespoons butter
- 1 medium onion, chopped
- 3 garlic cloves, minced
- ½ cup white wine or reduced-sodium chicken broth
- 3 pounds turnips, peeled and cut into 1-inch cubes
- 1 carton (32 ounces) reduced-sodium chicken broth
- 1 medium potato, peeled and cubed
- 1 cup half-and-half cream
- ½ teaspoon salt
- ½ teaspoon ground nutmeg
- ½ teaspoon olive oil
- 3 cups fresh baby spinach

1. In a Dutch oven, heat butter over medium-high heat. Add onion; cook and stir until tender. Add garlic; cook 1 minute longer. Stir in wine. Bring to a boil; cook until liquid is reduced by half.

2. Add turnips, broth and potato. Bring to a boil. Reduce heat; simmer, uncovered, 20-25 minutes or until vegetables are tender. Cool slightly.

3. In a food processor, process soup in batches until smooth. Return all to pan. Stir in cream, salt and nutmeg; heat through.

4. Meanwhile, in a large nonstick skillet, heat oil over medium-high heat. Add spinach; cook and stir just until wilted. Serve with soup.

Make It Bacon

Time to fire up the skillet and let the crackle of crispy bacon draw folks into the kitchen. Take a salad or sandwich from ho-hum to hero by just adding a few strips of this all-time favorite ingredient.

BACON CHEESEBURGER MEATBALL SUBS

I took two of my favorite foods, meatballs and bacon cheeseburgers, and rolled them into one delicious sandwich!

—CYNDY GERKEN NAPLES, FL

PREP: 40 MIN. • **BAKE:** 20 MIN. • **MAKES:** 8 SANDWICHES

- 2 **eggs, lightly beaten**
- 1 **tablespoon Worcestershire sauce**
- 2 **medium onions, finely chopped**
- ⅔ **cup seasoned bread crumbs**
- ⅓ **cup grated Parmesan cheese**
- 3 **tablespoons minced fresh parsley or 1 tablespoon dried parsley flakes**
- 8 **garlic cloves, minced**
- 2 **tablespoons minced fresh basil or 2 teaspoons dried basil**
- 1 **tablespoon minced fresh oregano or 1 teaspoon dried oregano**

- ⅛ **teaspoon kosher salt**
- ⅛ **teaspoon pepper**
- ⅛ **teaspoon crushed red pepper flakes**
- ¾ **pound ground beef**
- ⅔ **pound ground veal**
- ⅔ **pound ground pork**
- 24 **cubes cheddar cheese (½-inch each)**
- 8 **cooked bacon strips, cut into thirds**
- 8 **lettuce leaves**
- 8 **submarine buns, split and toasted**
- 1 **cup barbecue sauce, warmed**

1. In a large bowl, combine the first 12 ingredients. Crumble the meats over the mixture and mix well; divide into 24 portions.

2. Wrap each cheese cube with a cut bacon strip. Shape one portion of meat mixture around each bacon-wrapped cheese cube. Place meatballs on a greased rack in a shallow baking pan.

3. Bake, uncovered, at 400° for 20-25 minutes or until a thermometer reads 160°. Drain on paper towels. Serve on lettuce-lined buns with barbecue sauce.

FENNEL-BACON PASTA SALAD

I love when a recipe turns out to be easy to prepare but elegant enough to serve at a formal dinner. The pasta is best served warm, but letting it chill is another yummy option.

—JULIAN WONG LA JOLLA, CA

PREP: 15 MIN. • **COOK:** 20 MIN. • **MAKES:** 16 SERVINGS

- 1 **package (16 ounces) spiral pasta**
- 6 **thick-sliced bacon strips, chopped**
- 3 **small fennel bulbs, thinly sliced**
- 1½ **cups walnut halves**
- 1¼ **cups (5 ounces) crumbled Stilton cheese, divided**
- 1 **teaspoon coarsely ground pepper**
- ¾ **teaspoon salt**

1. Cook pasta according to package directions.

2. Meanwhile, in a large skillet, cook bacon over medium heat until crisp. Remove the bacon with a slotted spoon; drain on paper towels. Remove drippings, reserving 3 tablespoons. Saute fennel in reserved drippings for 4-6 minutes or until crisp-tender. Add walnuts; cook for 3-4 minutes longer or until toasted.

3. Drain pasta, reserving ⅓ cup pasta water. Add pasta, bacon and ¾ cup cheese to fennel mixture; sprinkle with pepper and salt. Toss lightly until cheese is melted, adding enough reserved pasta water to coat pasta. Serve warm with remaining cheese. Refrigerate leftovers.

BLT WITH PEPPERED BALSAMIC MAYO

Here's my twist on a classic, well-loved sandwich. Creamy avocado, balsamic mayo and crisp salad greens make this BLT legendary in my book. For a lighter take, I'll sometimes use turkey bacon instead.

—**AMI BOYER** SAN FRANCISCO, CA

START TO FINISH: 25 MIN. • **MAKES:** 4 SERVINGS

- 8 bacon strips, halved
- ½ cup mayonnaise
- 1 tablespoon balsamic vinegar
- ½ teaspoon pepper
- ⅛ teaspoon salt
- 8 slices bread, toasted
- 2 cups spring mix salad greens
- 8 cherry tomatoes, sliced
- 1 medium ripe avocado, peeled and sliced

1. In a large skillet, cook bacon over medium heat until crisp. Remove to paper towels to drain.

2. In a small bowl, mix mayonnaise, vinegar, pepper and salt. Spread half of the mixture over four toast slices. Layer with bacon, salad greens, tomatoes and avocado. Spread remaining mayonnaise over remaining toast; place over top.

LEMONY TORTELLINI BACON SALAD

Mealtime shouldn't be complicated. We especially love this simple salad on warm nights. Adding a glass of iced tea or lemonade on the side is just right.

—**SAMANTHA VICARS** KENOSHA, WI

START TO FINISH: 20 MIN. • **MAKES:** 4 SERVINGS

- 2 cups frozen cheese tortellini (about 8 ounces)
- 4 cups fresh broccoli florets
- ¾ cup mayonnaise
- 1 tablespoon balsamic vinegar
- 2 teaspoons lemon juice
- ¾ teaspoon dried oregano
- ¼ teaspoon salt
- 1 package (5 ounces) spring mix salad greens
- 4 bacon strips, cooked and crumbled

1. In a large saucepan, cook tortellini according to package directions, adding broccoli during the last 5 minutes of cooking. Meanwhile, in a small bowl, mix mayonnaise, vinegar, lemon juice, oregano and salt.

2. Drain tortellini and broccoli; gently rinse with cold water. Transfer to a large bowl. Add dressing; toss to coat. Serve over salad greens; sprinkle with bacon.

GARLIC SHRIMP & ORZO SALAD

I enjoy cold pasta salads and rice salads, so I decided to make one with orzo, a rice-shaped pasta. Feel free to add other favorite veggies, like asparagus and green beans, and serve with rolls or pita bread.
—**VALONDA SEWARD** COARSEGOLD, CA

PREP: 25 MIN. + CHILLING • **COOK:** 10 MIN. • **MAKES:** 4 SERVINGS

- 1 pound uncooked large shrimp, peeled and deveined
- ¼ cup olive oil
- 2 garlic cloves, minced
- ¼ teaspoon salt
- ¼ teaspoon pepper
- ¼ cup white wine

SALAD
- ¾ cup uncooked orzo pasta
- 1 medium tomato, seeded and chopped
- 1 small green pepper, chopped
- ½ cup chopped peeled cucumber
- ¼ cup chopped red onion
- 1 tablespoon minced fresh cilantro
- 1 can (2¼ ounces) sliced ripe olives, drained, optional
- 2 tablespoons lemon juice
- 1 tablespoon olive oil
- ¼ teaspoon salt
- ¼ teaspoon pepper

1. In a large bowl, combine the first five ingredients; toss to coat. Refrigerate, covered, up to 30 minutes.
2. Heat a large skillet over medium-high heat. Using a slotted spoon, add shrimp; cook and stir 2 minutes. Add wine; cook and stir 1-2 minutes longer or until shrimp turn pink. Remove to a shallow dish; refrigerate, covered, until cold.
3. Cook orzo according to package directions. Drain; rinse with cold water. Transfer to a large bowl. Add vegetables, cilantro, chilled shrimp and olives if desired. In a small bowl, whisk the remaining ingredients until blended. Drizzle over salad; toss to coat. Refrigerate until serving.

HEARTY BREADED FISH SANDWICHES

Fishing for a burger alternative? Consider it caught. A hint of cayenne is cooled by a creamy yogurt and mayo sauce that will put your local drive-thru to shame.
—**TASTE OF HOME** TEST KITCHEN

START TO FINISH: 30 MIN. • **MAKES:** 4 SERVINGS

- ½ cup dry bread crumbs
- ½ teaspoon garlic powder
- ½ teaspoon cayenne pepper
- ½ teaspoon dried parsley flakes
- 4 cod fillets (6 ounces each)
- 4 whole wheat hamburger buns, split
- ¼ cup plain yogurt
- ¼ cup fat-free mayonnaise
- 2 teaspoons lemon juice
- 2 teaspoons sweet pickle relish
- ¼ teaspoon dried minced onion
- 4 lettuce leaves
- 4 slices tomato
- 4 slices sweet onion

1. In a shallow bowl, combine the bread crumbs, garlic powder, cayenne and parsley. Coat fillets with bread crumb mixture.
2. Moisten a paper towel with cooking oil; using long-handled tongs, lightly coat the grill rack. Grill cod, covered, over medium heat or broil 4 in. from the heat for 4-5 minutes on each side or until fish flakes easily with a fork. Grill buns over medium heat for 30-60 seconds or until toasted.
3. Meanwhile, in a small bowl, combine the yogurt, mayonnaise, lemon juice, relish and minced onion; spread over bun bottoms. Top with cod, lettuce, tomato and onion; replace bun tops.

CARROT SOUP WITH ORANGE & TARRAGON

A pretty orange color, delicious hint of citrus and garden-fresh flavor make this soup a requested dish at my celebrations. Try sprinkling individual bowls with fresh tarragon before serving.

—**PHYLLIS SCHMALZ** KANSAS CITY, KS

PREP: 20 MIN. • **COOK:** 20 MIN. • **MAKES:** 8 SERVINGS (2 QUARTS)

- 2 **pounds fresh carrots, sliced**
- 2 **medium onions, chopped**
- 2 **tablespoons butter**
- 6 **cups reduced-sodium chicken broth**
- 1 **cup orange juice**
- 2 **tablespoons brandy**
- 4 **teaspoons minced fresh tarragon or ½ teaspoon dried tarragon**
- 1 **teaspoon salt**
- 1 **teaspoon pepper**
- 8 **tarragon sprigs**

1. In a Dutch oven, saute carrots and onion in butter for 8-10 minutes or until onion is tender. Add the broth; bring to a boil. Reduce heat; simmer, uncovered, for 10-12 minutes or until carrots are very tender. Cool slightly.

2. In a blender, process soup in batches until smooth. Return all to pan; stir in the orange juice, brandy and minced tarragon. Bring to a boil. Reduce heat; simmer, uncovered, for 5 minutes to allow flavors to blend. Season with salt and pepper. Garnish with tarragon sprigs before serving.

APPLE-GORGONZOLA ENDIVE SALAD

Curly endive is slightly bitter, making it a good match for sweet and crunchy apples. The dressing recipe came from my grandma, so it's extra special.

—**PAT FERJANCSIK** SANTA ROSA, CA

PREP: 20 MIN. + CHILLING • **MAKES:** 10 SERVINGS

- 1¼ **cups heavy whipping cream**
- ⅔ **cup red wine vinegar**
- 1 **teaspoon salt**
- 1 **teaspoon pepper**
- 5 **medium red apples, thinly sliced (about 5 cups)**
- 2 **cups (8 ounces) crumbled Gorgonzola cheese**
- 10 **cups torn curly endive**

In a large bowl, whisk cream, vinegar, salt and pepper until blended. Stir in apples and cheese. Refrigerate, covered, at least 1 hour. Serve apple mixture over endive.

REMOVE APPLE SEEDS IN A FLASH

Once you've cut a fresh apple in half to use in a recipe, use the small end of a melon baller to easily scoop out the core.

—**HELEN N.** SUN CITY CENTER, FL

ZESTY CHICKEN TORTELLINI SOUP

I love knowing I can warm up this soup when I get home. Don't hesitate to toss in any veggies you happen to have on hand.
—**NANCY LATULIPPE** SIMCOE, ON

PREP: 40 MIN. • **COOK:** 10 MIN. + FREEZING
MAKES: 6 SERVINGS (2½ QUARTS)

- 4 **cups reduced-sodium chicken broth**
- 4 **cups reduced-sodium beef broth**
- 6 **boneless skinless chicken thighs (about 1½ pounds)**
- 4 **medium carrots, sliced**
- 2 **celery ribs, sliced**
- 1 **small onion, chopped**
- 1 **envelope reduced-sodium onion soup mix**
- 1½ **teaspoons dried parsley flakes**
- ½ **teaspoon garlic powder**
- ½ **teaspoon crushed red pepper flakes**
- ½ **teaspoon poultry seasoning**
- ½ **teaspoon pepper**
- 2½ **cups frozen cheese tortellini**

1. In a Dutch oven, bring chicken broth and beef broth to a boil; reduce heat. Add chicken and poach, uncovered, for 25-30 minutes or until a thermometer reads 170°. Remove chicken; cool slightly.

2. Add the carrots, celery, onion, soup mix, parsley and seasonings to broth. Bring to a boil. Reduce heat; cover and simmer for 10-15 minutes or until vegetables are tender.

3. Cool soup. Meanwhile, chop chicken. Add tortellini and chicken to soup. Transfer to freezer containers; freeze for up to 3 months.

TO USE FROZEN SOUP *Thaw in the refrigerator overnight. Place in a saucepan; bring to a boil. Reduce heat; cook, uncovered, for 5-10 minutes or until heated through and tortellini are tender.*

PESTO-DIJON EGG SALAD SANDWICHES

Turn your standby egg salad into your new lunch favorite. Honey Dijon mustard and pesto add a sensational spin, and crisp veggies give it crunch.
—**CARRIE KENNEY** BATAVIA, OH

START TO FINISH: 20 MIN. • **MAKES:** 4 SERVINGS

- ½ **cup mayonnaise**
- ¼ **cup finely chopped celery**
- ¼ **cup finely chopped red onion**
- 2 **tablespoons honey Dijon mustard**
- 4 **teaspoons prepared pesto**
- 1 **garlic clove, minced**
- ½ **teaspoon salt**
- ¼ **teaspoon pepper**
- 8 **hard-cooked eggs, chopped**
- 8 **slices whole wheat bread, toasted**
- 4 **romaine leaves**
- 4 **slices tomato or ½ cup roasted sweet red peppers, cut into strips**

Combine the first eight ingredients in a small bowl. Gently stir in eggs. Spread over four toast slices; top with lettuce, tomato and remaining toast.

TRIPLE PEPPER STEAK SANDWICHES

This is a good way to use leftover grilled steak or chicken. Plus, the chipotle cream sauce can be made up to 3 days in advance.

—**ROBERT TAYLOR** SHAWNEE, KS

PREP: 40 MIN. • **COOK:** 5 MIN/BATCH • **MAKES:** 4 SERVINGS

- 2 boneless beef top loin steaks (1 inch thick and 8 ounces each)
- ¼ teaspoon salt
- ⅛ teaspoon pepper
- 1 large sweet onion, thinly sliced
- 1 cup sliced fresh mushrooms
- 1 poblano pepper, thinly sliced
- 2 tablespoons plus 2 teaspoons butter, divided
- 2 tablespoons chopped onion
- 1 garlic clove, minced
- ½ cup heavy whipping cream
- 1 chipotle pepper in adobo sauce, minced
- ½ teaspoon ground cumin
- ¼ teaspoon chicken bouillon granules
- 1 loaf (14 ounces) ciabatta bread
- 4 slices pepper jack cheese

1. Sprinkle the steaks with salt and pepper. Grill, covered, over medium heat or broil 3-4 in. from the heat for 7-9 minutes on each side or until meat reaches desired doneness (for medium-rare, a thermometer should read 145°; medium, 160°; well-done, 170°). Let stand for 5 minutes before slicing.

2. Meanwhile, in a large skillet, saute sliced onion, mushrooms and poblano pepper in 2 tablespoons butter until tender. Remove from the heat; stir in sliced steak.

3. In a small saucepan, saute chopped onion in remaining butter until tender. Add garlic; cook 1 minute longer. Stir in the cream, chipotle, cumin and bouillon; cook and stir until thickened.

4. Cut ciabatta in half horizontally, then cut into four equal portions. Place cheese on bottom bread slices; top with steak mixture, chipotle cream sauce and remaining bread. Cook on a panini maker or indoor grill for 3-4 minutes or until bread is browned and cheese is melted.

NOTE *Wear disposable gloves when cutting hot peppers; the oils can burn skin. Avoid touching your face.*

VEGETABLE MEATBALL SOUP

You can have this tasty soup on the table in less than 30 minutes. If you have leftover meatballs from a previous meal, toss 'em in.

—**SUSAN WESTERFIELD** ALBUQUERQUE, NM

START TO FINISH: 25 MIN. • **MAKES:** 6 SERVINGS (2 QUARTS)

- 1 package (12 ounces) frozen fully cooked Italian meatballs
- 2 cans (14½ ounces each) beef broth
- 2 cups frozen Italian vegetable blend
- 1 can (14½ ounces) Italian diced tomatoes, undrained
- 1½ cups water
- ⅓ cup small pasta shells
  Shredded Parmesan cheese, optional

In a Dutch oven, combine the meatballs, broth, vegetable blend, tomatoes, water and pasta. Bring to a boil. Reduce heat; simmer, uncovered, for 10-12 minutes or until pasta is tender. Garnish servings with cheese if desired.

SUN-DRIED TOMATO TURKEY BURGERS

This recipe always brings back warm memories of my mom's homemade sun-dried tomatoes in the summer. I've prepared it with both ground beef and ground turkey over time. Either way, it's fast and tastes great!

—**SAMMY STAAB** PENSACOLA, FL

START TO FINISH: 25 MIN. • **MAKES:** 6 SERVINGS

- 1 **large red onion**
- 1 **cup (4 ounces) crumbled feta cheese, divided**
- ⅔ **cup chopped oil-packed sun-dried tomatoes**
- ¼ **teaspoon salt**
- ¼ **teaspoon pepper**
- 2 **pounds lean ground turkey**
- 6 **ciabatta rolls, split**

1. Cut onion in half. Finely chop one half and thinly slice the remaining half. Combine ½ cup feta, sun-dried tomatoes, chopped onion, salt and pepper in a large bowl. Crumble turkey over mixture and mix well. Shape into six patties.

2. Grill burgers, covered, over medium heat or broil 4 in. from the heat for 5-7 minutes on each side or until a thermometer reads 165° and juices run clear.

3. Meanwhile, saute sliced onion in a small nonstick skillet coated with cooking spray until tender. Serve burgers on buns with onion and remaining feta.

FARMER'S MARKET CORN SALAD

I love fresh corn right off the cob (especially grilled), so I am always looking for innovative ways to serve it. This recipe takes the corn right off the cob and combines it with fresh basil.

—**CINDIE HARAS** JUPITER, FL

PREP: 25 MIN. • **COOK:** 10 MIN. • **MAKES:** 6 SERVINGS

- 6 **medium ears sweet corn**
- 3 **tablespoons butter, melted**
- ½ **cup chopped cucumber**
- ½ **cup fresh or frozen shelled edamame, thawed**
- ½ **cup julienned radishes**
- ¼ **cup fresh basil leaves, thinly sliced**

DRESSING
- ¼ **cup olive oil**
- 3 **tablespoons sherry vinegar**
- 1 **tablespoon white balsamic vinegar**
- ½ **teaspoon salt**
  Dash pepper

1. Brush corn with butter. Grill corn, covered, over medium heat for 10-12 minutes or until lightly browned, turning and basting occasionally.

2. Cut corn from cobs; transfer to a large bowl. Add vegetables and basil. In a small bowl, whisk dressing ingredients. Pour over vegetables; toss to coat.

HEARTY BUTTERNUT SQUASH SOUP

The squash, meat, beans and veggies in a bowl of this soup makes it my go-to fall recipe. It's full of freshness.

—**JAYE BEELER** GRAND RAPIDS, MI

PREP: 20 MIN. • **COOK:** 40 MIN. • **MAKES:** 12 SERVINGS (4½ QUARTS)

- 1 pound bulk Italian sausage
- 1 medium onion, chopped
- 1 medium sweet red pepper, chopped
- 4 garlic cloves, minced
- 1 large butternut squash (about 5 pounds), peeled, seeded and cut into 1-inch pieces
- 1 package (16 ounces) frozen corn, divided
- 4 cups water
- 1 tablespoon chicken base
- 2 cans (15½ ounces each) great northern beans, rinsed and drained
- 2 cans (14½ ounces each) fire-roasted diced tomatoes, undrained
- 1 teaspoon salt
- ¼ teaspoon pepper
  Heavy whipping cream and minced fresh parsley, optional

1. In a stockpot, cook sausage, onion and red pepper over medium heat 9-11 minutes or until sausage is no longer pink and onion is tender, breaking up sausage into crumbles. Add garlic; cook 1 minute longer. Remove with a slotted spoon; discard drippings.

2. Add squash, 1½ cups corn, water and chicken base to same pan; bring to a boil. Reduce heat; simmer, covered, 15-20 minutes or until squash is tender.

3. Remove soup from heat; cool slightly. Process in batches in a blender until smooth. Return to pot. Add beans, tomatoes, salt, pepper, sausage mixture and remaining corn; heat through. If desired, drizzle servings with cream and sprinkle with parsley.

FREEZE OPTION *Freeze cooled soup in freezer containers. To use, partially thaw in refrigerator overnight. Heat through in a saucepan, stirring occasionally and adding a little water if necessary.*

NEBRASKA'S STUFFED BEEF SANDWICHES

When I moved to Nebraska, a friend introduced me to this German-Russian beef sandwich, and it quickly became a most-requested meal at my home.

—DOLLY CROGHAN MEAD, NE

PREP: 35 MIN. + RISING • **BAKE:** 20 MIN. • **MAKES:** 12 SERVINGS

- 4½ cups all-purpose flour, divided
- ¼ cup sugar
- 2 packages (¼ ounce each) active dry yeast
- 1 teaspoon salt
- ¾ cup milk
- ½ cup water
- ½ cup shortening
- 2 eggs

FILLING

- 2 pounds lean ground beef (90% lean)
- 2 medium onions, chopped
- 4 cups chopped cabbage
- 2 teaspoons seasoned salt
- 1 teaspoon garlic powder
- 1 teaspoon pepper

1. Place 1¾ cups flour, sugar, yeast and salt in a large bowl. Heat the milk, water and shortening to 120°-130°. Pour over flour mixture; add the eggs. Beat with an electric mixer on low speed until blended. Beat 3 additional minutes on high. Stir in the remaining flour; knead until smooth and elastic, about 6-8 minutes.

2. Place dough in a greased bowl; cover and let rise in a warm place until doubled, about 1 hour.

3. Meanwhile, in a large skillet, cook beef and onions over medium heat until meat is no longer pink; drain. Add the cabbage, seasoned salt, garlic powder and pepper; cook until cabbage is wilted.

4. Punch the dough down; divide into 12 portions and cover with plastic wrap. Working with one piece at a time, roll into a 6-in. square. Place ¾ cup of the meat mixture in the center of each square. Fold the dough over filling, forming a rectangle. Pinch edges tightly to seal and place on greased baking sheets.

5. Bake at 350° for 18-20 minutes or until golden brown. Serve hot.

BEEF BARLEY SOUP WITH ROASTED VEGETABLES

The beauty of this soup is I can roast the vegetables separately in the oven while it simmers on the stovetop. Then I simply add the veggies during the last minutes of cooking.

—GAYLA SCOTT WEST JEFFERSON, NC

PREP: 25 MIN. • **COOK:** 1 HOUR • **MAKES:** 8 SERVINGS (3 QUARTS)

- ¼ cup all-purpose flour
- 1 teaspoon salt
- ½ teaspoon pepper
- 1 pound beef stew meat (¾-inch cubes)
- 5 tablespoons olive oil, divided
- 1 large portobello mushroom, stem removed, chopped
- 1 medium onion, chopped
- 1 fennel bulb, chopped
- 1 garlic clove, minced
- 8 cups beef stock
- 2 cups water
- 2 cups cubed peeled butternut squash
- 1 large baking potato, peeled and cubed
- 2 large carrots, cut into ½-inch slices
- ⅔ cup quick-cooking barley
- 2 teaspoons minced fresh thyme
  Dash ground nutmeg
- ¼ cup minced fresh parsley

1. In a small bowl, mix the flour, salt and pepper; sprinkle over beef and toss to coat. In a Dutch oven, heat 2 tablespoons oil over medium heat. Add beef; brown evenly. Remove from the pan.

2. In the same pan, heat 1 tablespoon oil over medium-high heat. Add the mushroom, onion and fennel; cook and stir for 4-5 minutes or until tender. Stir in garlic; cook 1 minute longer. Add stock and water, stirring to loosen browned bits from pan. Return beef to pan. Bring to a boil; reduce heat. Cover and simmer for 40-60 minutes or until meat is tender.

3. Meanwhile, place the squash, potato and carrots on a greased 15x10x1-in. baking pan; drizzle with remaining oil and toss to coat. Bake at 425° for 20-25 minutes or until vegetables are almost tender, stirring twice.

4. Add the barley, thyme, nutmeg and roasted vegetables to soup; return to a boil. Reduce heat; cover and simmer for 10-12 minutes or until barley is tender. Sprinkle with the parsley.

TURKEY SLOPPY JOES WITH AVOCADO SLAW

Sloppy joes are a suppertime staple, but my friends always say this avocado slaw makes them seem brand new. The creamy slaw is wonderful with the tangy sandwich filling. Try them; you'll agree!

—JACYN SIEBERT WALNUT CREEK, CA

PREP: 15 MIN. • **COOK:** 20 MIN. • **MAKES:** 6 SERVINGS

- 1 pound ground turkey
- 1 medium onion, chopped
- 1 envelope sloppy joe mix
- 1 can (6 ounces) tomato paste
- 1¼ cups water

SLAW

- 1 medium ripe avocado, peeled and cubed
- 1 tablespoon olive oil
- 2 teaspoons lemon juice
- ½ teaspoon ground cumin
- ¼ teaspoon salt
- ¼ teaspoon pepper
- 2½ cups coleslaw mix
- 6 hamburger buns, split

1. In a large skillet, cook turkey and onion over medium heat 7-8 minutes or until turkey is no longer pink and onion is tender, breaking up turkey into crumbles; drain.

2. Stir in sloppy joe mix, tomato paste and water. Bring to a boil. Reduce heat; simmer, uncovered, 8-10 minutes or until thickened, stirring occasionally.

3. Meanwhile, place avocado, oil, lemon juice, cumin, salt and pepper in a blender; cover and process until smooth. Transfer to a small bowl; stir in coleslaw mix. Spoon meat mixture onto bun bottoms and top with slaw. Replace tops.

GARDEN QUINOA SALAD

Healthy and amazing, what's not to like about this salad? Serve it hot or cold, and enjoy the leftovers while they're still fresh!

—PATRICIA NIEH PORTOLA VALLEY, CA

START TO FINISH: 30 MIN. • **MAKES:** 4 SERVINGS

- 1½ cups quinoa, rinsed and well drained
- 3 cups water
- 1 pound fresh asparagus, cut into 2-inch pieces
- ½ pound fresh sugar snap peas
- ½ pound fresh green beans, trimmed
- 2 tablespoons olive oil
- 2 tablespoons lemon juice
- 2 tablespoons minced fresh parsley
- 1 teaspoon grated lemon peel
- ¾ teaspoon salt
- 1 cup cherry tomatoes, halved
- 3 tablespoons salted pumpkin seeds or pepitas

1. In a large saucepan, cook and stir quinoa over medium-high heat 3-5 minutes or until toasted. Add water; bring to a boil. Reduce heat; simmer, covered, 12-15 minutes or until liquid is absorbed. Transfer to a large bowl.

2. Meanwhile, in a large saucepan, bring 4 cups water to a boil. Add asparagus and snap peas; cook, uncovered, 2-4 minutes or just until crisp-tender. Remove vegetables and immediately drop into ice water.

3. Return water to a boil. Add the green beans; cook for 3-4 minutes or until crisp-tender. Remove beans and drop into ice water. Drain vegetables; pat dry.

4. In a small bowl, whisk oil, lemon juice, parsley, lemon peel and salt. Add tomatoes and blanched vegetables to quinoa; drizzle with dressing and toss to combine. Top with pumpkin seeds.

GRILLED GOAT CHEESE & ARUGULA SANDWICHES

To create a more grown-up grilled cheese sandwich, I threw in appetizing goat cheese and peppery arugula. I enjoy a similar combination on pizza, and it works here, too.
—**JESS APFE** BERKELEY, CA

START TO FINISH: 30 MIN. • **MAKES:** 4 SERVINGS

- ½ cup sun-dried tomato pesto
- 8 slices sourdough bread
- 1½ cups roasted sweet red peppers, drained and patted dry
- 8 slices part-skim mozzarella cheese
- ½ cup crumbled goat cheese
- 1 cup fresh arugula
- ¼ cup butter, softened

1. Spread pesto over four slices of bread. Layer with peppers, mozzarella cheese, goat cheese and arugula; top with the remaining bread. Spread outsides of sandwiches with butter.

2. In a large skillet, toast sandwiches over medium heat 3-4 minutes on each side or until golden brown and cheese is melted.

CREAMY DILLED CUCUMBER SALAD

This crunchy, savory side dish, a Norwegian favorite, was a staple at all of our family gatherings. It's perfect for when you want a change-of-pace salad.
—**PATTY LANOUE STEARNS** TRAVERSE CITY, MI

PREP: 20 MIN. + CHILLING • **MAKES:** 6 SERVINGS

- 2 English cucumbers, thinly sliced
- 1 teaspoon salt
- 1½ cups (12 ounces) sour cream
- ¼ cup thinly sliced red onion
- ¼ cup snipped fresh dill
- 2 tablespoons white wine vinegar
- 2 garlic cloves, minced
- 1 teaspoon sugar
- 1 teaspoon coarsely ground pepper

1. Place cucumbers in a colander over a bowl; sprinkle with salt and toss. Let stand 15 minutes. Squeeze and blot dry with paper towels.

2. In a large bowl, combine the remaining ingredients; stir in cucumbers. Refrigerate, covered, at least 1 hour.

HEARTY PUMPKIN CHILI WITH POLENTA

If you want, make this healthy chili a day ahead. It reheats nicely, and the polenta stays good in the fridge for a few days, but make sure you keep it in an airtight container.

—**WENDY RUSCH** TREGO, WI

PREP: 30 MIN. • **COOK:** 45 MIN. • **MAKES:** 6 SERVINGS

- 1 pound ground beef
- 2 celery ribs, finely chopped
- 1 medium onion, finely chopped
- 1 small sweet red pepper, finely chopped
- 2 garlic cloves, minced
- 1 can (29 ounces) tomato sauce
- 1 can (15 ounces) crushed tomatoes
- 1 can (15 ounces) solid-pack pumpkin
- 1 tablespoon plus 2 teaspoons sugar, divided
- 1 tablespoon chili powder
- 1½ teaspoons pumpkin pie spice
- ½ teaspoon plus ¾ teaspoon salt, divided
- ½ teaspoon pepper
- 1½ cups 2% milk
- ½ cup heavy whipping cream
- ¼ cup butter, cubed
- ¾ cup yellow cornmeal
- 1 can (15 ounces) black beans, rinsed and drained

1. In a Dutch oven, cook the first five ingredients over medium heat 8-10 minutes or until beef is no longer pink and vegetables are tender, breaking up beef into crumbles; drain.

2. Stir in tomato sauce, tomatoes, pumpkin, 1 tablespoon sugar, chili powder, pie spice, ½ teaspoon salt and pepper; bring to a boil. Reduce heat; simmer, uncovered, 45 minutes, stirring occasionally.

3. Meanwhile, in a large heavy saucepan, bring milk, cream, butter and remaining sugar and salt to a boil. Reduce heat to a gentle boil; slowly whisk in cornmeal. Cook and stir with a wooden spoon 2-3 minutes or until polenta is thickened and pulls away cleanly from sides of pan (mixture will be very thick).

4. Pour into a greased 9-in.-square baking pan. Let stand until firm, about 30 minutes.

5. Stir beans into chili; heat through. Cut polenta into six pieces. Serve with chili.

WINTER COUNTRY SOUP

My soup will warm your family up on the chilliest nights. Featuring smoked sausage, beans and other vegetables, it's a hearty way to start a meal, or let it be a satisfying lunch all by itself.

—**JEANNETTE SABO** LEXINGTON PARK, MD

PREP: 15 MIN. • **COOK:** 40 MIN. • **MAKES:** 12 SERVINGS (3 QUARTS)

- 1 package (14 ounces) smoked sausage, cut into ¼-inch slices
- 1 large sweet red pepper, cut into ½-inch pieces
- 8 shallots, chopped
- 1 tablespoon butter
- 8 cups chopped fresh kale
- 8 cups vegetable broth
- 3 cups frozen corn
- 1 can (15½ ounces) great northern beans, rinsed and drained
- ½ teaspoon cayenne pepper
- ¼ teaspoon pepper
- ¾ cup uncooked orzo pasta

1. In a Dutch oven, saute the sausage, red pepper and shallots in butter until vegetables are tender.

2. Add kale; cover and cook for 2-3 minutes or until kale is wilted. Stir in the broth, corn, beans, cayenne and pepper. Bring to a boil. Reduce heat; simmer, uncovered, for 20 minutes. Return to a boil. Stir in orzo. Cook for 8-10 minutes longer or until pasta is tender.

CHILI-RUBBED STEAK & BREAD SALAD

We love skirt steak in our house. To make it into a meal, I created a ranch-inspired bread salad.

—DEVON DELANEY WESTPORT, CT

PREP: 35 MIN. + STANDING • **GRILL:** 15 MIN. • **MAKES:** 6 SERVINGS

- 2 **teaspoons chili powder**
- 2 **teaspoons brown sugar**
- ½ **teaspoon salt**
- ½ **teaspoon pepper**
- 1 **beef top sirloin steak (1 inch thick and 1¼ pounds)**
- 2 **cups cubed multigrain bread**
- 2 **tablespoons olive oil**
- 1 **cup ranch salad dressing**
- 2 **tablespoons finely grated horseradish**
- 1 **tablespoon prepared mustard**
- 3 **large tomatoes, cut into 1-inch pieces**
- 1 **medium cucumber, cut into 1-inch pieces**
- 1 **small red onion, halved and thinly sliced**

1. Mix chili powder, brown sugar, salt and pepper; rub over steak. Let stand for 15 minutes.

2. Meanwhile, toss bread cubes with oil. In a large skillet, toast bread over medium heat 8-10 minutes or until crisp and lightly browned, stirring frequently. In a small bowl, whisk salad dressing, horseradish and mustard.

3. Grill steak, covered, over medium heat or broil 4 in. from heat 6-8 minutes on each side or until meat reaches desired doneness (for medium-rare, a thermometer should read 145°; medium, 160°; well-done, 170°). Let stand 5 minutes.

4. In a large bowl, combine tomatoes, cucumber, onion and toasted bread. Add ½ cup dressing mixture; toss to coat. Slice steak; serve with salad and remaining dressing.

GARLICKY CHEDDAR CHEESE BISQUE

I came up with a cheddar cheese soup a while ago and decided to give it a boost with a variety of root vegetables. Crushed pita chips and fresh parsley make fun garnishes.

—PATRICIA HARMON BADEN, PA

PREP: 30 MIN. • **COOK:** 40 MIN. • **MAKES:** 6 SERVINGS

- 1 **tablespoon butter**
- 1 **tablespoon canola oil**
- 1 **medium leek (white portion only), sliced**
- ½ **cup chopped carrot**
- ½ **cup chopped celery**
- ½ **cup chopped peeled parsnip**
- 1 **teaspoon salt**
- ½ **teaspoon pepper**
- 6 **garlic cloves, minced**
- 2 **cans (14½ ounces each) chicken broth**
- ⅔ **cup dry white wine**
- 2 **tablespoons cornstarch**
- ¼ **cup cold water**
- 1 **can (12 ounces) evaporated milk**
- 2 **cups (8 ounces) shredded sharp white cheddar cheese**
  Crushed baked pita chips
  Minced fresh parsley

1. In a large saucepan, heat butter and oil over medium heat. Add vegetables, salt and pepper; cook and stir 7-8 minutes or until vegetables are crisp-tender. Add the garlic; cook 1-2 minutes longer.

2. Stir in broth and wine; bring to a boil. Reduce heat; simmer, uncovered, 15-20 minutes or until vegetables are tender. Remove from heat; cool slightly. Meanwhile, in a small bowl, mix cornstarch and water until smooth.

3. Process soup in batches in a food processor until smooth. Return all to pan. Stir in evaporated milk and cornstarch mixture; bring to a boil. Reduce heat; simmer, uncovered, until thickened and bubbly, stirring frequently. Add cheese; cook and stir until cheese is blended. Top servings with crushed pita chips and parsley.

CHICKEN SALAD PARTY SANDWICHES

My famous chicken salad arrives at the party chilled in a plastic container. When it's eventually time to set out the food, I stir in the pecans and assemble the sandwiches. They're great for buffet-style potlucks.

—**TRISHA KRUSE** EAGLE, ID

START TO FINISH: 20 MIN. • **MAKES:** 15 SERVINGS

- 4 **cups cubed cooked chicken breast**
- 1½ **cups dried cranberries**
- 2 **celery ribs, finely chopped**
- 2 **green onions, thinly sliced**
- ¼ **cup chopped sweet pickles**
- 1 **cup fat-free mayonnaise**
- ½ **teaspoon curry powder**
- ¼ **teaspoon coarsely ground pepper**
- ½ **cup chopped pecans, toasted**
- 15 **whole wheat dinner rolls**
  Torn leaf lettuce
  Frilled toothpicks, optional

1. In a large bowl, combine the first five ingredients. In a small bowl, combine the mayonnaise, curry and pepper. Add to chicken mixture; toss to coat. Chill until serving.
2. Stir pecans into chicken salad. Serve on rolls lined with lettuce. Secure with toothpicks if desired.

ALL-SPICED UP RASPBERRY AND MUSHROOM SALAD

Here's a refreshing salad for summertime or really any time. Make a unique homemade vinaigrette with just raspberry vinegar, olive oil, jalapeno jelly and allspice.

—**ROXANNE CHAN** ALBANY, CA

START TO FINISH: 30 MIN. • **MAKES:** 4 SERVINGS

- 2 **tablespoons raspberry vinegar**
- 2 **tablespoons olive oil, divided**
- 1 **tablespoon red jalapeno pepper jelly**
- ¼ **teaspoon ground allspice**
- 1 **pound small fresh mushrooms, halved**
- 4 **cups spring mix salad greens**
- 1 **cup fresh raspberries**
- 2 **tablespoons chopped red onion**
- 2 **tablespoons minced fresh mint**
- 2 **tablespoons sliced almonds, toasted**
- ¼ **cup crumbled goat cheese**

1. In a small bowl, whisk vinegar, 1 tablespoon oil, pepper jelly and allspice until blended. In a large skillet, heat remaining oil over medium-high heat. Add mushrooms; cook and stir until tender; cool slightly.
2. In a large bowl, combine salad greens, raspberries, onion, mint and almonds. Just before serving, add mushrooms and vinaigrette; toss to combine. Top with cheese.
NOTE *To toast nuts, spread in a 15x10x1-in. baking pan. Bake at 350° for 5-10 minutes or until lightly browned, stirring occasionally. Or, spread in a dry nonstick skillet and heat over low heat until lightly browned, stirring occasionally.*

Main Dishes

Whether you're craving saucy ribs, cheesy pasta, comforting meat loaf, festive ham or something else, find just the recipe you're looking for here. Your home crowd will love these, so be prepared to serve seconds!

RICH CHICKEN ALFREDO PIZZA

After a busy day, settle in for a family-pleasing meal of homemade pizza. With a prebaked crust and simple Alfredo sauce, it's easy and appetizing all at the same time.

—**TAMMY HANKS** GAINSVILLE, FL

PREP: 30 MIN. • **BAKE:** 15 MIN.
MAKES: 1 PIZZA (8 MAIN DISH SERVINGS OR 12 APPETIZER SLICES)

- 2½ teaspoons butter
- 1 garlic clove, minced
- 1½ cups heavy whipping cream
- 3 tablespoons grated Parmesan cheese
- ½ teaspoon salt
- ¼ teaspoon pepper
- 1 tablespoon minced fresh parsley
- 1 prebaked 12-inch thin pizza crust
- 1 cup cubed cooked chicken breast
- 1 cup thinly sliced baby portobello mushrooms
- 1 cup fresh baby spinach
- 2 cups (8 ounces) shredded part-skim mozzarella cheese

1. In a small saucepan over medium heat, melt butter. Add garlic; cook and stir for 1 minute. Add cream; cook until liquid is reduced by half, about 15-20 minutes. Add the Parmesan cheese, salt and pepper; cook and stir until thickened. Remove from the heat; stir in parsley. Cool slightly.

2. Place crust on an ungreased baking sheet; spread with cream mixture. Top with chicken, mushrooms, spinach and mozzarella cheese. Bake at 450° for 15-20 minutes or until cheese is melted and crust is golden brown.

ANDOUILLE-STUFFED PEPPERS

I was inspired by the important role of green peppers in Cajun dishes when I created my spiced-up recipe. For a healthier take, substitute chicken sausage or cubed cooked chicken breast for the andouille.

—**SARAH LARSON** CARLSBAD, CA

PREP: 40 MIN. • **BAKE:** 40 MIN. • **MAKES:** 4 SERVINGS

- 1 package (8 ounces) jambalaya mix
- 4 small green peppers
- ¾ pound fully cooked andouille sausage links, chopped
- 1 jalapeno pepper, seeded and minced
- 1 can (16 ounces) tomato juice
  Louisiana-style hot sauce, optional

1. Prepare jambalaya mix according to package directions. Meanwhile, cut peppers lengthwise in half; remove seeds.

2. In a large skillet, cook and stir sausage over medium-high heat until browned. Add jalapeno; cook 1 minute longer.

3. Stir sausage mixture into prepared jambalaya. Spoon into pepper halves. Place in a greased 13x9-in. baking dish; pour tomato juice over and around peppers.

4. Bake, uncovered, at 350° for 40-45 minutes or until peppers are tender. Serve with hot sauce if desired.

NOTE *Wear disposable gloves when cutting hot peppers; the oils can burn skin. Avoid touching your face.*

GRILLED STEAKS WITH CILANTRO SAUCE

Fresh herbs made into a zesty sauce transform these steaks into a grilling star.

—**LYNNE KEAST** MONTE SERENO, CA

PREP: 25 MIN. • **GRILL:** 15 MIN.
MAKES: 8 SERVINGS (3 CUPS SAUCE)

- 2 **cups fresh parsley leaves**
- 2 **cups fresh cilantro leaves**
- 1 **cup fresh mint leaves**
- 8 **garlic cloves, chopped**
- 1¾ **teaspoons kosher salt, divided**
- ½ **teaspoon plus ¾ teaspoon freshly ground pepper, divided**
- 2 **cups olive oil**
- ⅔ **cup red wine vinegar**
- 2 **tablespoons lemon juice**
- ½ **teaspoon crushed red pepper flakes**
- 4 **pounds beef flat iron steaks or top sirloin steaks (1 inch thick)**

1. Place herbs, garlic, 1 teaspoon salt and ½ teaspoon pepper in a food processor; pulse until herbs are chopped. Gradually add oil, vinegar, lemon juice and pepper flakes, processing just until blended.

2. Sprinkle the steaks with remaining salt and pepper. Grill, covered, over medium heat or broil 4 in. from heat 6-8 minutes on each side or until meat reaches desired doneness (for medium-rare, a thermometer should read 145°; medium, 160°; well-done, 170°). Cut steaks into ¼-in. slices; serve with sauce.

EASY CHEDDAR CHICKEN POTPIE

My kids love chicken potpie, and I really like that this is so quick to put together with frozen veggies and store-bought gravy. To make it even less complicated, I decided to top it with a biscuit crust instead of homemade pastry.

—**LINDA DREES** PALESTINE, TX

PREP: 20 MIN. • **BAKE:** 25 MIN. • **MAKES:** 6 SERVINGS

- 1 **package (16 ounces) frozen vegetables for stew, thawed and coarsely chopped**
- 1 **jar (12 ounces) chicken gravy**
- 2 **cups (8 ounces) shredded cheddar cheese**
- 2 **cups cubed cooked chicken**
- 1 **cup biscuit/baking mix**
- ¼ **teaspoon dried thyme**
- 2 **eggs**
- ¼ **cup 2% milk**

1. Combine vegetables and gravy in a large saucepan. Bring to a boil. Reduce heat; stir in cheese and chicken. Cook and stir until cheese is melted. Pour into a greased 11x7-in. baking dish.

2. Combine biscuit mix and thyme in a small bowl. In another bowl, whisk eggs and milk; stir into dry ingredients just until moistened. Drop by tablespoonfuls over chicken mixture; spread gently.

3. Bake, uncovered, at 375° for 23-27 minutes or until golden brown. Let stand for 5 minutes before serving.

ALL-AMERICAN MEAT LOAF

There are many variations on meat loaf, but my family loves it when I serve this classic stick-to-your-ribs version.

—MARGIE WILLIAMS MT. JULIET, TN

PREP: 30 MIN. • **BAKE:** 50 MIN. + STANDING
MAKES: 2 LOAVES (8 SERVINGS EACH)

- 1 large green pepper, chopped
- 1 large onion, chopped
- 2 teaspoons olive oil
- 4 garlic cloves, minced
- 2 eggs, lightly beaten
- 1 cup 2% milk
- 6 slices bread, cubed
- 1½ cups (6 ounces) shredded cheddar cheese
- 2¼ teaspoons dried rosemary, crushed
- 2 teaspoons salt
- 1 teaspoon pepper
- 2 pounds lean ground beef (90% lean)
- 1 pound ground pork
- 1½ cups ketchup
- ¼ cup packed brown sugar
- 2 teaspoons cider vinegar

1. Saute green pepper and onion in oil in a large skillet until tender. Add garlic; cook 1 minute longer. Transfer to a large bowl; cool to room temperature.
2. Preheat the oven to 350°. Add eggs, milk, bread, cheese, rosemary, salt and pepper to sauteed vegetables. Crumble beef and pork over mixture and mix well.
3. Pat into two greased 9x5-in. loaf pans. Combine ketchup, brown sugar and vinegar in a small bowl. Spread over tops.
4. Bake, uncovered, 50-55 minutes or until no pink remains and a thermometer reads 160°. Let stand for 10 minutes before slicing.

TURKEY TORTELLINI TOSS

I had frozen tortellini on hand and didn't have a clue what I was going to make. After scanning my cupboards and refrigerator, this tasty recipe was created.

—LEO PARR NEW ORLEANS, LA

START TO FINISH: 30 MIN. • **MAKES:** 4 SERVINGS

- 2 cups frozen cheese tortellini (about 8 ounces)
- 1 pound ground turkey
- 2 medium zucchini, halved lengthwise and sliced
- 2 garlic cloves, minced
- 1½ cups cherry tomatoes, halved
- 1 teaspoon dried oregano
- ½ teaspoon salt
- ¼ teaspoon crushed red pepper flakes
- 1 cup shredded Asiago cheese, divided
- 1 tablespoon olive oil

1. Cook tortellini according to package directions.
2. Meanwhile, in a large skillet, cook turkey, zucchini and garlic over medium heat 7-9 minutes or until turkey is no longer pink, breaking up turkey into crumbles; drain. Add tomatoes, oregano, salt and pepper flakes; cook 2 minutes longer. Stir in ¾ cup cheese.
3. Drain tortellini; add to skillet and toss to combine. Drizzle with oil; sprinkle with remaining cheese.

APRICOT-GINGERSNAP HAM

I've been told my ham is as much a feast for the eyes as it is for the taste buds. The apricot, brown sugar and gingersnaps all together brings out the best in the dish.

—MELANIE WOODEN RENO, NV

PREP: 20 MIN. • **BAKE:** 2 HOURS
MAKES: 15 SERVINGS (3½ CUPS SAUCE)

- 1 spiral-sliced fully cooked bone-in ham (7 to 9 pounds)
- 1½ cups apricot preserves
- ½ cup packed brown sugar
- ⅓ cup Dijon mustard
- 1½ cups crushed gingersnap cookies (about 30 cookies)
- 3 cups chicken broth
- ½ teaspoon salt
- ¼ teaspoon pepper
- 3 tablespoons cornstarch
- ½ cup cold water

1. Line a shallow roasting pan with heavy-duty foil. Place ham on a rack in prepared pan. Cover and bake at 325° for 1½ hours.

2. Combine the preserves, brown sugar and mustard, reserving ¼ cup of mixture for sauce. Spread over ham. Press cookie crumbs onto ham.

3. Bake, uncovered, 30-45 minutes longer or until a thermometer reads 140°. Remove meat to a serving platter and keep warm, reserving ⅓ cup drippings.

4. Combine the broth, salt, pepper, reserved ham drippings and reserved apricot mixture in a small saucepan. Combine cornstarch and water until smooth. Stir into saucepan. Bring to a boil; cook and stir for 2 minutes or until thickened. Serve with ham.

PACK IN BROWN SUGAR

Taste of Home recipes specifically call for packed brown sugar in the ingredients because the moisture in brown sugar traps unneeded air between the crystals.

OVEN-BARBECUED SALMON

When the South Carolina heat drove me indoors and away from my grill, I changed my favorite over-the-coals recipe to be baked in the oven. It's equally good either way!
—**MANDY RIVERS** LEXINGTON, SC

START TO FINISH: 25 MIN. • **MAKES:** 5 SERVINGS

- 5 **salmon fillets (6 ounces each)**
- 3 **tablespoons orange juice**
- 2 **tablespoons lemon juice**
- 2 **tablespoons brown sugar**
- 1 **tablespoon each chili powder and paprika**
- ½ **teaspoon salt**
- ½ **teaspoon garlic powder**
- ½ **teaspoon ground cumin**

1. Preheat the oven to 425°. Place the salmon in a greased 15x10x1-in. baking pan; drizzle with orange and lemon juices.

2. In a small bowl, mix remaining ingredients; sprinkle over fillets. Bake 13-15 minutes or until fish flakes easily with a fork.

HAM & CHEESE PENNE

This dish is so versatile, you'll love it from the first time you try it! You can easily take the recipe and make it your own by changing up the cheeses or veggie.

—DONNA BAILEY ORELAND, PA

PREP: 25 MIN. • **BAKE:** 20 MIN. • **MAKES:** 6 SERVINGS

- 1 package (16 ounces) ziti
- ¼ cup butter, cubed
- ¼ cup all-purpose flour
- 2 cups 2% milk
- 2 cups (8 ounces) shredded white cheddar cheese
- ¼ cup grated Parmesan cheese
- 1 teaspoon garlic powder
- ½ teaspoon pepper
- 3 cups cubed fully cooked ham
- 1 package (10 ounces) frozen chopped spinach, thawed and squeezed dry

1. Prepare ziti according to package directions. Meanwhile, in a Dutch oven, melt butter. Stir in flour until smooth; gradually add milk. Bring to a boil; cook and stir for 2 minutes or until thickened. Reduce heat; add the cheeses, garlic powder and pepper. Cook and stir until the cheese is melted.

2. Drain ziti; add to sauce mixture. Stir in ham and spinach. Transfer to a greased 13x9-in. baking dish. Bake, uncovered, at 375° for 20-25 minutes or until heated through.

GRILLED PINEAPPLE PORK & VEGETABLES

The pork takes just an hour to marinate, so you can enjoy some free time before taking this carefree meal to the grill. The end result is so good.

—TASTE OF HOME TEST KITCHEN

PREP: 25 MIN. + MARINATING • **GRILL:** 15 MIN. • **MAKES:** 5 SERVINGS

- 1 can (8 ounces) unsweetened pineapple chunks, undrained
- ¼ cup olive oil, divided
- 2 garlic cloves, peeled and halved
- 2 teaspoons ground cumin
- 2 teaspoons dried oregano
- ¾ teaspoon pepper, divided
- ¾ teaspoon salt, divided
- 2 pounds pork tenderloin, cut into ¾-inch slices
- 1 pound fresh asparagus, trimmed
- 4 medium carrots, halved lengthwise
- 1 large sweet red pepper, halved
- 1 bunch green onions, trimmed

1. Place the pineapple, 2 tablespoons oil, garlic, cumin, oregano, ½ teaspoon pepper and ¼ teaspoon salt in a blender; cover and process until blended. Place in a large resealable plastic bag; add pork. Seal bag and turn to coat; refrigerate 1 hour.

2. Drain and discard marinade. Moisten a paper towel with cooking oil; using long-handled tongs, lightly coat the grill rack. Grill, uncovered, over medium heat for 3-4 minutes on each side or until a thermometer reads 145°. Let stand for 5 minutes before serving.

3. Place vegetables in a grill wok or basket. Brush with remaining oil; sprinkle with remaining salt and pepper.

4. Grill, uncovered, over medium heat for 6-8 minutes or until tender, stirring frequently. Cut vegetables into 2-in. pieces. Serve with pork.

NOTE *If you do not have a grill wok or basket, use a disposable foil pan. Poke holes in the bottom of the pan with a meat fork to allow liquid to drain.*

One-Dish Entrees

No one likes washing a bunch of dishes after an enjoyable meal, which is exactly why one-dish recipes can save the day. Throw a few ingredients together in a pot or pan, and dinner will be ready in a flash!

ROASTED KIELBASA & VEGETABLES

This is the ultimate one-pan meal. It's healthy and filling all at the same time.

—MARIETTA SLATER JUSTIN, TX

PREP: 20 MIN. • **BAKE:** 40 MIN. • **MAKES:** 6 SERVINGS

- 3 medium sweet potatoes, peeled and cut into 1-inch pieces
- 1 large sweet onion, cut into 1-inch pieces
- 4 medium carrots, cut into 1-inch pieces
- 2 tablespoons olive oil
- 1 pound smoked kielbasa or Polish sausage, halved and cut into 1-inch pieces
- 1 medium yellow summer squash, cut into 1-inch pieces
- 1 medium zucchini, cut into 1-inch pieces
- ¼ teaspoon salt
- ¼ teaspoon pepper
  Dijon mustard, optional

1. Preheat the oven to 400°. Divide the sweet potatoes, onion and carrots between two greased 15x10x1-in. baking pans. Drizzle with oil; toss to coat. Roast for 25 minutes, stirring occasionally.
2. Add kielbasa, squash and zucchini to pans; sprinkle with salt and pepper. Roast 15-20 minutes longer or until vegetables are tender. Transfer to a serving bowl; toss to combine. If desired, serve with mustard.

SAUSAGE CHICKEN JAMBALAYA

Comforting, spicy and a cinch to prepare, this jambalaya is a terrific one-pot meal for feeding a crowd.

—BETTY BENTHIN GRASS VALLEY, CA

PREP: 20 MIN. • **COOK:** 30 MIN. • **MAKES:** 9 SERVINGS

- 6 fully cooked spicy chicken sausage links (3 ounces each), cut into ½-inch slices
- ½ pound chicken tenderloins, cut into ½-inch slices
- 1 tablespoon olive oil
- 3 celery ribs, chopped
- 1 large onion, chopped
- 2¾ cups chicken broth
- 1 can (14½ ounces) diced tomatoes, undrained
- 1½ cups uncooked long grain rice
- 1 teaspoon dried thyme
- 1 teaspoon Cajun seasoning

1. In a large saucepan, saute sausage and chicken in oil for 5 minutes. Add celery and onion; saute 6-8 minutes longer or until vegetables are tender. Stir in the broth, tomatoes, rice, thyme and Cajun seasoning.
2. Bring to a boil. Reduce heat; cover and simmer for 15-20 minutes or until rice is tender. Let stand for 5 minutes.

BAKED CHEDDAR EGGS & POTATOES

I love having breakfast for dinner, especially this combo of eggs with potatoes and cheese started in a skillet and then popped in the oven to bake. It's a perfect meal-in-one.
—**NADINE MERHEB** TUCSON, AZ

PREP: 20 MIN. • **BAKE:** 15 MIN. • **MAKES:** 4 SERVINGS

- 3 **tablespoons butter**
- 1½ **pounds red potatoes, chopped**
- ¼ **cup minced fresh parsley**
- 2 **garlic cloves, minced**
- ¾ **teaspoon kosher salt**
- ⅛ **teaspoon pepper**
- 8 **eggs**
- ½ **cup shredded extra-sharp cheddar cheese**

1. Preheat the oven to 400°. In a 10-in. ovenproof skillet, heat butter over medium-high heat. Add potatoes; cook and stir until golden brown and tender. Stir in parsley, garlic, salt and pepper. With back of a spoon, make four wells in the potato mixture; break two eggs into each well.
2. Bake 9-11 minutes or until egg whites are completely set and yolks begin to thicken but are not hard. Sprinkle with cheese; bake 1 minute or until cheese is melted.

MAKEOVER EASY-DOES-IT SPAGHETTI

All you need is a Dutch oven to make this meal with a simple homemade sauce. Allspice adds a new taste to this recipe, but you can use Italian seasoning instead.
—**CAROL BENZEL-SCHMIDT** STANWOOD, WA

PREP: 10 MIN. • **COOK:** 25 MIN. • **MAKES:** 4 SERVINGS

- 1 **pound lean ground beef (90% lean)**
- 1¾ **cups sliced fresh mushrooms**
- 3 **cups tomato juice**
- 1 **can (14½ ounces) no-salt-added diced tomatoes, drained**
- 1 **can (8 ounces) no-salt-added tomato sauce**
- 1 **tablespoon dried minced onion**
- ½ **teaspoon salt**
- ½ **teaspoon garlic powder**
- ½ **teaspoon ground mustard**
- ¼ **teaspoon pepper**
- ⅛ **teaspoon ground allspice**
- ⅛ **teaspoon ground mace, optional**
- 6 **ounces uncooked multigrain spaghetti, broken into pieces**
  Fresh mozzarella cheese pearls or shaved Parmesan cheese, optional

1. In a Dutch oven, cook beef and mushrooms over medium heat until meat is no longer pink; drain. Add tomato juice, tomatoes, tomato sauce, onion and seasonings.
2. Bring to a boil. Stir in spaghetti. Simmer, covered, for 12-15 minutes or until spaghetti is tender. If desired, serve with cheese.

BACON-SWISS PENNE

I was fortunate to inherit my grandmother's recipe book, which includes the instructions for this rich and cheesy casserole. I've been eating it for years...and still can't get enough.
—**JOSEPH SORTOR** TAMPA, FL

PREP: 35 MIN. • **BAKE:** 30 MIN. • **MAKES:** 10 SERVINGS

- 12 ounces uncooked penne pasta
- 13 bacon strips
- 1½ pounds boneless skinless chicken breasts, cut into 1-inch cubes
- 3 tablespoons butter
- 6 green onions, chopped
- 3 tablespoons all-purpose flour
- 4 cups 2% milk
- 3 cups (12 ounces) shredded cheddar cheese
- 1½ cups shredded Swiss cheese
- 1½ cups frozen peas, thawed
- ¾ teaspoon pepper
- ½ teaspoon dried thyme

TOPPING
- ¾ cup dry bread crumbs
- 2 tablespoons butter, melted

1. Cook penne according to package directions.
2. Meanwhile, in a large skillet, cook the bacon in batches over medium heat until crisp. Remove to paper towels; drain, reserving 4 teaspoons drippings. Crumble bacon and set aside.
3. Saute chicken in butter and drippings until no longer pink. Add onions; cook 1 minute longer. Stir in flour until blended; gradually add milk. Bring to a boil; cook and stir for 2 minutes or until thickened. Stir in the cheeses, peas, pepper, thyme and bacon.
4. Drain penne; add to chicken mixture and toss to coat. Transfer to a greased 13x9-in. baking dish. In a small bowl, combine bread crumbs and butter; sprinkle over top. Bake casserole, uncovered, at 350° for 30-35 minutes or until golden brown.

DECONSTRUCTED PEAR PORK CHOPS

You'll be tempted to eat this main dish straight out of the pan! It'll definitely wow your guests.
—**TASTE OF HOME** TEST KITCHEN

START TO FINISH: 30 MIN. • **MAKES:** 4 SERVINGS

- 1 package (6 ounces) corn bread stuffing mix
- 4 boneless pork loin chops (6 ounces each)
- ½ teaspoon pepper
- ¼ teaspoon salt
- 2 tablespoons butter
- 2 medium pears, chopped
- 1 medium sweet red pepper, chopped
- 2 green onions, thinly sliced

1. Prepare stuffing mix according to package directions. Meanwhile, sprinkle chops with pepper and salt. In a large skillet, brown pork chops in butter. Sprinkle with pears and red pepper.
2. Top with stuffing and onions. Cook, uncovered, over medium heat for 8-10 minutes or until a thermometer reads 145°.

LAYERED POTATO BEEF CASSEROLE

Beef and potatoes in a casserole? Talk about comfort food! After a little bit of prep time, you'll have 50 minutes to relax before dinner.
—**MARGIE WILLIAMS** MT. JULIET, TN

PREP: 25 MIN. • **BAKE:** 50 MIN. • **MAKES:** 6 SERVINGS

- 3 tablespoons butter, divided
- 2 tablespoons all-purpose flour
- ¾ teaspoon dried rosemary, crushed
- ¼ teaspoon pepper
- ⅛ teaspoon salt
- 2 cups 2% milk
- 2 cups (8 ounces) shredded sharp cheddar cheese
- 4 cups leftover beef stew
- 4 medium Yukon potatoes, thinly sliced
- ⅓ cup crushed butter-flavored crackers (about 8 crackers)
- 1 tablespoon dried parsley flakes
- ¼ teaspoon garlic powder

1. Melt 2 tablespoons butter in a large saucepan. Stir in the flour, rosemary, pepper and salt until blended; gradually add milk. Bring to a boil; cook and stir for 2 minutes or until thickened. Remove from the heat; stir in the cheese until melted.

2. Spoon 2 cups stew into a greased 2½ qt. baking dish. Layer with half of the potatoes and sauce mixture. Layer with remaining stew, potatoes and sauce.

3. Cover and bake at 400° for 45-50 minutes or until potatoes are tender. In a microwave, melt the remaining butter. Stir in the crackers, parsley and garlic powder. Sprinkle over casserole. Bake, uncovered, 5-10 minutes longer or until bubbly and topping is golden brown. Let stand for 10 minutes before serving.

HOMEMADE PASTA

Try your hand at preparing homemade pasta with this easy-to-work-with dough, you don't even need a pasta maker. The spinach and parsley give it a nice color.

—TASTE OF HOME TEST KITCHEN

PREP: 30 MIN. + STANDING • **COOK:** 10 MIN./BATCH
MAKES: 8 SERVINGS

- 1 package (10 ounces) frozen chopped spinach, thawed and squeezed dry
- ¼ cup packed fresh parsley sprigs
- 3½ to 4 cups all-purpose flour
- ½ teaspoon salt
- 4 eggs
- 3 tablespoons water
- 1 tablespoon olive oil
  Marinara sauce

1. Place spinach and parsley in a food processor; cover and process until finely chopped. Add 3½ cups flour and salt; process until blended. Add the eggs, water and oil. Process for 15-20 seconds or until dough forms a ball.

2. Turn onto a floured surface; knead for 8-10 minutes or until smooth and elastic, adding remaining flour if necessary. Cover and let rest for 30 minutes. Divide into fourths.

3. On a floured surface, roll each portion to ¹⁄₁₆-in. thickness. Dust top of dough with flour to prevent sticking; cut into ¼-in. slices. Separate the slices; allow noodles to dry on kitchen towels for at least 1 hour before cooking.

4. To cook, fill a Dutch oven three-fourths full with water. Bring to a boil. Add noodles in batches; cook, uncovered, for 8-10 minutes or until tender. Drain. Serve with sauce.

PORK TENDERLOIN MEDALLIONS WITH STRAWBERRY SAUCE

Pork tenderloin paired with strawberries is an appetizing pair, made even more special with a tangy feta garnish. Serve with roasted spring vegetables for a satisfying dinner.

—KATIE WOLLGAST FLORISSANT, MO

PREP: 15 MIN. • **COOK:** 20 MIN. • **MAKES:** 8 SERVINGS

- 1½ cups reduced-sodium beef broth
- 2 cups chopped fresh strawberries, divided
- ½ cup white wine vinegar
- ¼ cup packed brown sugar
- ¼ cup reduced-sodium soy sauce
- 3 garlic cloves, minced
- 2 pork tenderloins (1 pound each), cut into ½-inch slices
- 1 teaspoon garlic powder
- ½ teaspoon salt
- ½ teaspoon pepper
- 2 tablespoons canola oil
- 2 tablespoons cornstarch
- 2 tablespoons cold water
- ½ cup crumbled feta cheese
- ½ cup chopped green onions

1. In a large saucepan, combine broth, 1 cup strawberries, vinegar, brown sugar, soy sauce and garlic; bring to a boil. Reduce heat; simmer, uncovered, 15 minutes or until slightly thickened. Strain mixture and set aside liquid, discarding solids.

2. Sprinkle pork with garlic powder, salt and pepper. In a large skillet, heat oil over medium heat. Brown pork on both sides. Remove and keep warm.

3. Add broth mixture to the same skillet; bring to a boil. Combine cornstarch and water until smooth and gradually stir into skillet.

4. Return pork to skillet. Bring to a boil. Reduce heat; cook and stir 2 minutes or until sauce is thickened and pork is tender. Serve pork with sauce. Top with feta cheese, onions and remaining strawberries.

MOM'S SWEDISH MEATBALLS

Mom fixed these meatballs for all sorts of family dinners, potluck suppers and PTA meetings. Combine the aromas of browning meat and onions caramelizing, and everyone will be ready to eat.

—**MARYBETH MANK** MESQUITE, TX

PREP: 30 MIN. • **COOK:** 40 MIN. • **MAKES:** 6 SERVINGS

- ¾ cup seasoned bread crumbs
- 1 medium onion, chopped
- 2 eggs, lightly beaten
- ⅓ cup minced fresh parsley
- 1 teaspoon coarsely ground pepper
- ¾ teaspoon salt
- 2 pounds ground beef

GRAVY
- ½ cup all-purpose flour
- 2¾ cups 2% milk
- 2 cans (10½ ounces each) condensed beef consomme, undiluted
- 1 tablespoon Worcestershire sauce
- 1 teaspoon coarsely ground pepper
- ¾ teaspoon salt

NOODLES
- 1 package (16 ounces) egg noodles
- ¼ cup butter, cubed
- ¼ cup minced fresh parsley

1. In a large bowl, combine the first six ingredients. Add the beef; mix lightly but thoroughly. Shape into 1½-in. meatballs (about 36). In a large skillet, brown meatballs in batches. Using a slotted spoon, remove to paper towels to drain, reserving drippings in pan.

2. For gravy, stir flour into drippings; cook and stir until light brown (do not burn). Gradually whisk in milk until smooth. Stir in the consomme, Worcestershire sauce, pepper and salt. Bring to a boil; cook and stir for 2 minutes or until thickened.

3. Return meatballs to pan. Cook, uncovered, for 15-20 minutes longer or until meatballs are cooked through, stirring occasionally.

4. Meanwhile, cook noodles according to package directions. Drain; toss with butter. Serve with meatball mixture; sprinkle with parsley.

CHICKPEA POTPIES

My family loves potpies, and with this recipe, no one even misses the meat. It's that good.

—**ANNETTE WOOFENDEN** MIDDLEBORO, MA

PREP: 15 MIN. • **BAKE:** 25 MIN. • **MAKES:** 4 SERVINGS

- 1 small onion, chopped
- 6 tablespoons butter
- 2 garlic cloves, minced
- 6 tablespoons all-purpose flour
- ½ teaspoon salt
- ¼ teaspoon pepper
- 3 cups vegetable broth
- 2 cups frozen mixed vegetables, thawed
- 1 can (15 ounces) garbanzo beans or chickpeas, rinsed and drained
- 1¼ cups frozen cubed hash brown potatoes
- ¼ cup heavy whipping cream
- ¾ teaspoon Italian seasoning
- 1 sheet refrigerated pie pastry

1. Saute onion in butter in a large saucepan until tender. Add garlic; cook 1 minute longer. Stir in the flour, salt and pepper until blended. Gradually add broth; bring to a boil. Cook and stir for 2 minutes or until thickened.

2. Stir in the vegetables, garbanzo beans, potatoes, cream and Italian seasoning. Divide mixture among four ungreased 10-oz. ramekins.

3. Unroll pastry; divide into four portions. Roll out each portion to fit ramekins; place pastry over filling. Trim, seal and flute edges. Cut slits in pastry. Place ramekins on a baking sheet.

4. Bake at 400° for 25-30 minutes or until the pastry is golden brown.

CAJUN FISH TACOS

Classic fish tacos often feature deep-fried fish, a corn tortilla, cabbage and a thin mayo-based sauce. But we found that fish + pita bread = total yumminess in this streamlined version using lemon-flavored fish with a Cajun twist.

—TASTE OF HOME TEST KITCHEN

START TO FINISH: 25 MIN. • **YIELD:** 4 SERVINGS

- 2 packages (7.6 ounces each) frozen lemon butter grilled fish fillets
- 3 cups broccoli coleslaw mix
- ½ cup thinly sliced sweet orange pepper
- ½ cup mayonnaise
- 1 tablespoon lemon juice
- 1 teaspoon sugar
- 1¾ teaspoons Cajun seasoning, divided
- 4 whole pita breads, warmed
  Lemon wedges, optional

1. Cook fish according to package directions. Meanwhile, in a small bowl, combine the coleslaw mix, pepper, mayonnaise, lemon juice, sugar and 1½ teaspoons Cajun seasoning.

2. Slice fillets. Spoon coleslaw mixture onto pita breads; top with fish. Sprinkle with remaining Cajun seasoning. Serve with lemon wedges if desired.

CRAB LASAGNA ROLL-UPS

A creamy, delicate filling is rolled up into lasagna noodles for a simple and satisfying main dish. Garlic bread on the side rounds out the meal.

—FRAN RODGERS LAKE GENEVA, WI

PREP: 20 MIN. • **BAKE:** 30 MIN. • **MAKES:** 6 SERVINGS

- 2 eggs, lightly beaten
- 2 cups (16 ounces) 4% cottage cheese
- ¼ cup grated Parmesan cheese
- 2 tablespoons Italian seasoning
- 2 tablespoons minced fresh parsley
- 1 teaspoon dried oregano
- ½ teaspoon dried basil
- ½ teaspoon dried thyme
- ¼ teaspoon garlic powder
- 1 package (8 ounces) imitation crabmeat, flaked
- 12 lasagna noodles, cooked and drained
- 2 cans (8 ounces each) tomato sauce

In a large bowl, combine the eggs, cheeses and seasonings. Add crab; mix well. Place about ⅓ cup on each noodle; roll up. Place seam side down in a 13x9-in. baking dish coated with cooking spray. Top with tomato sauce. Cover and bake at 350° for 30-40 minutes or until heated through.

SMOKY CRANBERRY RIBS

I love cranberries and freeze them when they're in season to enjoy all year-round. Living near New Jersey's cranberry bogs inspires me to develop new and delicious ways to use them, as in this recipe.

—**CHRISTINE WENDLAND** BROWNS MILLS, NJ

PREP: 25 MIN. + CHILLING • **GRILL:** 2 HOURS • **MAKES:** 6 SERVINGS

- 4½ teaspoons paprika
- 4 teaspoons salt
- 2 teaspoons fennel seed
- 1½ teaspoons pepper
- 1 teaspoon onion powder
- 1 teaspoon caraway seeds
- 1 teaspoon ground allspice
- ½ teaspoon garlic powder
- ½ teaspoon rubbed sage
- 6 pounds pork baby back ribs

SAUCE
- 1½ cups fresh or frozen cranberries, thawed
- 1½ cups packed dark brown sugar
- 1 cup cider vinegar
- 1 small sweet onion, chopped
- ¼ cup ketchup

1. In a spice grinder or with a mortar and pestle, combine the first nine ingredients; grind until fennel and caraway seeds are crushed. Set aside 4 teaspoons for sauce.

2. Rub remaining spice mixture over ribs. Cover and refrigerate for at least 1 hour.

3. Wrap ribs in a large piece of heavy-duty foil (about 28x18 in.); seal tightly. Prepare grill for indirect heat, using a drip pan. Place ribs over drip pan and grill, covered, over indirect medium heat for 1½ to 2 hours or until tender.

4. In a small saucepan, combine the cranberries, brown sugar, vinegar, onion and reserved spice mixture. Cook over medium heat until berries pop, about 15 minutes; cool slightly. Transfer to a blender; add ketchup. Cover and process until smooth. Set aside 1 cup sauce for serving.

5. Moisten a paper towel with cooking oil; using long-handled tongs, lightly coat the grill rack. Carefully remove ribs from foil. Place over direct heat; baste with some of the sauce. Grill, covered, over medium heat for 20-30 minutes or until browned, turning and basting occasionally. Serve with reserved sauce.

SPAGHETTI SQUASH WITH BALSAMIC VEGETABLES

In this spaghetti squash dinner, the veggies can be prepped while the squash is cooking in the microwave.

—**DEANNA MCDONALD** KALAMAZOO, MI

PREP: 20 MIN. • **COOK:** 15 MIN. • **MAKES:** 6 SERVINGS

- 1 medium spaghetti squash (about 4 pounds)
- 1 cup chopped carrots
- 1 small red onion, halved and sliced
- 1 tablespoon olive oil
- 4 garlic cloves, minced
- 1 can (15½ ounces) great northern beans, rinsed and drained
- 1 can (14½ ounces) diced tomatoes, drained
- 1 can (14 ounces) water-packed artichoke hearts, rinsed, drained and halved
- 1 medium zucchini, chopped
- 3 tablespoons balsamic vinegar
- 2 teaspoons minced fresh thyme or ½ teaspoon dried thyme
- ¼ teaspoon salt
- ¼ teaspoon pepper
- ½ cup pine nuts, toasted

1. Cut squash in half lengthwise; discard seeds. Place the squash cut side down on a microwave-safe plate. Microwave, uncovered, on high for 15-18 minutes or until tender.

2. Meanwhile, in a large nonstick skillet, saute carrots and onion in oil until tender. Add garlic; cook 1 minute. Stir in beans, tomatoes, artichokes, zucchini, vinegar, thyme, salt and pepper. Cook and stir over medium heat 8-10 minutes or until heated through.

3. When squash is cool enough to handle, use a fork to separate strands. Serve with the bean mixture. Sprinkle with nuts.

CREAMY HAM & CHEESE CASSEROLE

I felt so proud when I created this recipe. Throwing together leftover ham, convenient cooking creme and garlic-herb seasoning make this pasta toss so delicious.

—**BETSY L. HOWARD** KIRKWOOD, MO

PREP: 15 MIN. • **BAKE:** 20 MIN. • **MAKES:** 4 SERVINGS

- 8 ounces uncooked wide egg noodles
- 3 cups cubed fully cooked ham
- 1 can (10¾ ounces) condensed cream of chicken soup, undiluted
- 1 carton (10 ounces) Philadelphia original cooking creme
- 1 cup 2% milk
- ½ teaspoon garlic-herb seasoning blend
- ¼ teaspoon pepper
- 2 cups (8 ounces) shredded Monterey Jack cheese

1. Cook noodles according to package directions. Meanwhile, combine the ham, soup, cooking creme, milk and seasonings in a large bowl.

2. Drain noodles and add to ham mixture; mix well. Transfer to a 13x9-in. baking dish coated with cooking spray; sprinkle with cheese.

3. Bake, uncovered, at 350° for 20-25 minutes or until heated through.

BAKED ORANGE ROUGHY AND RICE

It might sound too good to be true, but you really can make this delectable fish dinner with just one dish. Your family will be lining up to dig in once they see the beautiful results!

—*TASTE OF HOME* TEST KITCHEN

PREP: 10 MIN. • **BAKE:** 30 MIN. • **MAKES:** 4 SERVINGS

- 2 cups uncooked instant rice
- 1 package (16 ounces) frozen broccoli-cauliflower blend, thawed
- 4 orange roughy fillets (6 ounces each)
- 1 can (14½ ounces) chicken broth
- 1 can (14½ ounces) fire-roasted diced tomatoes, undrained
- 1 teaspoon garlic powder
- 1 teaspoon lemon-pepper seasoning
- ¼ to ½ teaspoon cayenne pepper
- ½ cup shredded cheddar cheese

1. Place rice in a greased 13x9-in. baking dish. Layer with the vegetables and fish. Pour the broth and tomatoes over the top; sprinkle with seasonings.

2. Cover and bake at 375° for 25-30 minutes or until fish flakes easily with a fork and rice is tender. Sprinkle with cheese; bake 5 minutes longer or until cheese is melted.

PEPPERONI PIZZA CASSEROLE

Loaded with all the goodness you love in pizza, this noodle bake is sure to be a winner with all ages. You can use ground beef instead of turkey if you prefer.

—**DEB STALEY** MOUNT VERNON, IL

PREP: 25 MIN. • **BAKE:** 30 MIN.
MAKES: 2 CASSEROLES (6 SERVINGS EACH)

- 1 package (16 ounces) egg noodles
- 2 pounds ground turkey
- ⅓ cup chopped onion
- 1 jar (24 ounces) meatless spaghetti sauce
- 1 can (10 ounces) diced tomatoes and green chilies
- 1 can (8 ounces) mushroom stems and pieces, drained
- 2 cups (8 ounces) shredded part-skim mozzarella cheese
- 2 cups (8 ounces) shredded cheddar cheese
- 1 cup (4 ounces) shredded Parmesan cheese
- 3 ounces sliced turkey pepperoni

1. In a Dutch oven, cook noodles according to package directions; drain.

2. Meanwhile, in a large skillet, cook turkey and onion over medium heat until meat is no longer pink; drain. Stir in the spaghetti sauce and tomatoes. Bring to a boil. Reduce heat; simmer, uncovered, for 5 minutes. Stir in noodles.

3. Transfer to two greased 13x9-in. baking dishes. Sprinkle each with mushrooms, cheeses and pepperoni.

4. Bake, uncovered, at 350° for 30-35 minutes or until heated through and cheeses have melted. Let stand for 5 minutes before serving.

ROAST BEEF POTPIE

Everyone will want a piece of this pie, and you'll appreciate that it starts with packaged beef roast and refrigerated pie pastry.

—**PATRICIA MYERS** MARYVILLE, TN

PREP: 30 MIN. • **BAKE:** 30 MIN. • **MAKES:** 6 SERVINGS

- 10 fresh baby carrots, chopped
- 6 small red potatoes, cubed
- 1 medium onion, chopped
- 2 tablespoons olive oil
- 1 package (17 ounces) refrigerated beef roast au jus, coarsely chopped
- 2 tablespoons minced fresh cilantro
- ¼ teaspoon salt
- ¼ teaspoon pepper
- ⅓ cup all-purpose flour
- 2¼ cups reduced-sodium beef broth
- 1 sheet refrigerated pie pastry
- 1 egg, beaten

1. In a large skillet, saute the carrots, potatoes and onion in oil until crisp-tender. Add the beef roast, cilantro, salt and pepper. Combine flour and broth until smooth; gradually stir into the pan. Bring to a boil; cook and stir for 2 minutes or until thickened.

2. Transfer to a 9-in. deep-dish pie plate. Place pie pastry over filling. Trim, seal and flute edges. Cut slits in pastry; brush with egg. Bake at 375° for 30-35 minutes or until golden brown.

HOW TO PREP CILANTRO

To easily trim fresh cilantro from its stems, hold the bunch, then angle the blade of a chef's knife almost parallel with the stems. With short, downward strokes, shave off the leaves.

SAUCY PORK CHOP SKILLET

Served over brown rice or whole grain noodles, this quick skillet dinner is healthier than most comfort food. I make it quite a bit for my family of six; it's a challenge to feed a large family on a budget, and this meal is affordable. Add a salad and fruit and you have a filling meal.

—**DONNA ROBERTS** MANHATTAN, KS

START TO FINISH: 30 MIN. • **MAKES:** 6 SERVINGS

- 3 cups instant brown rice
- 2 teaspoons canola oil
- 6 boneless pork loin chops (6 ounces each)
- 1 small onion, sliced
- 1 cup canned diced tomatoes
- 1 cup reduced-sodium beef broth
- 1 tablespoon dried parsley flakes
- ½ teaspoon salt
- ¼ teaspoon pepper
- ⅛ teaspoon dried basil
- ⅛ teaspoon dried oregano
- 2 tablespoons all-purpose flour
- ½ cup water

1. Cook rice according to package directions. Meanwhile, in a large nonstick skillet coated with cooking spray, heat oil over medium-high heat. Brown pork chops on both sides. Remove from the pan.

2. Cook and stir onion in drippings over medium-high heat until tender. Stir in the tomatoes, broth, parsley and seasonings. Bring to a boil. Return pork to skillet. Reduce heat; simmer, covered, for 6-8 minutes or until a thermometer inserted in pork reads 145°.

3. Remove pork to a serving plate. Mix flour and water until smooth; stir into pan. Bring to a boil; cook and stir 2 minutes or until thickened. Pour over pork; serve with rice.

PASTRY CHICKEN A LA KING

My mom made this when I was growing up. She always made it smell and look so divine, I'd forget that peas were in it and clean my plate.

—**PATTY LANOUE STEARNS** TRAVERSE CITY, MI

PREP: 25 MIN. • **COOK:** 20 MIN. • **MAKES:** 6 SERVINGS

- 1 package (10 ounces) frozen puff pastry shells
- 3 tablespoons butter
- 1 cup sliced fresh mushrooms
- 1 medium sweet red pepper, finely chopped
- 1 celery rib, finely chopped
- 1 small onion, finely chopped
- 3 tablespoons all-purpose flour
- 2 cups 2% milk
- 2 egg yolks
- 2 tablespoons heavy whipping cream
- ¼ teaspoon lemon juice
- ½ teaspoon salt
- ¼ teaspoon paprika
- ¼ teaspoon pepper
- 2 cups cubed cooked chicken
- 1 cup frozen petite peas

1. Bake pastry shells according to package directions.

2. Meanwhile, in a large skillet, heat butter over medium-high heat. Add mushrooms, red pepper, celery and onion; cook and stir until tender. Stir in the flour until blended; gradually add milk. Bring to a boil; cook and stir 2 minutes or until thickened.

3. In a small bowl, mix egg yolks and cream. Stir a small amount of hot mixture into egg yolk mixture; return all to pan, stirring constantly. Add lemon juice, salt, paprika and pepper; cook and stir over low heat for 2 minutes or until thickened. Add chicken and peas; heat through. Serve over pastry shells.

CHILI MAC & CHEESE

This Southwestern twist on the ultimate comfort food tastes great, and you don't need to do much to get it ready.
—**MARY AGUILAR** SHELBY, OH

PREP: 30 MIN. • **BAKE:** 20 MIN. • **MAKES:** 8 SERVINGS

- **2 packages (7¼ ounces each) macaroni and cheese dinner mix**
- **2 pounds ground beef**
- **1 small onion, chopped**
- **1 can (14½ ounces) diced tomatoes, undrained**
- **1 can (10 ounces) diced tomatoes and green chilies, undrained**
- **1 can (8 ounces) tomato sauce**
- **2 tablespoons chili powder**
- **1 teaspoon garlic salt**
- **½ teaspoon ground cumin**
- **¼ teaspoon crushed red pepper flakes**
- **¼ teaspoon pepper**
- **2 cups (16 ounces) sour cream**
- **1½ cups (6 ounces) shredded Mexican cheese blend, divided**

1. Preheat the oven to 350°. Set aside cheese packets from dinner mixes. In a large saucepan, bring 2 quarts water to a boil. Add macaroni; cook 8-10 minutes or until tender.
2. Meanwhile, in a Dutch oven, cook and stir beef and onion over medium heat 8-10 minutes or until beef is no longer pink; drain. Stir in tomatoes, tomatoes and green chilies, tomato sauce and seasonings. Drain macaroni; add to beef mixture. Stir in the contents of cheese packets, sour cream and 1 cup cheese.
3. Transfer to a greased 13x9-in. baking dish; top with remaining cheese. Bake, uncovered, 20-25 minutes or until bubbly.

MANGO CHUTNEY PORK ROAST

This isn't a traditional Bahamian recipe, but we've adapted this dish throughout the years to give it a tropical flavor. The chutney is fantastic on nearly any meat. You might consider making an extra batch for tacos the next night.

—PAMELA VITTI KNOWLES HENDERSONVILLE, NC

PREP: 15 MIN. • **BAKE:** 1 HOUR + STANDING
MAKES: 6 SERVINGS (2 CUPS CHUTNEY)

- 1 **tablespoon butter**
- 1 **boneless pork loin roast (2 to 3 pounds)**
- ½ **teaspoon each salt, pepper and ground ginger**

MANGO CHUTNEY
- 2 **medium mangoes, peeled and cubed**
- ¼ **cup finely chopped red onion**
- ¼ **cup finely chopped sweet red pepper**
- 1 **jalapeno pepper, seeded and minced**
- 2 **tablespoons white vinegar**
- 1 **tablespoon grated fresh gingerroot**
- ⅛ **teaspoon each salt, ground turmeric and ground cloves**

1. In a large skillet, heat butter over medium-high heat. Brown the pork on all sides. Sprinkle with the salt, pepper and ginger.

2. Place on a rack in a shallow roasting pan. Bake at 350° for 1 to 1½ hours or until a thermometer reads 145°. Remove roast from oven; tent with foil. Let stand for 10 minutes before slicing.

3. Meanwhile, in a large saucepan, combine all chutney ingredients. Cook, uncovered, over medium heat for 8-10 minutes to allow flavors to blend, stirring occasionally. Serve with pork.

CREAMY CHIPOTLE PASTA WITH SAUSAGE

After one taste of the hearty and spicy sauce, you'll find yourself making this recipe often.

—*TASTE OF HOME* TEST KITCHEN

START TO FINISH: 30 MIN. • **MAKES:** 6 SERVINGS

- 1 pound Italian turkey sausage links, cut into ¾-inch slices
- ½ pound sliced fresh mushrooms
- 1 medium sweet red pepper, chopped
- 2 teaspoons olive oil
- 1 tablespoon brown sugar
- 1 tablespoon minced chipotle pepper in adobo sauce
- 2 teaspoons chili powder
- ¾ teaspoon salt
- ½ teaspoon dried marjoram
- 1½ cups heavy whipping cream
- 1½ cups (6 ounces) shredded Mexican cheese blend, divided
- 2 cups frozen peas
  Hot cooked thin spaghetti

1. Cook sausage in a large skillet over medium heat until no longer pink; drain. Remove and keep warm.

2. Saute mushrooms and red pepper in oil in the same pan until tender. Stir in the brown sugar, chipotle pepper, chili powder, salt and marjoram; cook 1 minute longer.

3. Add cream, stirring to loosen browned bits from pan. Bring to a boil; cook and stir for 2-3 minutes or until slightly thickened. Reduce heat.

4. Add 1 cup cheese; cook and stir until melted. Stir in sausage and peas; heat through. Serve with spaghetti. Sprinkle with remaining cheese.

SAVORY TOMATO-BRAISED TILAPIA

When I shared this recipe with a few friends, it was a huge hit! One friend makes it often now, which I think is a testament to how good it is.

—**NANCY SHIVELY** SHOREWOOD, IL

START TO FINISH: 30 MIN. • **MAKES:** 4 SERVINGS

- 4 tilapia fillets (6 ounces each)
- ¼ teaspoon seasoned salt
- 1 tablespoon lemon juice
- 2 tablespoons olive oil
- 1 small red onion, chopped
- 1 can (10 ounces) diced tomatoes and green chilies, undrained
- ¾ cup chopped roasted sweet red peppers
- ½ cup chicken broth
- ¼ cup tomato paste
- 1 teaspoon garlic powder
- 1 teaspoon dried oregano
  Hot cooked pasta, optional

1. Sprinkle fillets with seasoned salt; drizzle with lemon juice. In a large skillet, heat oil over medium-high heat. Add onion; cook and stir until tender. Add tomatoes, peppers, broth, tomato paste, garlic powder and oregano; cook and stir 2-3 minutes longer.

2. Place fillets over tomato mixture; cook, covered, for 6-8 minutes or until fish flakes easily with a fork. If desired, serve with pasta.

REUBEN QUICHE

Deli flavors combine in this one-of-a-kind quiche. Serve some Thousand Island dressing on the side for an authentic taste.
—**BARBARA NOWAKOWSKI** NORTH TONAWANDA, NY

PREP: 25 MIN. • **BAKE:** 25 MIN. • **MAKES:** 6 SERVINGS

- 1 cup plus 3 tablespoons finely crushed Rye Triscuits or other crackers
- 1 tablespoon rye or all-purpose flour
- 2 tablespoons plus 1½ teaspoons butter, melted

FILLING
- 5 green onions, chopped
- 1 tablespoon butter
- 1½ cups (6 ounces) shredded Swiss cheese, divided
- 1 package (2½ ounces) deli corned beef, cut into 2-inch strips
- ½ cup sauerkraut, well drained
- 4 eggs
- 1 cup half-and-half cream
- 1 tablespoon all-purpose flour
- ½ teaspoon ground mustard
- ¼ teaspoon salt

1. In a small bowl, combine the cracker crumbs, flour and butter; press onto the bottom and up the sides of an ungreased 9-in. pie plate. Bake at 375° for 8-10 minutes or until edges are lightly browned.

2. Meanwhile, in a small skillet, saute onions in butter until tender; set aside. Sprinkle ½ cup cheese over crust. Top with corned beef, sauerkraut and remaining cheese. Whisk the eggs, cream, flour, mustard, salt and reserved onion mixture; pour over cheese.

3. Bake, uncovered, at 375° for 25-30 minutes or until a knife inserted near the center comes out clean. Let stand for 5 minutes before cutting.

TACO CORN BREAD CASSEROLE

Don't be scared of a little heat! A whole can of chilies adds a touch of fire to this corn bread casserole. For less heat, you can include just enough of the chilies for your taste.
—**LISA PAUL** TERRE HAUTE, IN

PREP: 15 MIN. • **BAKE:** 1 HOUR • **MAKES:** 8 SERVINGS

- 2 pounds ground beef
- 2 envelopes taco seasoning
- 2 cans (14½ ounces each) diced tomatoes, drained
- 1 cup water
- 1 cup cooked rice
- 1 can (4 ounces) chopped green chilies
- 2 packages (8½ ounces each) corn bread/muffin mix
- 1 can (8¾ ounces) whole kernel corn, drained
- 1 cup (8 ounces) sour cream
- 2 cups corn chips
- 2 cups (8 ounces) shredded Mexican or cheddar cheese, divided
- 1 can (2¼ ounces) sliced ripe olives, drained
  Shredded lettuce and chopped tomatoes, optional

1. Preheat the oven to 400°. In a Dutch oven, cook beef over medium heat 8-10 minutes or until no longer pink, breaking into crumbles; drain. Stir in taco seasoning. Add the tomatoes, water, rice and green chilies; heat through, stirring occasionally.

2. Meanwhile, prepare the corn bread mix according to package directions; stir in corn. Pour half of the batter into a greased 13x9-in. baking dish. Layer with half of the meat mixture, all the sour cream, half of the corn chips and 1 cup cheese. Top with remaining batter, remaining meat mixture, olives and remaining corn chips.

3. Bake, uncovered, 55-60 minutes or until cornbread is cooked through. Sprinkle with remaining cheese; bake 3-5 minutes longer or until cheese is melted. If desired, serve with lettuce and chopped tomatoes.

SPICY SHRIMP & PEPPERS WITH PASTA

Spice up any weeknight with this dish. It goes together in no time and features shrimp, veggies, whole-wheat pasta and just the right amount of kick.

—AMY MILLS SEBRING, FL

PREP: 20 MIN. • **COOK:** 25 MIN. • **MAKES:** 4 SERVINGS

- 1 cup sliced baby portobello mushrooms
- 1 medium sweet yellow pepper, cut into ½-inch pieces
- 1 medium green pepper, cut into ½-inch pieces
- 1 shallot, minced
- 2 tablespoons olive oil
- 1 garlic clove, minced
- ½ teaspoon crushed red pepper flakes
- 1 can (28 ounces) crushed tomatoes
- 1 teaspoon Italian seasoning
- ½ teaspoon salt
- 6 ounces uncooked whole wheat linguine
- 1 pound uncooked medium shrimp, peeled and deveined
- 3 tablespoons minced fresh parsley or 1 tablespoon dried parsley flakes

1. In a large nonstick skillet coated with cooking spray, saute the mushrooms, peppers and shallot in oil until tender. Add garlic and pepper flakes; cook 1 minute longer.
2. Stir in the tomatoes, Italian seasoning and salt. Bring to a boil. Reduce heat; simmer, uncovered, for 12-15 minutes or until vegetables are tender.
3. Meanwhile, cook linguine according to package directions. Add shrimp to sauce; cook and stir for 5-7 minutes or until shrimp turn pink.
4. Drain linguine; stir into sauce. Heat through. Sprinkle with parsley.

BEER CAN CHICKEN

This is a stand-up chicken that you'll be proud to serve at any family gathering. Treated to a savory rub, then roasted over a beer can for added moisture, it's so tasty you'll want to call dibs on the leftovers right away.

—SHIRLEY WARREN THIENSVILLE, WI

PREP: 20 MIN. • **GRILL:** 1¼ HOURS + STANDING • **MAKES:** 4 SERVINGS

- 4 teaspoons chicken seasoning
- 2 teaspoons sugar
- 2 teaspoons chili powder
- 1½ teaspoons paprika
- 1¼ teaspoons dried basil
- ¼ teaspoon pepper
- 1 broiler/fryer chicken (3 to 4 pounds)
- 1 tablespoon canola oil
- 2 lemon slices
- 1 can (12 ounces) beer or nonalcoholic beer

1. In a small bowl, combine the first six ingredients. Gently loosen skin from the chicken. Brush chicken with oil. Sprinkle 1 teaspoon of spice mixture into cavity. Rub the remaining spice mixture over and under the skin. Place lemon slices in neck cavity. Tuck wing tips behind the back.
2. Prepare grill for indirect heat, using a drip pan. Pour out half of the beer, reserving for another use. Poke additional holes in top of the can with a can opener. Holding the chicken with legs pointed down, lower chicken over the can so it fills the body cavity.
3. Place chicken over drip pan; grill, covered, over indirect medium heat for 1¼ to 1½ hours or until a thermometer reads 180°. Remove chicken from grill; cover and let stand for 10 minutes. Remove chicken from can.
NOTE *This recipe was tested with McCormick's Montreal Chicken Seasoning. Look for it in the spice aisle.*

2. Meanwhile, mix rub seasonings; rub over steaks. Grill steaks, covered, over medium heat or broil 4 in. from heat 8-10 minutes on each side or until meat reaches desired doneness (for medium-rare, a thermometer should read 145°; medium, 160°; well-done, 170°). Let stand 5 minutes before cutting each steak into thirds.

3. Place steaks on a platter. Top with tomatoes; drizzle with any remaining beer mixture.

HONEY-BEER BRAISED RIBS

Braised in beer with a sweet honey finish, these tender ribs will be the talk of the table. Serve them with baked potatoes, green beans and a salad for a memorable meal.

—TERRY SERENA MCMURRAY, PA

PREP: 3½ HOURS • **GRILL:** 10 MIN. • **MAKES:** 6 SERVINGS

- ½ **cup packed brown sugar**
- 1 **teaspoon pepper**
- ¾ **teaspoon salt**
- 6 **pounds pork baby back ribs**
- ¼ **cup honey**
- 1 **bottle (12 ounces) dark beer or beef broth**
- ¼ **cup cider vinegar**
- 1 **bottle (18 ounces) barbecue sauce**

1. Combine the brown sugar, pepper and salt; rub over ribs. Place ribs bone side down on a rack in a large shallow roasting pan. Drizzle with honey.

2. Combine beer and vinegar; pour around ribs. Spoon some of the beer mixture over ribs. Cover tightly with foil and bake at 325° for 1 hour. Reduce heat to 250°; bake 2 hours longer or until tender.

3. Moisten a paper towel with cooking oil; using long-handled tongs, lightly coat the grill rack. Drain ribs. Grill, covered, over medium heat for 10-15 minutes or until browned, turning and basting occasionally with barbecue sauce. Serve with remaining barbecue sauce.

GRILLED STEAKS WITH MARINATED TOMATOES

The flavor of the tomatoes improves after they marinate overnight. I could eat them all by themselves! Our family likes these steaks best served with cheesy potatoes or glazed green beans.

—ANNA DAVS SPRINGFIELD, MO

PREP: 25 MIN. + MARINATING • **GRILL:** 20 MIN. • **MAKES:** 6 SERVINGS

- ¼ **cup light beer**
- 3 **tablespoons raspberry vinaigrette**
- 3 **tablespoons olive oil**
- 1 **tablespoon torn fresh basil**
- 1 **tablespoon cider vinegar**
- 2 **teaspoons garlic powder**
- 2 **teaspoons coriander seeds, crushed**
- 1½ **teaspoons minced fresh oregano**
- 1 **teaspoon sugar**
- ½ **teaspoon salt**
- ½ **teaspoon pepper**
- 3 **large tomatoes, sliced**

RUB

- 2 **teaspoons Montreal steak seasoning**
- 2 **teaspoons chili powder**
- 1 **teaspoon salt**
- 1 **teaspoon celery seed**
- 1 **teaspoon smoked paprika**
- ½ **teaspoon pepper**
- 2 **beef top sirloin steaks (1 inch thick and 1 pound each)**

1. In a small bowl, whisk the first 11 ingredients until blended. Place tomatoes in a 13x9-in. dish; pour beer mixture over top. Cover and refrigerate at least 1 hour.

PAPRIKA CHICKEN THIGHS

This is one of my favorite family meals. The gravy is ideal over rice, grits or mashed potatoes.

—**JUDY ARMSTRONG** PRAIRIEVILLE, LA

PREP: 15 MIN. • **BAKE:** 50 MIN. • **MAKES:** 8 SERVINGS

- ¼ **cup butter**
- 3 **tablespoons all-purpose flour**
- 2 **tablespoons paprika**
- 1 **teaspoon poultry seasoning**
- 8 **bone-in chicken thighs, skin removed**
- ½ **teaspoon salt**
- ½ **teaspoon pepper**
- 1 **can (10¾ ounces) condensed cream of mushroom soup, undiluted**
- 1 **cup 2% milk**
- 8 **ounces sliced fresh mushrooms**
- 2 **tablespoons minced fresh parsley**
  Hot cooked rice, optional

1. In a small saucepan, melt butter over medium heat. Remove from the heat; stir in the flour, paprika and poultry seasoning. Sprinkle chicken with salt and pepper; place in an ungreased 13x9-in. baking dish. Spread butter mixture over chicken.

2. In a bowl, whisk soup and milk; stir in mushrooms. Pour over chicken. Bake, covered, at 350° for 35 minutes. Uncover; bake 15-20 minutes longer or until a thermometer inserted in chicken reads 180°. Sprinkle with parsley. If desired, serve with rice.

Slow Cooker

A slow cooker can be your best friend in the kitchen. Come home to a hot meal after a busy day, or maybe use it to free up some space in the oven. After all, what's easier than being able to set it and forget it for a few hours?

CAROLINA-STYLE PORK BARBECUE

I'm originally from North Carolina, and my husband swears my authentic Carolina barbecue is the best he has ever had!

—KATHRYN RANSOM WILLIAMS SPARKS, NV

PREP: 30 MIN. • **COOK:** 6 HOURS • **MAKES:** 14 SERVINGS

- 1 boneless pork shoulder butt roast (4 to 5 pounds)
- 2 tablespoons brown sugar
- 2 teaspoons salt
- 1 teaspoon paprika
- ½ teaspoon pepper
- 2 medium onions, quartered
- ¾ cup cider vinegar
- 4 teaspoons Worcestershire sauce
- 1 tablespoon sugar
- 1 tablespoon crushed red pepper flakes
- 1 teaspoon garlic salt
- 1 teaspoon ground mustard
- ½ teaspoon cayenne pepper
- 14 hamburger buns, split
- 1¾ pounds deli coleslaw

1. Cut roast into quarters. Mix brown sugar, salt, paprika and pepper; rub over meat. Place the meat and onions in a 5-qt. slow cooker.

2. In a small bowl, whisk vinegar, Worcestershire sauce, sugar and seasonings; pour over roast. Cook, covered, on low 6-8 hours or until meat is tender.

3. Remove roast; cool slightly. Reserve 1½ cups cooking juices; discard remaining juices. Skim fat from reserved juices. Shred pork with two forks. Return the pork and reserved juices to slow cooker; heat through. Serve on buns with coleslaw.

EASY SLOW COOKER MAC & CHEESE

My sons always cheer, "You're the best mom in the world!" whenever I make this creamy mac and cheese perfection. You can't beat a response like that!

—HEIDI FLEEK HAMBURG, PA

PREP: 25 MIN. • **COOK:** 1 HOUR • **MAKES:** 8 SERVINGS

- 2 cups uncooked elbow macaroni
- 1 can (10¾ ounces) condensed cheddar cheese soup, undiluted
- 1 cup 2% milk
- ½ cup sour cream
- ¼ cup butter, cubed
- ½ teaspoon onion powder
- ¼ teaspoon white pepper
- ⅛ teaspoon salt
- 1 cup (4 ounces) shredded cheddar cheese
- 1 cup (4 ounces) shredded fontina cheese
- 1 cup (4 ounces) shredded provolone cheese

1. Cook macaroni according to package directions for al dente. Meanwhile, in a large saucepan, combine soup, milk, sour cream, butter and seasonings; cook and stir over medium-low heat until blended. Stir in the cheeses until melted.

2. Drain macaroni; transfer to a greased 3-qt. slow cooker. Stir in cheese mixture. Cook, covered, on low 1-2 hours or until heated through.

CHAI TEA

A wonderful sweet-spicy aroma wafts from the slow cooker as this chai tea cooks away.

—CRYSTAL BRUNS ILIFF, CO

PREP: 20 MIN. • **COOK:** 8 HOURS • **MAKES:** 12 SERVINGS (3 QUARTS)

- 3½ ounces fresh gingerroot, peeled and thinly sliced
- 25 whole cloves
- 15 cardamom pods, crushed
- 3 cinnamon sticks (3 inches)
- 3 whole peppercorns
- 3½ quarts water
- 8 individual black tea bags
- 1 can (14 ounces) sweetened condensed milk

1. Place the ginger, cloves, cardamom, cinnamon sticks and peppercorns on a double thickness of cheesecloth; bring up corners of cloth and tie with string to form a bag. Add spice bag and water to a 5- or 6-qt. slow cooker. Cover and cook on low for 8 hours.

2. Add tea bags; cover and steep for 3-5 minutes. Discard tea bags and spice bag. Stir in milk; heat through. Serve warm.

HOST THE PERFECT APPETIZER PARTY

When planning an appetizer party, look for recipes that can be made ahead to avoid last-minute fuss. Be sure to label the beverages and food so guests will be more likely to try everything.

TROPICAL COMPOTE DESSERT

To make a more adult version of this recipe, use brandy instead of the extra tropical fruit juice.

—TASTE OF HOME TEST KITCHEN

PREP: 15 MIN. • **COOK:** 2¼ HOURS • **MAKES:** 6 SERVINGS

- 1 jar (23½ ounces) mixed tropical fruit
- 1 jalapeno pepper, seeded and chopped
- ¼ cup sugar
- 1 tablespoon chopped crystallized ginger
- ¼ teaspoon ground cinnamon
- 1 can (15 ounces) mandarin oranges, drained
- 1 jar (6 ounces) maraschino cherries, drained
- 1 medium firm banana, sliced
- 6 individual round sponge cakes
- 6 tablespoons flaked coconut, toasted

1. Drain tropical fruit, reserving ¼ cup liquid. Combine the tropical fruit and jalapeno in a 1½-qt. slow cooker. Combine the sugar, ginger, cinnamon and reserved juice; pour over fruit. Cover and cook on low for 2 hours. Stir in the mandarin oranges, cherries and banana; cook 15 minutes longer.

2. Place sponge cakes on dessert plates; top with compote. Sprinkle with coconut.

NOTE *Wear disposable gloves when cutting hot peppers; the oils can burn skin. Avoid touching your face.*

SLOW-ROASTED CHICKEN WITH VEGETABLES

The combined smell of rosemary and garlic is mouthwatering, and this recipe could not be easier. Just a few minutes of early prep and you'll come home to a delicious dinner. Even if you're not an experienced cook, this will make you look like a pro.

—ANITA BELL HERMITAGE, TN

PREP: 15 MIN. • **COOK:** 6 HOURS + STANDING • **MAKES:** 6 SERVINGS

- 2 medium carrots, halved lengthwise and cut into 3-inch pieces
- 2 celery ribs, halved lengthwise and cut into 3-inch pieces
- 8 small red potatoes, quartered
- ¾ teaspoon salt, divided
- ⅛ teaspoon pepper
- 1 medium lemon, halved
- 2 garlic cloves, crushed
- 1 broiler/fryer chicken (3 to 4 pounds)
- 1 tablespoon dried rosemary, crushed
- 1 tablespoon lemon juice
- 1 tablespoon olive oil
- 2½ teaspoons paprika

1. Place carrots, celery and potatoes in a 6-qt. slow cooker; toss with ¼ teaspoon salt and pepper. Place lemon halves and garlic in chicken cavity. Tuck wings under chicken; tie drumsticks together. Place chicken over vegetables in slow cooker, breast side up. Mix rosemary, lemon juice, oil, paprika and remaining salt; rub over chicken.

2. Cook, covered, on low 6-8 hours or until a thermometer inserted in thickest part of thigh reads 170°-175°; and vegetables are tender.

3. Remove chicken to a serving platter; tent with foil. Let stand 15 minutes before carving. Serve with vegetables.

HEARTY SPLIT PEA SOUP

We started a 39-day soup challenge, figuring if *Survivor* contestants could last for 39 days on little food, we could survive on soup! This became a family favorite during our challenge.

—DEBRA KEIL OWASSO, OK

PREP: 30 MIN. • **COOK:** 7 HOURS • **MAKES:** 6 SERVINGS (2¼ QUARTS)

- 1 large onion, chopped
- 1 cup chopped celery
- 1 cup chopped fresh carrots
- 2 tablespoons olive oil
- 1 teaspoon dried thyme
- 1 package (16 ounces) dried green split peas, rinsed
- 4 cups vegetable broth
- 2 cups water
- 6 ounces Canadian bacon, chopped
- ¼ teaspoon pepper

1. In a large skillet, saute the onion, celery and carrots in oil until tender. Add thyme; cook 1 minute longer.

2. Transfer to a 5-qt. slow cooker. Add the peas, broth and water. Cover and cook on low for 7-8 hours or until the peas are tender.

3. Cool slightly. In a blender, process half of the soup until smooth. Return all to the slow cooker. Add bacon and pepper; heat through.

CHOCOLATE PEANUT DROPS

got this recipe from a friend who originally got it from her sister.
was surprised these chocolaty candies came from a slow cooker.
You can get several dozen candies from just one batch.
—**ANITA BELL** HERMITAGE, TN

PREP: 20 MIN. • **COOK:** 1½ HOURS + STANDING
MAKES: ABOUT 11 DOZEN

- **4 ounces German sweet chocolate, chopped**
- **1 package (12 ounces) semisweet chocolate chips**
- **4 packages (10 to 12 ounces each) white baking chips**
- **2 jars (16 ounces each) lightly salted dry roasted peanuts**

1. In a 6-qt. slow cooker, layer ingredients in order listed
(do not stir). Cover and cook on low for 1½ hours. Stir to
combine. (If chocolate is not melted, cover and cook
15 minutes longer; stir. Repeat in 15-minute increments
until chocolate is melted.)
2. Drop mixture by rounded tablespoonfuls onto waxed
paper. Let stand until set. Store in an airtight container at
room temperature.

CHOCOLATE PEANUT BARK *Cook chocolate mixture
as directed; spread into two 15x10x1-in. waxed paper-lined
baking pans. Refrigerate 30 minutes or until firm. Cut into
bite-sized pieces.*

GLAZED SPICED CARROTS

Glazed carrots are a classic side dish for special occasions.
This recipe leaves your oven and stovetop free for other
cooking creations.
—*TASTE OF HOME* TEST KITCHEN

PREP: 10 MIN. • **COOK:** 6 HOURS • **MAKES:** 6 SERVINGS

- **2 pounds fresh baby carrots**
- **½ cup peach preserves**
- **¼ cup packed brown sugar**
- **½ cup butter, melted**
- **1 teaspoon vanilla extract**
- **½ teaspoon ground cinnamon**
- **¼ teaspoon salt**
- **⅛ teaspoon ground nutmeg**
- **2 tablespoons cornstarch**
- **2 tablespoons water**
  Toasted chopped pecans, optional

1. Place carrots in a 3-qt. slow cooker. Combine the
preserves, brown sugar, butter, vanilla, cinnamon, salt and
nutmeg. Combine cornstarch and water until smooth;
stir into preserve mixture. Pour over carrots.
2. Cover and cook on low for 6-8 hours or until tender.
Stir carrots; sprinkle with pecans if desired.

SLOW-COOKED REUBEN BRATS

Sauerkraut gives these beer-simmered brats a big boost, but it's the special chili sauce and melted cheese that puts them over the top. Top your favorite burger with some of the chili sauce; you won't be sorry!

—**ALANA SIMMONS** JOHNSTOWN, PA

PREP: 30 MIN. • **COOK:** 7¼ HOURS • **MAKES:** 10 SERVINGS

- 10 **uncooked bratwurst links**
- 3 **cans (12 ounces each) light beer or nonalcoholic beer**
- 1 **large sweet onion, sliced**
- 1 **can (14 ounces) sauerkraut, rinsed and well drained**
- ¾ **cup mayonnaise**
- ¼ **cup chili sauce**
- 2 **tablespoons ketchup**
- 1 **tablespoon finely chopped onion**
- 2 **teaspoons sweet pickle relish**
- 1 **garlic clove, minced**
- ⅛ **teaspoon pepper**
- 10 **hoagie buns, split**
- 10 **slices Swiss cheese**

1. In a large skillet, brown bratwurst in batches; drain. In a 5-qt. slow cooker, combine beer, sliced onion and sauerkraut; top with bratwurst. Cook, covered, on low 7-9 hours or until sausages are cooked through.

2. Preheat the oven to 350°. In a small bowl, mix the mayonnaise, chili sauce, ketchup, chopped onion, relish, garlic and pepper until blended. Spread over cut sides of buns; top with cheese, bratwurst and sauerkraut mixture. Place on an ungreased baking sheet. Bake 8-10 minutes or until cheese is melted.

ROOT BEER BBQ RIBS

This is a winner! The root beer soaks into the ribs while slow cooking and gives them a fantastic taste. You won't be disappointed with the end result.
—**MAIRYN S** SANDY, UT

PREP: 25 MIN. • **COOK:** 6 HOURS • **MAKES:** 5 SERVINGS

- 1 **cup root beer**
- 1 **cup ketchup**
- ¼ **cup orange juice**
- 3 **tablespoons Worcestershire sauce**
- 2 **tablespoons molasses**
- 1 **teaspoon onion powder**
- 1 **teaspoon garlic powder**
- ½ **teaspoon ground ginger**
- ½ **teaspoon paprika**
- ¼ **teaspoon crushed red pepper flakes**
- 4½ **pounds pork baby back ribs**
- 1 **teaspoon salt**
- ½ **teaspoon pepper**

1. In a small saucepan, combine the first 10 ingredients. Bring to a boil over medium heat. Reduce heat; simmer, uncovered, for 10 minutes or until sauce is reduced to 2 cups. Set aside.

2. Cut ribs into five serving-size pieces; sprinkle with salt and pepper. Place in a 5- or 6-qt. slow cooker. Pour sauce over ribs. Cover and cook on low for 6-8 hours or until meat is tender. Serve with sauce.

HAM AND BLACK BEAN SOUP

I originally made this soup for my black-bean-loving husband, but I ended up loving it just as much. Even better, the compliments kept coming when some neighbors stopped over and stayed for supper.
—**LAURA MEURER** GREEN BAY, WI

PREP: 25 MIN. • **COOK:** 4 HOURS
MAKES: 8 SERVINGS (ABOUT 2 QUARTS)

- 3 **cans (15 ounces each) black beans, rinsed and drained**
- 2 **cans (14½ ounces each) beef broth**
- 1 **can (14½ ounces) diced tomatoes, undrained**
- 1½ **cups cubed fully cooked ham**
- 1 **can (4 ounces) chopped green chilies**
- ¼ **cup red wine vinegar**
- 1 **large onion, chopped**
- 3 **garlic cloves, minced**
- 1 **teaspoon dried oregano**
- 1 **teaspoon dried thyme**
- 1 **teaspoon pepper**

In a 3-qt. slow cooker, combine all ingredients. Cover and cook on high for 4-5 hours or until onion is tender.

CREAMY CHICKEN & BROCCOLI STEW

This recipe is so easy to make, but no one would ever guess. My husband, who doesn't like many chicken dishes, requests it regularly.
—**MARY WATKINS** LITTLE ELM, TX

PREP: 15 MIN. • **COOK:** 6 HOURS • **MAKES:** 8 SERVINGS

- 8 **bone-in chicken thighs, skin removed (about 3 pounds)**
- 1 **cup Italian salad dressing**
- ½ **cup white wine or chicken broth**
- 6 **tablespoons butter, melted, divided**
- 1 **tablespoon dried minced onion**
- 1 **tablespoon garlic powder**
- 1 **tablespoon Italian seasoning**
- ¾ **teaspoon salt, divided**
- ¾ **teaspoon pepper, divided**
- 1 **can (10¾ ounces) condensed cream of mushroom soup, undiluted**
- 1 **package (8 ounces) cream cheese, softened**
- 2 **cups frozen broccoli florets, thawed**
- 2 **pounds red potatoes, quartered**

1. Place chicken in a 4-qt. slow cooker. Combine the salad dressing, wine, 4 tablespoons butter, onion, garlic powder, Italian seasoning, ½ teaspoon salt and ½ teaspoon pepper in a small bowl; pour over chicken.
2. Cover and cook on low for 5 hours. Skim fat. Combine the soup, cream cheese and 2 cups of liquid from slow cooker in a small bowl until blended; add to slow cooker.
3. Cover and cook 45 minutes longer or until chicken is tender, adding the broccoli during the last 30 minutes of cooking.
4. Meanwhile, place potatoes in a large saucepan and cover with water. Bring to a boil. Reduce heat; cover and simmer for 15-20 minutes or until tender. Drain and return to pan. Mash potatoes with the remaining butter, salt and pepper. Serve with chicken and broccoli mixture.

AMARETTO CHERRIES WITH DUMPLINGS

Treat everyone to a truly comforting dessert: warm tart cherries drizzled with amaretto and topped with fluffy dumplings. A scoop of vanilla ice cream is the perfect finishing touch.
—**TASTE OF HOME** TEST KITCHEN

PREP: 15 MIN. • **COOK:** 7¾ HOURS • **MAKES:** 6 SERVINGS

- 2 **cans (14½ ounces each) pitted tart cherries**
- ¾ **cup sugar**
- ¼ **cup cornstarch**
- ⅛ **teaspoon salt**
- ¼ **cup amaretto or ½ teaspoon almond extract**

DUMPLINGS

- 1 **cup all-purpose flour**
- ¼ **cup sugar**
- 1 **teaspoon baking powder**
- ½ **teaspoon grated lemon peel**
- ⅛ **teaspoon salt**
- ⅓ **cup 2% milk**
- 3 **tablespoons butter, melted**
  Vanilla ice cream, optional

1. Drain cherries, reserving ¼ cup juice. Place cherries in a 3-qt. slow cooker.
2. In a small bowl, mix sugar, cornstarch and salt; stir in reserved juice until smooth. Stir into cherries. Cook, covered, on high 7 hours. Drizzle amaretto over the cherry mixture.
3. For dumplings, in a small bowl, whisk flour, sugar, baking powder, lemon peel and salt. In another bowl, whisk milk and melted butter. Add to flour mixture; stir just until moistened.
4. Drop by tablespoonfuls on top of hot cherry mixture. Cook, covered, 45 minutes or until a toothpick inserted in center of dumplings comes out clean. If desired, serve warm with ice cream.

PEPPERONI PIZZA SOUP

My husband and I used to own a pizzeria, where this dish was always popular. We've since sold the restaurant, but I still make the soup for potlucks and other gatherings.
—**ESTELLA PETERSON** MADRAS, OR

PREP: 20 MIN. • **COOK:** 8¼ HOURS
MAKES: 6 SERVINGS (2¼ QUARTS)

- 2 cans (14½ ounces each) Italian stewed tomatoes, undrained
- 2 cans (14½ ounces each) reduced-sodium beef broth
- 1 small onion, chopped
- 1 small green pepper, chopped
- ½ cup sliced fresh mushrooms
- ½ cup sliced pepperoni, halved
- 1½ teaspoons dried oregano
- ⅛ teaspoon pepper
- 1 package (9 ounces) refrigerated cheese ravioli
  Shredded part-skim mozzarella cheese and sliced ripe olives

1. In a 4-qt. slow cooker, combine the first eight ingredients. Cook, covered, on low 8-9 hours.
2. Stir in ravioli; cook, covered, on low 15-30 minutes or until pasta is tender. Top servings with cheese and olives.

LOADED MASHED POTATOES

My mom always made cream cheese mashed potatoes for Thanksgiving. I'm carrying on the tradition with a recipe I tailored for the slow cooker. I usually make them a day ahead, freeing up oven space on the big day.
—**ANN NOLTE** RIVERVIEW, FL

PREP: 25 MIN. + CHILLING • **COOK:** 3 HOURS • **MAKES:** 10 SERVINGS

- 3 pounds potatoes (about 9 medium), peeled and cubed
- 1 package (8 ounces) cream cheese, softened
- 1 cup (8 ounces) sour cream
- ½ cup butter, cubed
- ¼ cup 2% milk
- 1½ cups (6 ounces) shredded cheddar cheese
- 1½ cups (6 ounces) shredded pepper jack cheese
- ½ pound bacon strips, cooked and crumbled
- 4 green onions, chopped
- ½ teaspoon onion powder
- ½ teaspoon garlic powder

1. Place potatoes in a Dutch oven and cover with water. Bring to a boil. Reduce heat; cover and cook for 10-15 minutes or until tender. Drain. Mash potatoes with cream cheese, sour cream, butter and milk. Stir in the cheeses, bacon, onions and seasonings. Transfer to a large bowl; cover and refrigerate overnight.
2. Transfer to a greased 3- or 4-qt. slow cooker. Cover and cook on low for 3 to 3½ hours.

Slow-Cooked Apps

Relax, the slow cooker has you covered for your next party or gathering. Set these recipes up and you'll have plenty of extra time for handling other matters. Then it's time to snack away!

JALAPENO SPINACH DIP

Spinach dip is always a party hit, and this version is as easy as it is delicious. Just mix and your work is done.

—**MICHAELA DEBELIUS** WADDELL, AZ

PREP: 10 MIN. • **COOK:** 2 HOURS
MAKES: 16 SERVINGS (¼ CUP EACH)

- 2 **packages (10 ounces each) frozen chopped spinach, thawed and squeezed dry**
- 2 **packages (8 ounces each) cream cheese, softened**
- 1 **cup grated Parmesan cheese**
- 1 **cup half-and-half cream**
- ½ **cup finely chopped onion**
- ¼ **cup chopped seeded jalapeno peppers**
- 2 **teaspoons Worcestershire sauce**
- 2 **teaspoons hot pepper sauce**
- 1 **teaspoon garlic powder**
- 1 **teaspoon dill weed**
  Tortilla chips

In a 1½-qt. slow cooker, combine the first 10 ingredients.

Cover and cook on low for 2-3 hours or until heated through. Serve with chips.

NOTE *Wear disposable gloves when cutting hot peppers; the oils can burn skin. Avoid touching your face.*

SLOW-COOKED SMOKIES

I like to include these little sausages smothered in barbecue sauce on all my party and picnic menus.

—**SUNDRA HAUCK** BOGALUSA, LA

PREP: 5 MIN. • **COOK:** 6 HOURS • **MAKES:** 8 SERVINGS

- 1 **package (1 pound) miniature smoked sausages**
- 1 **bottle (28 ounces) barbecue sauce**
- 1¼ **cups water**
- 3 **tablespoons Worcestershire sauce**
- 3 **tablespoons steak sauce**
- ½ **teaspoon pepper**

In a 3-qt. slow cooker, combine all ingredients. Cover and cook on low for 5-6 hours or until heated through. Serve with a slotted spoon.

BUFFALO WING DIP

If you love spicy wings, you'll love this dip. It's super cheesy and really has the taste of Buffalo wings.
—*TASTE OF HOME* TEST KITCHEN

PREP: 20 MIN. • **COOK:** 2 HOURS • **MAKES:** 6 CUPS

- 2 packages (8 ounces each) cream cheese, softened
- ½ cup ranch salad dressing
- ½ cup sour cream
- 5 tablespoons crumbled blue cheese
- 2 cups shredded cooked chicken
- ½ cup Buffalo wing sauce
- 2 cups (8 ounces) shredded cheddar cheese, divided
- 1 green onion, sliced
  Tortilla chips

1. In a small bowl, combine the cream cheese, dressing, sour cream and blue cheese. Transfer to a 3-qt. slow cooker. Layer with chicken, wing sauce and 1 cup cheese. Cover and cook on low for 2-3 hours or until heated through.

2. Sprinkle with remaining cheese and onion. Serve with tortilla chips.

SWEET & SPICY PEANUTS

With a caramel-like coating, these crunchy peanuts also get a zip from the hot sauce. They make a tasty snack any time of day.
—*TASTE OF HOME* TEST KITCHEN

PREP: 10 MIN. • **COOK:** 1½ HOURS + COOLING • **MAKES:** 4 CUPS

- 3 cups salted peanuts
- ½ cup sugar
- ⅓ cup packed brown sugar
- 2 tablespoons hot water
- 2 tablespoons butter, melted
- 1 tablespoon Sriracha Asian hot chili sauce or hot pepper sauce
- 1 teaspoon chili powder

1. Place peanuts in a greased 1½-qt. slow cooker. In a small bowl, combine the sugars, water, butter, hot sauce and chili powder. Pour over peanuts. Cover and cook on high for 1½ hours, stirring once.

2. Spread on waxed paper to cool. Store in an airtight container.

PUMPKIN CRANBERRY BREAD PUDDING

Savor the best of fall with this scrumptious bread pudding, served warm with a sweet vanilla sauce. Yum!

—**JUDITH BUCCIARELLI** NEWBURGH, NY

PREP: 15 MIN. • **COOK:** 3 HOURS
MAKES: 8 SERVINGS (1⅓ CUPS SAUCE)

- 8 slices cinnamon bread, cut into 1-inch cubes
- 4 eggs, beaten
- 2 cups 2% milk
- 1 cup canned pumpkin
- ¼ cup packed brown sugar
- ¼ cup butter, melted
- 1 teaspoon vanilla extract
- ½ teaspoon ground cinnamon
- ¼ teaspoon ground nutmeg
- ½ cup dried cranberries

SAUCE
- 1 cup sugar
- ⅔ cup water
- 1 cup heavy whipping cream
- 2 teaspoons vanilla extract

1. Place bread in a greased 3- or 4-qt. slow cooker. In a large bowl, combine the eggs, milk, pumpkin, brown sugar, butter, vanilla, cinnamon and nutmeg; stir in cranberries. Pour over bread cubes. Cover and cook on low for 3-4 hours or until a knife inserted near the center comes out clean.

2. For sauce, in a large saucepan, bring sugar and water to a boil over medium heat. Cook until sugar is dissolved and mixture turns a golden amber color, about 20 minutes. Gradually stir in cream until smooth. Remove from the heat; stir in vanilla. Serve warm with bread pudding.

SLOW-COOKED FISH STEW

I love fish and chowder, so this stew is a favorite of mine. It's made without cream or whole milk for a healthier take. Feel free to top servings with a little grated cheddar.

—**JANE WHITTAKER** PENSACOLA, FL

PREP: 25 MIN. • **COOK:** 6½ HOURS • **MAKES:** 8 SERVINGS (3 QUARTS)

- 1 pound potatoes (about 2 medium), peeled and finely chopped
- 1 package (10 ounces) frozen corn, thawed
- 1½ cups frozen lima beans, thawed
- 1 large onion, finely chopped
- 1 celery rib, finely chopped
- 1 medium carrot, finely chopped
- 4 garlic cloves, minced
- 1 bay leaf
- 1 teaspoon lemon-pepper seasoning
- 1 teaspoon dried parsley flakes
- 1 teaspoon dried rosemary, crushed
- ½ teaspoon salt
- 1½ cups vegetable or chicken broth
- 1 can (10¾ ounces) condensed cream of celery soup, undiluted
- ½ cup white wine or additional vegetable broth
- 1 pound cod fillets, cut into 1-inch pieces
- 1 can (14½ ounces) diced tomatoes, undrained
- 1 can (12 ounces) fat-free evaporated milk

1. In a 5-qt. slow cooker, combine the first 15 ingredients. Cook, covered, on low 6-8 hours or until potatoes are tender.

2. Remove bay leaf. Stir in cod, tomatoes and milk; cook, covered, 30-35 minutes longer or until fish just begins to flake easily with a fork.

HOT HAM SANDWICHES

I came up with this recipe when trying to re-create a hometown restaurant's sandwich. Serve these sandwiches in a buffet line because they don't really need condiments...and folks will eat them up.

—**SUSAN REHM** GRAHAMSVILLE, NY

PREP: 10 MIN. • **COOK:** 4 HOURS • **MAKES:** 12 SERVINGS

- 3 **pounds thinly sliced deli ham (about 40 slices)**
- 2 **cups apple juice**
- ⅔ **cup packed brown sugar**
- ½ **cup sweet pickle relish**
- 2 **teaspoons prepared mustard**
- 1 **teaspoon paprika**
- 12 **kaiser rolls, split**
  Additional sweet pickle relish, optional

1. Separate ham slices and place in a 3-qt. slow cooker. In a small bowl, combine the apple juice, brown sugar, relish, mustard and paprika. Pour over ham.

2. Cover and cook on low for 4-5 hours or until heated through. Place 3-4 slices of ham on each roll. Serve with additional relish if desired.

NO-FUSS BEEF ROAST

You just need a few ingredients to make this tangy roast that feeds a bunch. The gravy is tasty on top of mashed potatoes, too.

—**JEANIE BEASLEY** TUPELO, MS

PREP: 10 MIN. • **COOK:** 6 HOURS • **MAKES:** 8 SERVINGS

- 1 **boneless beef chuck roast (3 to 4 pounds)**
- 1 **can (14½ ounces) stewed tomatoes, cut up**
- 1 **can (10¾ ounces) condensed cream of mushroom soup, undiluted**
- 1 **envelope Lipton beefy onion soup mix**
- ¼ **cup cornstarch**
- ½ **cup cold water**

1. Cut roast in half. Transfer to a 5-qt. slow cooker. In a small bowl, combine the tomatoes, soup and soup mix; pour over meat. Cover and cook on low for 6-8 hours or until meat is tender.

2. Remove meat to a serving platter; keep warm. Skim the fat from cooking juices; transfer to a large saucepan. Bring liquid to a boil. Combine cornstarch and water until smooth; stir into the pan. Bring to a boil; cook and stir for 2 minutes or until thickened. Serve with roast.

DON'T PEEK!

Unless the recipe instructs you to stir in or add ingredients, don't peek under the slow cooker lid. Every time you open it, steam escapes and you add 15 to 30 minutes of cooking time to the recipe.

SPICED AMBROSIA PUNCH

The flavor of chai tea inspired this twist on a basic spiced cider punch. Using apricot and peach nectars gives everyone a little surprise.
—AYSHA SCHURMAN AMMON, ID

PREP: 15 MIN. • **COOK:** 3 HOURS
MAKES: 10 SERVINGS (¾ CUP EACH)

- 3½ cups apple cider or juice
- 3 cups apricot nectar
- 1 cup peach nectar or additional apricot nectar
- ¼ cup water
- 3 tablespoons lemon juice
- ½ teaspoon ground cardamom
- ½ teaspoon ground nutmeg
- 2 cinnamon sticks (3 inches)
- 1 teaspoon finely chopped fresh gingerroot
- 1 teaspoon grated orange peel
- 8 whole cloves
  Lemon or orange slices, optional

1. In a 3- or 4-qt. slow cooker, combine the first seven ingredients. Place cinnamon sticks, ginger, orange peel and cloves on a double thickness of cheesecloth. Gather corners of cloth to enclose seasonings; tie securely with string. Place bag in slow cooker.
2. Cook, covered, on low 3-4 hours or until heated through. Remove and discard spice bag. Serve warm, with lemon or orange slices, if desired.

ELVIS' PUDDING CAKE

I love eating peanut butter and banana together, and this slow cooker pudding cake is just like eating an Elvis sandwich, only sweeter. Banana chips add a surprisingly crunchy texture. Find them near the dried fruit in your grocery store.
—LISA RENSHAW KANSAS CITY, MO

PREP: 10 MIN. • **COOK:** 3 HOURS + STANDING • **MAKES:** 12 SERVINGS

- 3 cups cold 2% milk
- 1 package (3.4 ounces) instant banana cream pudding mix
- 1 package banana cake mix (regular size)
- ½ cup creamy peanut butter
- 2 cups peanut butter chips
- 1 cup chopped dried banana chips

1. In a small bowl, whisk the milk and pudding mix for 2 minutes. Let stand for 2 minutes or until soft-set. Transfer to a greased 5-qt. slow cooker.
2. Prepare cake mix batter according to package directions, adding peanut butter before mixing. Pour over pudding. Cover and cook on low for 3 to 3½ hours or until a toothpick inserted near the center comes out with moist crumbs.
3. Sprinkle with peanut butter chips; cover and let stand for 15-20 minutes or until partially melted. Top with the banana chips.

¼ cup lime juice
4 garlic cloves, minced
1 teaspoon ground cumin
½ teaspoon pepper
¼ teaspoon salt
⅛ teaspoon cayenne pepper
1 cup olive oil

1. In a bowl, combine the first six ingredients. Crumble sausage over mixture and mix well.
2. With skin side down, pound turkey breast with a meat mallet to ½-in. thickness. Sprinkle with salt and pepper. Spread sausage mixture over turkey to within 1 in. of edges. Roll up jelly-roll style, starting with a short side; tie at 1½-in. to 2-in. intervals with kitchen string. Place in a 5-qt. oval slow cooker.
3. In a blender, combine the first nine sauce ingredients; cover and process until blended. While processing, gradually add oil in a steady stream. Pour over turkey.
4. Cover and cook on low for 5 hours or until a thermometer inserted in center reads 165°. Remove from slow cooker; cover and let stand for 10 minutes before slicing. Discard the string.
5. Meanwhile, skim fat from cooking juices; transfer juices to a small saucepan. Bring to a boil; cook until liquid is reduced by half. Serve with turkey.
BAKE OPTION *Place turkey roll in a 13x9-in. baking dish. Pour sauce over top. Bake, uncovered, at 400° for 70-80 minutes or until a thermometer inserted in center of stuffing reads 165°. (Cover loosely with foil during the last 20 minutes if turkey browns too quickly.) Remove from the oven; cover and let stand for 10 minutes before slicing. Discard string. Skim fat from cooking juices; serve juices with turkey.*

STUFFED TURKEY WITH MOJO SAUCE

I love Latin food, so I created this recipe that combines wonderful spices and fresh ingredients. This take on a traditional turkey dish uses chicken sausage instead of chorizo.
—**MELISSA LAUER** SAN ANTONIO, TX

PREP: 30 MIN. • **COOK:** 5 HOURS + STANDING
MAKES: 8 SERVINGS (ABOUT 1 CUP SAUCE)

1 medium green pepper, finely chopped
1 medium onion, finely chopped
2 garlic cloves, minced
2 teaspoons ground coriander
1 teaspoon ground cumin
⅛ teaspoon cayenne pepper
1 pound uncooked chicken sausage links, casings removed
1 fresh boneless turkey breast (4 pounds)
¼ teaspoon salt
¼ teaspoon pepper
MOJO SAUCE
1 cup orange juice
½ cup fresh cilantro leaves
¼ cup minced fresh oregano or 4 teaspoons dried oregano

SWEET & HOT BAKED BEANS

Baked beans just belong at a barbecue...or really any gathering. They're sweet with heat when you add pineapple and jalapenos.
—**ROBIN HAAS** CRANSTON, RI

PREP: 20 MIN. • **COOK:** 5 HOURS
MAKES: 12 SERVINGS (½ CUP EACH)

4 cans (15 ounces each) white kidney or cannellini beans, rinsed and drained
2 cans (8 ounces each) crushed pineapple, undrained
2 large onions, finely chopped
1 cup packed brown sugar
1 cup ketchup
10 bacon strips, cooked and crumbled
½ cup molasses
¼ cup canned diced jalapeno peppers
2 tablespoons white vinegar
4 garlic cloves, minced
4 teaspoons ground mustard
¼ teaspoon ground cloves

In a 3- or 4-qt. slow cooker, combine all ingredients. Cook, covered, on low 5-6 hours.

Breads, Rolls & More

Quick breads, muffins, biscuits, scones, yeast breads, coffee cakes... it's all here! It'll be hard to decide what's better: the aroma or the flavor when these golden breads emerge from the oven. Make it a day of baking fun and tasty results!

BREAD MACHINE PUMPKIN MONKEY BREAD

Leftovers of this pumpkin monkey bread reheat well on busy weekdays, and any extra sauce makes for an excellent pancake or waffle syrup.
—**EMILY MAIN** TONOPAH, AZ

PREP: 45 MIN. + RISING • **BAKE:** 20 MIN. + COOLING
MAKES: 18 SERVINGS

- 1 cup warm 2% milk (70° to 80°)
- ¾ cup canned pumpkin
- 2 tablespoons butter, softened
- ¼ cup sugar
- 1 teaspoon salt
- 1 teaspoon ground cinnamon
- ½ teaspoon ground ginger
- ¼ teaspoon ground cloves
- ¼ teaspoon ground nutmeg
- 4 to 4¼ cups all-purpose flour
- 2 teaspoons active dry yeast

SAUCE
- 1 cup butter, cubed
- 1 cup packed brown sugar
- 1 cup dried cranberries
- ¼ cup canned pumpkin
- 1 teaspoon ground cinnamon
- ½ teaspoon ground ginger
- ¼ teaspoon ground nutmeg
- ¼ teaspoon ground cloves

1. In a bread machine pan, place the first 11 ingredients in order suggested by manufacturer. Select the dough setting. Check dough after 5 minutes of mixing; add 1-2 tablespoons of water or flour if needed.
2. Meanwhile, in a large saucepan, combine sauce ingredients; cook and stir until blended. Remove from heat.

3. When dough cycle is completed, turn dough onto a lightly floured surface. Divide into 36 portions; shape into balls.
4. Arrange half of the balls in a greased 10-in. fluted tube pan; cover with half of the sauce. Repeat, being sure to thoroughly coat the top layer with sauce.
5. Let rise in a warm place until doubled, about 30 minutes. Preheat oven to 375°. Bake 20-25 minutes or until golden brown. Cover loosely with foil if top browns too quickly.
6. Cool in pan 10 minutes before inverting onto a serving plate. Serve warm.
NOTE *We recommend you do not use a bread machine's time-delay feature for this recipe.*

HAM AND CHEDDAR SCONES

This recipe first came from a friend of mine. I like that you can see the flecks of cheese, ham and green onions.
—**FELICITY LA RUE** PALMDALE, CA

PREP: 25 MIN. • **BAKE:** 20 MIN. • **MAKES:** 1 DOZEN

- 3 cups all-purpose flour
- ½ cup sugar
- 2 tablespoons baking powder
- ½ teaspoon salt
- 2 cups heavy whipping cream
- 1 cup diced fully cooked ham
- ½ cup diced cheddar cheese
- 4 green onions, thinly sliced

1. Preheat oven to 400°. In a large bowl, combine flour, sugar, baking powder and salt. Stir in cream just until moistened. Stir in ham, cheese and onions. Turn onto a floured surface; knead 10 times.
2. Transfer dough to a greased baking sheet. Pat into a 9-in. circle. Cut into 12 wedges, but do not separate. Bake 20-25 minutes or until golden brown. Serve warm.

RUSTIC COUNTRY BREAD

My husband loved the bread at a local sandwich shop. After experimenting, I have come close to duplicating the bread's taste and texture, much to his delight.
—**DEBRA KEIL** OWASSO, OK

PREP: 20 MIN. + RISING • **BAKE:** 20 MIN.
MAKES: 1 LOAF (8 WEDGES)

- 1 package (¼ ounce) active dry yeast
- 1½ teaspoons sugar
- 1 cup warm water (110° to 115°)
- 1 teaspoon salt
- 1 teaspoon balsamic vinegar
- 2 cups all-purpose flour
- 1 tablespoon olive oil
  Additional water

1. In a large bowl, dissolve yeast and sugar in warm water. Let stand 5 minutes. Add salt, vinegar and 1½ cups flour. Beat until smooth. Stir in enough remaining flour to form a soft dough (dough will be sticky).
2. Do not knead. Transfer to a greased bowl. Cover and let rise in a warm place until doubled, about 50 minutes.
3. Stir dough down. Transfer to a greased 9-in. pie plate. Cover and let rise in a warm place until doubled, about 35 minutes.
4. Preheat oven to 425°. Brush with oil. Bake 10 minutes. Reduce heat to 375°; bake 10-15 minutes longer or until golden brown, spritzing twice with additional water.

LEMON-RASPBERRY STREUSEL CAKE

Buttery almond streusel tops the luscious, raspberry-studded lemon cream in these very special bars.
—**JEANNE HOLT** MENDOTA HEIGHTS, MN

PREP: 25 MIN. • **BAKE:** 35 MIN. + COOLING • **MAKES:** 24 SERVINGS

- ⅓ cup shortening
- ⅓ cup butter, softened
- 1¼ cups sugar
- 3 eggs
- ½ teaspoon almond extract
- 2¼ cups all-purpose flour
- 1¼ teaspoons baking powder
- ½ teaspoon salt
- 1 package (8 ounces) cream cheese, softened
- ½ cup lemon curd
- ½ cup seedless raspberry jam
- 1 cup fresh raspberries

STREUSEL
- ⅔ cup all-purpose flour
- ⅓ cup sugar
- ⅓ cup sliced almonds, finely chopped
- ¼ cup cold butter

ICING
- 1 cup confectioners' sugar
- 4 teaspoons lemon juice

1. Preheat oven to 350°. In a large bowl, cream shortening, butter and sugar until light and fluffy. Beat in eggs and extract. Combine flour, baking powder and salt; gradually add to creamed mixture and mix well. Set aside 1 cup batter.
2. Spread remaining batter into a greased 13x9-in. baking pan. Combine cream cheese and lemon curd; spoon over batter. In a small bowl, beat jam; stir in raspberries. Drop by tablespoonfuls over lemon mixture. Drop the reserved batter by tablespoonfuls over top.
3. For streusel, in a small bowl, combine flour, sugar and almonds. Cut in butter until crumbly. Sprinkle over batter.
4. Bake 35-40 minutes or until a toothpick inserted in the center comes out clean. Cool on a wire rack.
5. Combine icing ingredients; drizzle over cake.

ALMOND & CRANBERRY COCONUT BREAD

Sure, this is an all-around great bread for all seasons, but the red bursts of cranberry gives the loaf an especially festive look for a special occasion.

—ROSEMARY JOHNSON IRONDALE, AL

PREP: 20 MIN. • **BAKE:** 1 HOUR + COOLING
MAKES: 2 LOAVES (16 SLICES EACH)

- 2 **cups flaked coconut**
- 1 **cup slivered almonds**
- 1 **cup butter, softened**
- 1 **cup sugar**
- 4 **eggs**
- 1 **cup (8 ounces) vanilla yogurt**
- 1 **teaspoon almond extract**
- 4½ **cups all-purpose flour**
- 3 **teaspoons baking powder**
- ½ **teaspoon salt**
- ½ **teaspoon baking soda**
- 1 **can (15 ounces) cream of coconut**
- 1 **cup dried cranberries**

1. Place coconut and almonds in an ungreased 15x10x1-in. pan. Bake at 350° for 10-15 minutes or until lightly toasted, stirring occasionally. Cool.

2. In a large bowl, cream butter and sugar until light and fluffy. Add eggs, one at a time, beating well after each addition. Beat in yogurt and extract until blended. Combine the flour, baking powder, salt and baking soda. Add to the creamed mixture alternately with cream of coconut, beating well after each addition. Fold in the cranberries, coconut and almonds.

3. Transfer to two greased and floured 9x5-in. loaf pans. Bake at 350° for 60-70 minutes or until a toothpick inserted near the center of the loaf comes out clean. Cool for 10 minutes before removing from pans to wire racks to cool completely.

MUSHROOM & ONION CRESCENTS

I knew these stuffed crescents were keepers when my husband ate most of the filling before I could roll it into the dough. I've learned to be sneaky when making them now!

—**CARRIE POMMIER** FARMINGTON, MN

PREP: 25 MIN. • **BAKE:** 10 MIN. • **MAKES:** 8 ROLLS

- 3 **tablespoons butter, divided**
- 1 **cup sliced baby portobello mushrooms**
- 1 **medium onion, halved and sliced**
- 3 **garlic cloves, minced**
- ⅓ **cup grated Parmesan cheese**
- 1 **tablespoon minced fresh parsley**
- 1 **tube (8 ounces) refrigerated reduced-fat crescent rolls**
- ½ **cup shredded part-skim mozzarella cheese**

1. Preheat oven to 375°. In a large skillet, heat 2 tablespoons butter over medium-high heat. Add mushrooms and onion; cook and stir 2-3 minutes or until softened. Reduce heat to medium-low; cook and stir 10-12 minutes or until onion is golden. Add garlic; cook 1 minute longer. Remove from heat; stir in Parmesan cheese and parsley.

2. Unroll crescent dough; separate into triangles. Place 1 tablespoon mushroom mixture at the wide end of each triangle; top with 1 tablespoon mozzarella cheese. Roll up and seal edges. Place 2 in. apart on an ungreased baking sheet, point side down; curve ends to form a crescent. Melt remaining butter; brush over tops.

3. Bake 10-12 minutes or until golden brown. Refrigerate any leftovers.

PEANUT BUTTER & JELLY BITES

My friend is an avid runner. After I heard that she craved a peanut butter and jelly sandwich during a race, I whipped up these easy-to-carry bites for her.

—**JENNIFER HEASLEY** YORK, PA

PREP: 25 MIN. • **BAKE:** 15 MIN. + COOLING • **MAKES:** 2 DOZEN

- 4 **ounces cream cheese, softened**
- ½ **cup strawberry jelly, divided**
- 2 **tubes (8 ounces each) refrigerated seamless crescent dough sheets**
- ½ **cup creamy peanut butter**
- 1 **cup confectioners' sugar**
- 5 **tablespoons 2% milk**

1. Preheat oven to 350°. In a small bowl, beat cream cheese and ¼ cup jelly until smooth. Unroll each sheet of crescent dough into a rectangle. Spread each with half of the filling to within ½ in. of edges. Roll up jelly-roll style, starting with a long side; pinch seam to seal. Cut each roll widthwise into 12 slices; place on parchment paper-lined baking sheets, cut side down.

2. Bake 12-15 minutes or until golden brown. Cool on pans 2 minutes. Remove to wire racks to cool.

3. In a small bowl, beat peanut butter, confectioners' sugar and milk until smooth. Drizzle over rolls; top with remaining jelly.

LET CREAM CHEESE SIT OUT A BIT

The key to softening cream cheese, butter or margarine is to keep it out at room temperature for a short time.

Baskets of Rolls!

Buttery, delicious, warm, melt-in-your-mouth good—there are many ways to describe fresh-baked rolls. We've rounded up the best of the best here to complement your next meal.

CORNMEAL DINNER ROLLS

A robust sidekick to chili, soups and stews, these biscuits can also stand alone with a simple pat of butter and drizzle of honey.
—**BRYNN RADER** OLYMPIA, WA

PREP: 35 MIN.+ RISING • **BAKE:** 15 MIN. • **MAKES:** 2½ DOZEN

- 2 **cups whole milk**
- ½ **cup sugar**
- ½ **cup butter, cubed**
- ⅓ **cup cornmeal**
- 1¼ **teaspoons salt**
- 1 **package (¼ ounce) active dry yeast**
- ¼ **cup warm water (110° to 115°)**
- 2 **eggs**
- 4¾ **to 5¾ cups all-purpose flour**

TOPPING

- 2 **tablespoons butter, melted**
- 1 **tablespoon cornmeal**

1. In a large saucepan, combine the milk, sugar, butter, cornmeal and salt. Bring to a boil over medium heat, stirring constantly. Reduce heat; cook and stir 5-8 minutes or until thickened. Cool to 110°-115°.

2. In a small bowl, dissolve yeast in warm water. In a large bowl, combine the eggs, cornmeal mixture, yeast mixture and 2 cups flour; beat until smooth. Stir in enough remaining flour to form a soft dough (dough will be sticky).

3. Turn onto a floured surface; knead until smooth and elastic, about 6-8 minutes. Place in a greased bowl, turning once to grease the top. Cover with plastic wrap; let rise in a warm place until doubled, about 1 hour.

4. Punch dough down. Turn onto a lightly floured surface; divide into 30 balls. Place 2 in. apart on greased baking sheets. Cover with a clean kitchen towel; let rise in a warm place until doubled, about 45 minutes.

5. Uncover rolls; brush with melted butter and sprinkle with cornmeal. Bake at 375° for 13-17 minutes or until golden brown. Remove from pans to wire racks; serve warm.

HONEY WHEAT ROLLS

Two things really stand out about these rolls: They're not difficult to make and they have the most wonderful honey flavor.
—**SANDY KLOCINSKI** SUMMERVILLE, SC

PREP: 40 MIN. + RISING • **BAKE:** 10 MIN. • **MAKES:** 2 DOZEN

- 2 **packages (¼ ounce each) active dry yeast**
- 1¾ **cups warm fat-free milk (110° to 115°)**
- 2 **eggs**
- ½ **cup honey**
- ¼ **cup mashed potatoes (without added milk and butter)**
- ¼ **cup butter, melted**
- 1 **teaspoon salt**
- 3 **cups whole wheat flour**
- 2¼ **to 2¾ cups all-purpose flour**

1. In a small bowl, dissolve yeast in warm milk. In a large bowl, combine 1 egg, honey, mashed potatoes, butter, salt, whole wheat flour, yeast mixture and 1½ cups all-purpose flour; beat on medium speed for 3 minutes. Stir in enough remaining flour to form a soft dough (dough will be sticky).

2. Turn onto a floured surface; knead until smooth and elastic, about 6-8 minutes. Place in a bowl coated with cooking spray, turning once to coat the top. Cover with plastic wrap and let rise in a warm place until doubled, about 1 hour.

3. Turn onto a floured surface; divide into 24 balls. Roll each into a 7-in. rope. Holding one end of rope, loosely wrap dough around, forming a coil. Tuck end under; pinch to seal. Place in muffin cups coated with cooking spray. Cover and let rise until doubled, about 30 minutes.

4. Beat remaining egg; brush over rolls. Bake at 400° for 9-11 minutes or until golden brown. Remove from pans to wire racks to cool.

WHOLE WHEAT POTATO ROLLS

This classic-with-a-twist recipe comes from my cousin. If you have leftovers, go ahead and freeze them for later.

—**DEVON VICKERS** GODDARD, KS

PREP: 30 MIN.+ RISING • **BAKE:** 10 MIN. • **MAKES:** 24 ROLLS

- 1 package (¼ ounce) active dry yeast
- 2 cups warm water (110° to 115°)
- ½ cup sugar
- ½ cup canola oil
- 2 eggs
- ⅓ cup mashed potato flakes
- 1½ teaspoons salt
- 2 cups all-purpose flour
- 4 to 4¾ cups whole wheat flour
- 2 tablespoons butter, melted
   Quick-cooking oats, optional

1. In a small bowl, dissolve yeast in warm water. In a large bowl, combine sugar, oil, eggs, potato flakes, salt, yeast mixture, all-purpose flour and 2½ cups whole wheat flour. Beat until smooth. Stir in enough remaining whole wheat flour to form a soft dough (dough will be sticky).

2. Turn onto a floured surface; knead until smooth and elastic, about 6-8 minutes. Place in a greased bowl, turning once to grease the top. Cover with plastic wrap and let rise in a warm place until doubled, about 1½ hours.

3. Punch down dough. Turn onto a lightly floured surface; divide and shape into 24 balls. Place 2 in. apart on greased baking sheets. Cover with kitchen towels; let rise in a warm place until doubled, about 30 minutes.

4. Preheat the oven to 375°. Brush tops with melted butter; if desired, sprinkle with oats. Bake 9-11 minutes or until lightly browned. Serve warm.

BACON CRESCENT ROLLS

A cinch to assemble, kids will love helping put together these three-ingredient bites. Better yet, it takes only 25 minutes to make this recipe.

—**JANE NEARING** INDIANAPOLIS, IN

START TO FINISH: 25 MIN. • **MAKES:** 8 SERVINGS

- 1 tube (8 ounces) refrigerated crescent rolls
- 6 bacon strips, cooked and crumbled
- 1 teaspoon onion powder

1. Separate crescent dough into eight triangles. Set aside 1 tablespoon of bacon. Sprinkle onion powder and remaining bacon over triangles; roll up and place point side down on an ungreased baking sheet. Sprinkle with the reserved bacon.

2. Bake at 375° for 10-15 minutes or until golden brown. Serve warm.

FREEZE OPTION *Freeze cooled rolls in resealable plastic freezer bags. To use, thaw rolls at room temperature or, if desired, microwave each roll on high 10-15 seconds or until heated through.*

DOUGHNUT MUFFINS

My mom and I went to a bakery every morning on the way to school and I got to pick out a different treat each day. That's how my affinity for doughnuts began. With this recipe, you get all the taste of a doughnut in an easy-to-bake muffin.

—**MORGAN BOTWINICK** RICHMOND, VA

PREP: 30 MIN. • **BAKE:** 20 MIN. • **MAKES:** 1 DOZEN

- ¾ cup butter, softened
- ⅔ cup packed brown sugar
- ¼ cup sugar
- 2 eggs
- 1¼ cups 2% milk
- 1 teaspoon vanilla extract
- 3 cups all-purpose flour
- 2½ teaspoons baking powder
- ¾ teaspoon salt
- ½ teaspoon ground nutmeg
- ½ teaspoon ground cinnamon
- ¼ teaspoon baking soda

COATING
- 1 cup coarse sugar
- 1 tablespoon ground cinnamon
- ⅓ cup butter, melted

1. Preheat oven to 350°. In a large bowl, cream butter and sugars until light and fluffy. Add eggs, one at a time, beating well after each addition. Gradually beat in milk and vanilla. In another bowl, whisk flour, baking powder, salt, nutmeg, cinnamon and baking soda. Add to creamed mixture; stir just until moistened.

2. Fill greased or paper-lined muffin cups with batter. Bake 18-20 minutes or until a toothpick inserted in center comes out clean. Cool 5 minutes before removing from pan to a wire rack.

3. Meanwhile, for coating, combine coarse sugar and cinnamon. Dip tops of warm muffins in butter, then coat in cinnamon-sugar.

SUN-DRIED TOMATO PROVOLONE BREAD

This quick bread, which was passed down from my mother, is packed with goodness. It not only goes well with soups and chowders, but it also makes a savory accompaniment to beef and chicken entrees.

—**MARIE RIZZIO** INTERLOCHEN, MI

PREP: 30 MIN. • **BAKE:** 40 MIN. + COOLING
MAKES: 3 MINI LOAVES (6 SLICES EACH)

- ⅓ cup oil-packed sun-dried tomatoes
- 2¼ cups all-purpose flour
- 2 teaspoons baking powder
- 2 teaspoons sugar
- 1¼ teaspoons dried basil
- 1 teaspoon salt
- ½ teaspoon baking soda
- ½ teaspoon coarsely ground pepper
- 2 eggs
- 1¼ cups buttermilk
- 3 tablespoons canola oil
- 1 cup (4 ounces) shredded provolone cheese
- ¼ cup minced fresh parsley

1. Preheat the oven to 350°. Drain tomatoes, reserving 2 tablespoons oil. Chop tomatoes and set aside.

2. In a large bowl, combine flour, baking powder, sugar, basil, salt, baking soda and pepper. In a small bowl, whisk eggs, buttermilk, oil and reserved sun-dried tomato oil. Stir into dry ingredients just until moistened. Fold in cheese, parsley and sun-dried tomatoes.

3. Transfer to three greased 5¾x3x2-in. loaf pans. Bake 40-45 minutes or until a toothpick inserted in center comes out clean. Cool 10 minutes before removing from pans to wire racks.

ASIAGO BAGELS

Discover a cheesy alternative to the usual sweet bread brunch offerings. There's no need to stop by a bakery when you can make bagels at home.

—TAMI KUEHL LOUP CITY, NE

PREP: 30 MIN. + STANDING • **BAKE:** 15 MIN. + COOLING
MAKES: 1 DOZEN

- 1 cup water (70° to 80°)
- 2 eggs
- ¼ cup plus 1 tablespoon olive oil
- 2 tablespoons honey
- ¾ cup shredded Asiago cheese, divided
- ⅓ cup nonfat dry milk powder
- 1½ teaspoons salt
- 1 teaspoon dried basil
- 2 cups whole wheat flour
- 1½ cups plus 2 tablespoons all-purpose flour
- 4 teaspoons active dry yeast
- 1 egg white
- 1 tablespoon water

1. In a bread machine pan, place the water, eggs, oil, honey, ½ cup cheese, milk powder, salt, basil, flours and yeast in order suggested by manufacturer. Select dough setting (check the dough after 5 minutes of mixing; add 1 to 2 tablespoons of water or flour if needed).

2. When cycle is completed, turn dough onto a lightly floured surface. Shape into 12 balls. Push thumb through centers to form a 1½-in. hole. Stretch and shape dough to form an even ring. Cover and let rest for 10 minutes; flatten bagels slightly.

3. Fill a Dutch oven two-thirds full with water; bring to a boil. Drop bagels, two at a time, into boiling water. Cook for 45 seconds; turn and cook 45 seconds longer. Remove with a slotted spoon; drain well on paper towels.

4. In a small bowl, combine egg white and water; brush over bagels. Sprinkle with remaining cheese. Place 2 in. apart on greased baking sheets. Bake at 400° for 15-20 minutes or until golden brown. Remove to wire racks to cool.

LIME MUFFINS WITH COCONUT STREUSEL

A dozen of these tempting gems will dazzle your brunch guests. The macadamia-coconut streusel is the perfect complement to the fresh lime flavor in the batter.

—TERESA GRISSOM ZIONSVILLE, IN

PREP: 30 MIN. • **BAKE:** 20 MIN. • **MAKES:** 1 DOZEN

- 2 cups all-purpose flour
- ¾ cup sugar
- 1 teaspoon baking powder
- ¾ teaspoon baking soda
- ½ teaspoon salt
- ¾ cup buttermilk
- ¾ cup (6 ounces) Key lime yogurt
- 1 egg
- ¼ cup butter, melted
- 2 teaspoons Key lime juice
- 1 teaspoon grated lime peel
- 1 teaspoon vanilla extract

TOPPING
- 3 tablespoons sugar
- 2 tablespoons all-purpose flour
- 2 tablespoons flaked coconut
- 2 tablespoons finely chopped macadamia nuts
- 2 tablespoons butter, melted

1. In a large bowl, combine the first five ingredients. In another bowl, combine the buttermilk, yogurt, egg, butter, lime juice, lime peel and vanilla. Stir into dry ingredients just until moistened. Fill greased muffin cups three-fourths full of batter.

2. In a small bowl, combine topping ingredients; sprinkle over muffins. Bake at 375° for 18-22 minutes or until a toothpick inserted in muffin comes out clean. Cool for 5 minutes before removing from pan to a wire rack. Serve muffins warm.

RUSTIC RYE BREAD

With a crusty top and firm texture, this gorgeous rye bread holds up well for sandwiches, but just a pat of butter will do the job, too.

—**HOLLY WADE** HARRISONBURG, VA

PREP: 20 MIN. + RISING • **BAKE:** 30 MIN. + COOLING
MAKES: 2 LOAVES (12 SLICES EACH)

 1 package (¼ ounce) active dry yeast
1¾ cups warm water (110° to 115°), divided
 ¼ cup packed brown sugar
 ¼ cup light molasses
 3 tablespoons caraway seeds
 2 tablespoons canola oil
 3 teaspoons salt
1¾ cups rye flour
 ¾ cup whole wheat flour
1¾ to 2¼ cups all-purpose flour

1. In a large bowl, dissolve the yeast in ¼ cup warm water. Add the brown sugar, molasses, caraway seeds, oil, salt and remaining water; mix well. Add the rye flour, whole wheat flour and 1¾ cups all-purpose flour. Beat until smooth. Stir in enough remaining all-purpose flour to form a firm dough.
2. Turn onto a lightly floured surface; knead until smooth and elastic, about 6-8 minutes. Place in a bowl coated with cooking spray, turning once to coat the top. Cover and let rise in a warm place until doubled, about 1 hour.
3. Punch dough down; shape into two round loaves. Place on a baking sheet coated with cooking spray. Cover and let rise until doubled, about 1 hour.
4. Bake at 350° for 30-35 minutes or until golden brown. Remove from pan to wire rack to cool.

CREAM-FILLED CHOCOLATE SUPREME MUFFINS

Because of her reputation for baking up yummy things, Mom used to sell muffins at my dad's workplace. These cupcake-like treats were always among my favorites.

—**SUSANNE SPICKER** NORTH OGDEN, UT

PREP: 30 MIN. • **BAKE:** 25 MIN. + COOLING • **MAKES:** 1 DOZEN

 3 cups all-purpose flour
 2 cups sugar
 ½ cup baking cocoa
 2 teaspoons baking soda
 1 teaspoon salt
 2 cups cold water
 ¾ cup canola oil
 1 egg
 2 tablespoons white vinegar
 2 teaspoons vanilla extract
FILLING
 4 ounces cream cheese, softened
 ¼ cup sugar
 ⅛ teaspoon salt
 2 tablespoons beaten egg
 ½ teaspoon vanilla extract
 ¾ cup milk chocolate chips
    Confectioners' sugar, optional

1. Preheat the oven to 350°. In a large bowl, combine flour, sugar, cocoa, baking soda and salt. In another bowl, combine water, oil, egg, vinegar and vanilla. Stir into dry ingredients just until moistened.
2. For filling, beat cream cheese, sugar and salt until smooth. Beat in egg and vanilla. Fold in chips.
3. Fill 12 paper-lined jumbo muffin cups half full with batter. Drop a rounded tablespoonful of cream cheese mixture into center of each; cover with remaining batter.
4. Bake 25-30 minutes or until a toothpick inserted in muffin comes out clean. Cool 5 minutes before removing from pans to wire racks to cool completely. Sprinkle with confectioners' sugar if desired.

CARAMEL APPLE SCONES

A drizzle of caramel round outs the apple and whole wheat goodness in these rustic scones.
—**ARLENE COOK** BAINBRIDGE, GA

PREP: 20 MIN. • **BAKE:** 15 MIN. + COOLING • **MAKES:** 4 SERVINGS

- ½ cup whole wheat flour
- ½ cup all-purpose flour
- 2 tablespoons brown sugar
- 1½ teaspoons baking powder
- ¼ teaspoon salt
- 3 tablespoons cold butter
- ¼ cup plus 2 tablespoons half-and-half cream
- 1 egg yolk
- 1½ teaspoons vanilla extract
- ⅔ cup shredded peeled apple
- 1 tablespoon caramel ice cream topping

1. In a small bowl, combine the flours, brown sugar, baking powder and salt. Cut in butter until mixture resembles coarse crumbs. In a small bowl, whisk the cream, egg yolk and vanilla; add to dry ingredients just until moistened. Stir in apple. Turn onto a floured surface; knead 10 times.
2. Pat into a 5-in. circle. Cut into four wedges. Separate wedges and place on an ungreased baking sheet. Bake at 400° for 15-20 minutes or until golden brown. Cool for 10 minutes. Drizzle with caramel topping.

BEERNANA BREAD

Beer is good, banana bread is good, and beernana bread is great! This recipe is a guaranteed crowd-pleaser.
—**STEVE CAYFORD** DUBUQUE, IA

PREP: 15 MIN. • **BAKE:** 55 MIN. + COOLING
MAKES: 1 LOAF (16 SLICES)

- 3 cups self-rising flour
- ¾ cup quick-cooking oats
- ½ cup packed brown sugar
- 1½ cups mashed ripe bananas (about 3 medium)
- 1 bottle (12 ounces) wheat beer
- ¼ cup maple syrup
- 2 tablespoons olive oil
- 1 tablespoon sesame seeds
- ¼ teaspoon kosher salt

1. Preheat oven to 375°. In a large bowl, mix flour, oats and brown sugar. In another bowl, mix bananas, beer and maple syrup until blended. Add to flour mixture; stir just until moistened.
2. Transfer to a greased 9x5-in. loaf pan. Drizzle with oil; sprinkle with sesame seeds and salt. Bake 55-60 minutes or until a toothpick inserted in center comes out clean. Cool in pan 10 minutes before removing to wire rack to cool.

HERBED DINNER ROLLS

To dress up everyday dinner rolls, brush herbed butter over the dough, then form accordion rolls. The smell is amazing!
—*TASTE OF HOME* TEST KITCHEN

PREP: 40 MIN. + CHILLING • **BAKE:** 20 MIN. • **MAKES:** 2 DOZEN

- 2 packages (¼ ounce each) active dry yeast
- ½ cup warm water (110° to 115°)
- 1 teaspoon plus ⅓ cup sugar, divided
- 1¼ cups warm 2% milk (110° to 115°)
- ½ cup butter, melted
- 2 eggs
- 1½ teaspoons salt
- 6 to 6½ cups all-purpose flour
- 3 tablespoons butter, softened
- 1 teaspoon Italian seasoning
- 1 egg white, beaten

1. In a large bowl, dissolve the yeast in warm water with 1 teaspoon sugar. Add milk, melted butter, eggs, salt, 3 cups flour and remaining sugar; beat until smooth. Stir in enough remaining flour to form a soft dough.
2. Turn onto a floured surface; knead until smooth and elastic, about 6-8 minutes. Place in a greased bowl, turning once to grease the top. Cover and let rise in a warm place until doubled, about 1 hour.
3. Punch dough down; place on a lightly floured surface. Divide into four portions. Roll each portion into a 14x6-in. rectangle. Combine softened butter and Italian seasoning; spread over dough.
4. Score each rectangle widthwise at 2-in. intervals. Using marks as a guide, fold dough accordion-style back and forth along score lines. Cut the folded dough into six 1-in. pieces. Place pieces cut side down in greased muffin cups. Cover loosely with plastic wrap. Refrigerate for 8 hours or overnight.
5. Preheat the oven to 375°. Uncover and let stand at room temperature 10 minutes before baking. Brush with egg white. Bake 18-22 minutes or until golden brown. Remove from pans to wire racks.
BASIL & OREGANO DINNER ROLLS *Substitute ½ teaspoon each dried oregano and basil for Italian seasoning.*

BUTTERMILK CORN BREAD

This tender corn bread can be made and baked in a half hour. There's a lot to like about this straightforward recipe.

—PATRICIA SWART GALLOWAY, NJ

START TO FINISH: 30 MIN. • **MAKES:** 8 SERVINGS

- 1 cup all-purpose flour
- 1 cup yellow cornmeal
- 1 tablespoon sugar
- 2 teaspoons baking powder
- 1 teaspoon baking soda
- ¼ teaspoon salt
- 2 eggs
- 1 cup buttermilk
- 3 tablespoons butter, melted

1. In a large bowl, combine the flour, cornmeal, sugar, baking powder, baking soda and salt. In a small bowl, whisk the eggs, buttermilk and butter. Stir into dry ingredients just until moistened.

2. Transfer to a 9-in. square baking pan coated with cooking spray. Bake at 400° for 15-20 minutes or until top is lightly browned and a toothpick inserted near the center comes out clean. Serve warm.

MINI MAPLE CINNAMON ROLLS

Maple syrup boosts the sweetness in these lovely cinnamon buns. I make the dough in my bread machine before popping the rolls in the oven.

—JUANITA CARLSEN NORTH BEND, OR

PREP: 20 MIN. + RISING • **BAKE:** 20 MIN. • **MAKES:** 2 DOZEN

- ⅔ cup milk
- ⅓ cup maple syrup
- ⅓ cup butter, softened
- 1 egg
- ¾ teaspoon salt
- 3 cups bread flour
- 1 package (¼ ounce) active dry yeast

TOPPING
- ½ cup packed brown sugar
- 2 tablespoons bread flour
- 4 teaspoons ground cinnamon
- 6 tablespoons cold butter

MAPLE ICING
- 1 cup confectioners' sugar
- 3 tablespoons butter, melted
- 3 tablespoons maple syrup
- 1 to 2 teaspoons milk

1. In a bread machine pan, place the first seven ingredients in order suggested by manufacturer. Select the dough setting (check dough after 5 minutes of mixing; add 1 to 2 tablespoons of water or bread flour if needed).

2. When the cycle is completed, turn dough onto a lightly floured surface. Roll into two 12x7-in. rectangles. In a small bowl, combine the brown sugar, flour and cinnamon; cut in butter until mixture resembles coarse crumbs. Sprinkle half

over each rectangle. Roll up jelly-roll style, starting from a long side; pinch seam to seal.

3. Cut each roll into 12 slices. Place cut side down in one greased 13x9-in. baking pan. Cover and let rise in a warm place until doubled, about 20 minutes.

4. Bake at 375° for 20-25 minutes or until golden brown. Cool on a wire rack for 5 minutes. Meanwhile, in a small bowl, combine the confectioners' sugar, butter, syrup and enough milk to achieve desired consistency. Spread over warm rolls.

NOTE *We recommend you do not use a bread machine's time-delay feature for this recipe.*

SAVORY BISCUIT-BREADSTICKS

I love to experiment in the kitchen with simple ingredients like refrigerated biscuits. The results usually are a big hit, like these super-fast breadsticks.

—BILLY HENSLEY MOUNT CARMEL, TN

START TO FINISH: 20 MIN. • **MAKES:** 10 BREADSTICKS

- ½ cup grated Parmesan cheese
- 2 teaspoons dried minced garlic
- ¼ teaspoon crushed red pepper flakes
- 1 tube (12 ounces) refrigerated buttermilk biscuits
- 2 tablespoons olive oil

Preheat oven to 400°. In a shallow bowl, mix cheese, garlic and pepper flakes. Roll each biscuit into a 6-in. rope. Brush lightly with oil; roll in cheese mixture. Place on a greased baking sheet. Bake 8-10 minutes or until golden brown.

2. Spoon a third of the batter into a greased and floured 10-in. tube pan. Combine brown sugar, flour and cinnamon; sprinkle half over batter. Top with half of the berries. Repeat layers. Top with remaining batter.

3. Bake 55-65 minutes or until a toothpick inserted near the center comes out clean. Cool 10 minutes before removing from pan to a wire rack to cool completely. Combine glaze ingredients; drizzle over warm coffee cake.

FLUFFY HERB DROP BISCUITS

I grow a lot of herbs so I can just go out to the garden and pick them as needed for different recipes. These biscuits contain fresh basil and rosemary.

—**MELISSA MCCABE** LONG BEACH, CA

START TO FINISH: 20 MIN. • **MAKES:** 1 DOZEN

- 2 **cups all-purpose flour**
- 2 **teaspoons baking powder**
- ½ **teaspoon salt**
- ¼ **teaspoon baking soda**
- ¾ **cup buttermilk**
- ⅓ **cup canola oil**
- 2 **tablespoons minced fresh basil**
- 2 **teaspoons minced fresh rosemary**

1. Preheat oven to 450°. In a large bowl, whisk flour, baking powder, salt and baking soda. In another bowl, whisk the buttermilk, oil, basil and rosemary; stir into dry ingredients just until moistened.

2. Drop by rounded tablespoonfuls 2 in. apart onto an ungreased baking sheet. Bake 10-12 minutes or until light brown. Serve warm.

BLUEBERRY SOUR CREAM COFFEE CAKE

Special breakfasts would not be the same at our house without this delicious coffee cake. Whenever I take it anywhere, folks rave about it.

—**SUSAN WALSCHLAGER** ANDERSON, IN

PREP: 25 MIN. • **BAKE:** 55 MIN. + COOLING • **MAKES:** 10-12 SERVINGS

- ¾ **cup butter, softened**
- 1½ **cups sugar**
- 4 **eggs**
- 1 **teaspoon vanilla extract**
- 3 **cups all-purpose flour**
- 1½ **teaspoons baking powder**
- ¾ **teaspoon baking soda**
- ¼ **teaspoon salt**
- 1 **cup (8 ounces) sour cream**

FILLING

- ¼ **cup packed brown sugar**
- 1 **tablespoon all-purpose flour**
- ½ **teaspoon ground cinnamon**
- 2 **cups fresh or frozen blueberries**

GLAZE

- 1 **cup confectioners' sugar**
- 2 **to 3 tablespoons 2% milk**

1. Preheat oven to 350°. In a large bowl, cream butter and sugar until light and fluffy. Add eggs, one at a time, beating well after each addition. Beat in vanilla. Combine the flour, baking powder, baking soda and salt; add to creamed mixture alternately with sour cream, beating well after each addition.

Meals in Minutes

Don't have lots of time on your hands? No problem! You can have dinner on the table in a half hour (or less!) with the help of this chapter. With so many tasty choices, your menu planning will be a breeze.

ITALIAN SAUSAGE & SUN-DRIED TOMATO PASTA

Flavor-packed sausage and sun-dried tomatoes are sure to liven up any simple pasta dish. I have a feeling that once you try this, it'll be a new favorite.

—DAWN SINGLETON EIGHTY FOUR, PA

START TO FINISH: 30 MIN. • **MAKES:** 8 SERVINGS

- 1 package (16 ounces) uncooked penne pasta
- 1½ pounds bulk Italian sausage
- ⅔ cup julienned soft sun-dried tomatoes (not packed in oil)
- 3 garlic cloves, thinly sliced
- 2 teaspoons fennel seed
- ¼ teaspoon crushed red pepper flakes
- ½ cup dry red wine or reduced-sodium chicken broth
- ½ cup heavy whipping cream
- 1 package (9 ounces) fresh spinach
- ¾ cup shredded Romano cheese, divided
- ⅔ cup crushed seasoned salad croutons

1. Cook pasta according to package directions for al dente.
2. Meanwhile, in a Dutch oven, cook sausage over medium-high heat 5-6 minutes or until no longer pink, breaking into crumbles. Stir in tomatoes, garlic, fennel seed and pepper flakes; cook 1 minute longer.
3. Add wine. Bring to a boil; cook 1-2 minutes or until liquid is almost evaporated. Stir in cream; cook 1 minute longer. Add spinach; cook and stir just until spinach is wilted.
4. Drain pasta; add to sausage mixture. Stir in ½ cup cheese. Sprinkle with crushed croutons and the remaining cheese.
NOTE *This recipe was tested with sun-dried tomatoes that are ready-to-use without soaking. When using other sun-dried tomatoes (not packed in oil), cover with boiling water and let stand until soft. Drain before using.*

SWEET-AND-SOUR MEAT LOAF

Put this zippy twist on your meat loaf dinner. It won't take long for this to become a most-requested meal in your home.

—DEB THOMPSON LINCOLN, NE

START TO FINISH: 25 MIN. • **MAKES:** 4 SERVINGS

- 1 egg, lightly beaten
- 5 tablespoons ketchup, divided
- 2 tablespoons prepared mustard
- ½ cup dry bread crumbs
- 2 tablespoons onion soup mix
- ¼ teaspoon salt
- ¼ teaspoon pepper
- 1 pound lean ground beef (90% lean)
- ¼ cup sugar
- 2 tablespoons brown sugar
- 2 tablespoons cider vinegar

1. In a large bowl, combine the egg, 2 tablespoons ketchup, mustard, bread crumbs, dry soup mix, salt and pepper. Crumble beef over mixture and mix well. Shape into an oval loaf.
2. Place in a shallow 1-qt. microwave-safe dish. Cover and microwave on high for 10-12 minutes or until no pink remains and a thermometer reads 160°; drain.
3. Meanwhile in a small bowl, combine the sugars, vinegar and remaining ketchup; drizzle over meat loaf. Cover and microwave on high for 2-3 minutes longer or until heated through. Let stand for 10 minutes before slicing.
NOTE *This recipe was tested in a 1,100-watt microwave.*

BLUE CHEESE-CRUSTED SIRLOIN STEAKS

My wife loves when I fix this steak for her. It's the ideal dish for Friday night after a long workweek.

—MICHAEL ROUSE MINOT, ND

START TO FINISH: 30 MIN. • **MAKES:** 4 SERVINGS

- 2 tablespoons butter, divided
- 1 medium onion, chopped
- 1 beef top sirloin steak (1 inch thick and 1½ pounds)
- ¾ teaspoon salt
- ½ teaspoon pepper
- ⅓ cup crumbled blue cheese
- 2 tablespoons soft bread crumbs

1. In a large ovenproof skillet, heat 1 tablespoon butter over medium heat. Add onion; cook and stir until tender. Transfer to a small bowl.

2. Cut steak into four equal portions; season with salt and pepper. In the same skillet, heat remaining butter over medium heat. Brown steaks, about 5 minutes on each side. Meanwhile, add blue cheese and bread crumbs to onion; mix well. Spread over steaks.

3. Broil steaks 4-6 in. from the heat for 3-5 minutes or until steaks reach desired doneness (for medium-rare, a thermometer should read 145°; medium, 160°; well-done, 170°).

BALSAMIC SIRLOIN STEAK *Mix 3 tablespoons balsamic vinegar and 3 teaspoons steak sauce. Season steak with ½ teaspoon coarsely ground pepper. Do not brown steaks; broil as directed 5-7 minutes on each side or until desired doneness is reached. Baste with steak sauce mixture when steak is turned over. Cut steak across the grain into ¼-in. slices. Place on a foil-lined baking sheet; drizzle with juices from cutting board and remaining steak sauce mixture. Top with 2 ounces Swiss cheese cut into thin strips. Broil 1 minute or until cheese is melted.*

DRESSED-UP SIRLOIN STEAK MIX *Mix 1 tablespoon olive oil, 1½ teaspoons minced garlic, 1 teaspoon dried oregano and 1 teaspoon pepper. Rub over both sides of steak. Brush with ¼ cup Catalina salad dressing. Do not brown steaks; broil as directed 5-7 minutes on each side or until desired doneness is reached. Serve with additional Catalina dressing if desired.*

TUNA CAKES WITH MUSTARD MAYO

These patties take the cake! The recipe starts off easy by using canned tuna. If you'd like, add more kick to the creamy mustard-mayo sauce with prepared horseradish.

—TASTE OF HOME TEST KITCHEN

START TO FINISH: 30 MIN. • **MAKES:** 4 SERVINGS

- 2 eggs
- 3 tablespoons minced fresh parsley, divided
- ½ teaspoon seafood seasoning
- 2 cans (5 ounces each) light water-packed tuna, drained and flaked
- ½ cup seasoned bread crumbs
- ½ cup shredded carrots
- 2 tablespoons butter, divided
- 1 package (12 ounces) frozen peas
- ¼ teaspoon pepper
- ⅓ cup mayonnaise
- 1 tablespoon Dijon mustard
- 1 teaspoon 2% milk

1. In a large bowl, combine the eggs, 2 tablespoons parsley and seafood seasoning. Stir in the tuna, bread crumbs and carrot. Shape into eight patties.

2. In a large skillet, brown patties in 1 tablespoon butter for 3-4 minutes on each side or until golden brown.

3. Meanwhile, microwave peas according to package directions. Stir in the pepper and remaining butter and parsley. Combine the mayonnaise, mustard and milk. Serve with tuna cakes and peas.

SPINACH QUESADILLAS

My family gave these cheesy quesadillas a solid positive rating. Give the spinach here a quick wilt so it's still a little crisp when it's time to eat.

—PAM KAISER MANSFIELD, MO

START TO FINISH: 25 MIN. • **MAKES:** 4 SERVINGS

- 4 cups fresh baby spinach
- 4 green onions, chopped
- 1 small tomato, chopped
- 2 tablespoons lemon juice
- 1 teaspoon ground cumin
- ¼ teaspoon garlic powder
- 1 cup (4 ounces) shredded reduced-fat Monterey Jack cheese or Mexican cheese blend
- ¼ cup reduced-fat ricotta cheese
- 6 flour tortillas (6 inches)
- ¼ cup fat-free sour cream

1. Place the first six ingredients in a large nonstick skillet; cook and stir over medium heat just until spinach is wilted. Remove from heat; stir in cheeses.

2. Top half of each tortilla with spinach mixture; fold other half over filling. Place on a griddle coated with cooking spray. Cook over medium heat 1-2 minutes on each side or until golden brown. Cut each quesadilla in half. Serve with sour cream.

BROILED FISH WITH TARRAGON SAUCE

A surprising, yummy hint of honey comes through in this delicious fish recipe. Serve it with crusty bread, mixed vegetables or rice to help soak up the tangy sauce. You can't go wrong with a dinner that's ready in under a half hour.

—ROBIN PRATT ATHENS, GA

START TO FINISH: 25 MIN. • **MAKES:** 8 SERVINGS

- 2 pounds cod or red snapper fillets
- 1 tablespoon cornstarch
- ½ cup cold water
- ½ cup honey
- ¼ cup white wine or chicken broth
- ¼ cup lemon juice
- 1 teaspoon garlic salt
- ½ teaspoon grated lemon peel
- 1 tablespoon minced fresh tarragon

1. Place fish on a lightly greased 15x10x1-in. baking pan. Broil 4 in. from the heat for 8-10 minutes or until fish flakes easily with a fork.

2. Meanwhile, in a small saucepan, whisk cornstarch and water until smooth. Stir in the honey, wine, lemon juice, garlic salt and lemon peel. Bring to a boil. Cook and stir for 3-5 minutes or until thickened. Remove from the heat; stir in tarragon. Serve with fish.

HEARTY SAUSAGE AND RICE SKILLET

At the end of the day, who wants a stack of dishes to wash? That's why this entree is a winner: It cooks up in one skillet.
—*TASTE OF HOME* TEST KITCHEN

START TO FINISH: 30 MIN. • **MAKES:** 5 SERVINGS

- 1 pound Italian turkey sausage links, cut into ½-inch slices
- ½ pound sliced fresh mushrooms
- 1 medium sweet yellow pepper, chopped
- 1 medium onion, chopped
- 2 teaspoons olive oil
- 1 can (14½ ounces) diced tomatoes with mild green chilies, undrained
- 2 cups fresh baby spinach, coarsely chopped
- 1½ cups water
- 1 can (8 ounces) tomato sauce
- 1 teaspoon dried oregano
- 1 teaspoon chili powder
- ½ teaspoon garlic salt
- 2 cups uncooked instant rice

1. Cook the sausage in a Dutch oven over medium heat until no longer pink; drain. Remove and keep warm. Saute the mushrooms, pepper and onion in oil in the same pan until tender.

2. Return sausage to pan. Stir in the tomatoes, spinach, water, tomato sauce and seasonings.

3. Bring to a boil; cook for 2 minutes. Stir in rice. Remove from the heat; cover and let stand for 5-7 minutes or until rice is tender. Fluff with a fork.

CHILI BEEF PASTA

Right after I got married, my aunt gave me her recipe for skillet spaghetti. It's been one of my main go-to recipes ever since. Over the years, I've tinkered with the ingredients and played with different seasonings to make it a healthier dish that my family still truly enjoys.
—**KRISTEN KILLIAN** DEPEW, NY

START TO FINISH: 30 MIN. • **MAKES:** 6 SERVINGS

- 1 pound lean ground beef (90% lean)
- 2 tablespoons dried minced onion
- 2 teaspoons dried oregano
- 2 teaspoons chili powder
- ½ teaspoon garlic powder
- ⅛ teaspoon salt
- 3 cups tomato juice
- 2 cups water
- 1 can (6 ounces) tomato paste
- 1 teaspoon sugar
- 8 ounces uncooked whole wheat spiral pasta
  Chopped tomatoes and minced fresh oregano, optional

1. In a Dutch oven, cook beef over medium heat for 6-8 minutes or until no longer pink, breaking into crumbles; drain. Stir in seasonings.

2. Add tomato juice, water, tomato paste and sugar to pan; bring to a boil. Stir in pasta. Reduce heat; simmer, covered, 20-22 minutes or until pasta is tender, stirring occasionally. If desired, top with tomatoes and oregano.

Family Favorites Made Easy

No need to make multiple dishes to appease everyone at the table. You'll get a big thumbs-up from the whole gang when you plate up one of these classics.

PRETZEL-CRUSTED CHICKEN WITH MIXED GREENS

The secret to crunchy success is grinding up the sourdough pretzel nuggets until they're finely crushed. Change up the flavor and use hot Buffalo wing or buttermilk ranch nuggets.
—**KERRI BALLIET** MEQUON, WI

START TO FINISH: 30 MIN. • **MAKES:** 4 SERVINGS (⅔ CUP SAUCE)

- 2 cups sourdough pretzel nuggets
- ½ cup all-purpose flour
- 2 eggs
- ¼ cup buttermilk
- 2 garlic cloves, minced
- ⅛ teaspoon pepper
- 4 boneless skinless chicken breast halves (5 ounces each)
- 5 tablespoons olive oil, divided
- ⅔ cup mayonnaise
- 2 tablespoons Dijon mustard
- 2 teaspoons cider vinegar
- ⅛ teaspoon salt
- ⅛ teaspoon pepper
- 1 package (5 ounces) spring mix salad greens

1. Place pretzels in a food processor; process until finely crushed. Place pretzels and flour in separate shallow bowls. In another shallow bowl, whisk the eggs, buttermilk, garlic and pepper. Pound chicken with a meat mallet to ¼-in. thickness. Dip both sides of chicken in flour, egg mixture and then pretzel crumbs.

2. In a large skillet, heat 3 tablespoons oil over medium heat. Add chicken; cook for 4-6 minutes on each side or no longer pink.

3. Meanwhile, in a small bowl, mix mayonnaise and mustard. Remove 2 tablespoons to another bowl for dressing; whisk in remaining oil, vinegar, salt and pepper.

4. Place salad greens in a large bowl. Drizzle with dressing; toss to coat. Serve with the chicken and remaining mayonnaise mixture.

MEATBALL HOAGIES WITH SEASONED FRIES

Try this fresh take on a classic combo, and you might never stop by a deli again. Including the apricot preserves and bacon give the sandwich a sweet-savory twist, and celery salt on the fries is a welcome surprise.
—**TASTE OF HOME** TEST KITCHEN

START TO FINISH: 30 MIN. • **MAKES:** 4 SERVINGS

- 4 cups frozen steak fries
- 1 tablespoon olive oil
- ½ teaspoon seasoned salt
- ¼ teaspoon celery salt
- 1 package (12 ounces) frozen fully cooked Italian meatballs, thawed
- 2 cups barbecue sauce
- ¼ cup apricot preserves
- 4 hoagie buns, split and toasted
- 4 large lettuce leaves
- 3 plum tomatoes, sliced
- 8 ready-to-serve fully cooked bacon strips, warmed
- 8 slices provolone cheese

1. Place steak fries in a single layer in a 15x10x1-in. baking pan. Drizzle with oil; sprinkle with seasonings. Toss to coat. Bake according to package directions.

2. Meanwhile, place meatballs, barbecue sauce and preserves in a large saucepan. Bring to a boil over medium heat; cook and stir 6-8 minutes or until heated through.

3. Layer bun bottoms with lettuce, tomatoes, bacon, meatball mixture and cheese; replace tops. Serve with fries.

BACON CHEESEBURGER SPAGHETTI

I run a daycare center, and it's hard to find foods that the kids will eat. I spruced up a variation of this simple recipe, and now the kids (and my husband) request it all the time!

—**NICHELLE NELL** ISLE, MN

START TO FINISH: 30 MIN. • **MAKES:** 6 SERVINGS

- 10 ounces uncooked spaghetti
- 1 pound lean ground beef (90% lean)
- ⅔ cup chopped onion
- 6 slices ready-to-serve fully cooked bacon, chopped
- 1½ cups ketchup
- 1 cup chopped dill pickles
- 1 cup barbecue sauce
- ½ cup prepared mustard
- 2 cups (8 ounces) shredded cheddar cheese

1. Cook spaghetti according to package directions. Meanwhile, in a large skillet, cook beef and onion over medium heat until meat is no longer pink; drain. Stir in the bacon, ketchup, pickles, barbecue sauce and mustard. Bring to a boil. Reduce heat; simmer, uncovered, for 5 minutes. Drain spaghetti; stir into meat mixture.
2. Sprinkle with cheese. Remove from the heat; cover and let stand until cheese is melted.
3. Serve immediately, or cool before placing in a freezer container. Cover and freeze for up to 3 months.
TO USE FROZEN CASSEROLE *Thaw in the refrigerator overnight. Place in a Dutch oven; heat through. Sprinkle with additional cheese.*

CREAMY RANCH MAC AND CHEESE

I gave creamy and comforting macaroni and cheese an update with this special ranch-flavored twist. My husband requests it often.

—**MICHELLE ROTUNNO** INDEPENDENCE, MO

START TO FINISH: 30 MIN. • **MAKES:** 8 SERVINGS

- 1 package (16 ounces) elbow macaroni
- 1 cup 2% milk
- 2 tablespoons butter
- 4½ teaspoons ranch salad dressing mix
- 1 teaspoon garlic pepper blend
- 1 teaspoon lemon-pepper seasoning
- ½ teaspoon garlic powder
- 1 cup (4 ounces) shredded Monterey Jack cheese
- 1 cup (4 ounces) shredded Colby cheese
- 1 cup (8 ounces) reduced-fat sour cream
- ½ cup crushed saltines
- ⅓ cup grated Parmesan cheese

1. Cook macaroni according to package directions. Meanwhile, in a Dutch oven, combine the milk, butter, dressing mix and seasonings; heat through. Stir in Monterey Jack and Colby cheeses until melted. Stir in sour cream.
2. Drain macaroni; stir into cheese sauce with the saltines. Sprinkle with Parmesan cheese.

SEAFOOD BISQUE

We live on the Gulf Coast, where fresh seafood is plentiful. I adapted several recipes to come up with my own unique bisque. It's great as a first course or an entree, and it can be made with just shrimp or crab.

—**PAT EDWARDS** DAUPHIN ISLAND, AL

START TO FINISH: 30 MIN. • **MAKES:** 10 SERVINGS (2½ QUARTS)

- 2 cans (10¾ ounces each) **condensed cream of mushroom soup, undiluted**
- 1 can (10¾ ounces) **condensed cream of celery soup, undiluted**
- 2⅔ cups **2% milk**
- 4 **green onions, chopped**
- ½ cup **finely chopped celery**
- 1 **garlic clove, minced**
- 1 teaspoon **Worcestershire sauce**
- ¼ teaspoon **hot pepper sauce**
- 1½ pounds **uncooked medium shrimp, peeled and deveined**
- 1 can (6 ounces) **crabmeat, drained, flaked and cartilage removed**
- 1 jar (4½ ounces) **whole mushrooms, drained**
- 3 tablespoons **Madeira wine or chicken broth**
- ½ teaspoon **salt**
- ½ teaspoon **pepper**
  Thinly sliced green onions, optional

In a Dutch oven, combine the first eight ingredients. Bring to a boil. Reduce heat; add the shrimp, crab and mushrooms. Simmer, uncovered, for 10 minutes. Stir in the wine, salt and pepper; cook 2-3 minutes longer. Top with onions if desired.

TACO-FILLED PEPPERS

Packed with vegetables, beef and beans, these stuffed peppers stand out from the others.

—**NANCY MCDONALD** BURNS, WY

START TO FINISH: 30 MIN. • **MAKES:** 4 SERVINGS

- 1 pound **ground beef**
- 1 envelope **taco seasoning**
- ¾ cup **canned kidney beans, rinsed and drained**
- 1 cup **salsa**
- 4 **medium green peppers**
- 1 **medium tomato, chopped**
- ½ cup **shredded cheddar cheese**
- ½ cup **sour cream**

1. In a large skillet, cook beef over medium heat until no longer pink; drain. Stir in the taco seasoning, kidney beans and salsa. Bring to a boil; reduce heat and simmer for 5 minutes.

2. Cut peppers in half lengthwise; remove stems and discard seeds. In a stockpot, cook peppers in boiling water for 3-5 minutes. Drain and rinse in cold water.

3. Spoon about ½ cup meat mixture into each pepper half. Place in an ungreased 13x9-in. baking dish. Cover and bake at 350° for 15-20 minutes or until the peppers are crisp-tender and filling is heated through. Top each with tomato and cheese. Serve with sour cream.

SHRIMP TORTELLINI PASTA TOSS

Cheese tortellini may seem indulgent, but when you bulk it up with shrimp and frozen veggies, it becomes a fast and tasty meal.
—*TASTE OF HOME* TEST KITCHEN

START TO FINISH: 20 MIN. • **MAKES:** 4 SERVINGS

- 1 package (9 ounces) refrigerated cheese tortellini
- 1 cup frozen peas
- 3 tablespoons olive oil, divided
- 1 pound uncooked shrimp (31-40 per pound), peeled and deveined
- 2 garlic cloves, minced
- ¼ teaspoon salt
- ¼ teaspoon dried thyme
- ¼ teaspoon pepper

1. Cook tortellini according to package directions, adding peas during the last 5 minutes of cooking.
2. Meanwhile, in a large nonstick skillet, heat 2 tablespoons oil over medium-high heat. Add shrimp; cook and stir 2 minutes. Add garlic; cook 1-2 minutes longer or until shrimp turn pink.
3. Drain tortellini mixture; add to skillet. Stir in salt, thyme, pepper and remaining oil; toss to coat.

SHRIMP ASPARAGUS FETTUCCINE *Bring 4 quarts water to a boil. Add 9 ounces refrigerated fettuccine and 1 cup cut fresh asparagus. Boil for 2-3 minutes or until pasta is tender. Proceed with the recipe as written but replace thyme with ¾ teaspoon dried basil.*

SOY SHRIMP WITH RICE NOODLES *Cook 8.8 ounces thin rice noodles according to package directions, adding 1 cup frozen shelled edamame during the last 4 minutes of cooking. Proceed with the recipe as written but replace thyme with ¼ cup reduced-sodium soy sauce and omit salt.*

PORK CHOPS WITH BLACKBERRY SAUCE

Yum! You need only 20 minutes to create this winning dish.
—**PRISCILLA GILBERT** INDIAN HARBOUR BEACH, FL

START TO FINISH: 20 MIN. • **MAKES:** 4 SERVINGS

- 4 bone-in pork loin chops (7 ounces each)
- ¼ cup seedless blackberry spreadable fruit
- 3 tablespoons ketchup
- ¼ teaspoon minced garlic
- ¼ teaspoon prepared mustard
- ¼ teaspoon cornstarch
- 1 tablespoon A.1. steak sauce

1. Broil chops 4-5 in. from the heat for 4-5 minutes on each side or until a thermometer reads 145°. Let stand for 5 minutes before serving.
2. Meanwhile, in a small saucepan, combine the spreadable fruit, ketchup, garlic and mustard. Bring to a boil. Combine cornstarch and steak sauce until smooth. Gradually stir into pan. Bring to a boil; cook and stir for 2 minutes or until thickened. Serve with pork chops.

MINCED GARLIC MADE EASY
Minced garlic that you can buy, garlic that's been finely chopped by hand and garlic that's been put through a press can all be used interchangeably in recipes, so go with what's most convenient for you.

ORANGE SALMON WITH SAUTEED SPINACH

I love orange marmalade and wanted a version of orange salmon without a heavy spice rub or brown sugar. I was quite pleased with the results.

—JANET CAICO HILLSBOROUGH, NC

START TO FINISH: 30 MIN. • **MAKES:** 4 SERVINGS

- 4 salmon fillets (4 ounces each)
- ¼ teaspoon plus ⅛ teaspoon pepper, divided
- ¼ teaspoon salt, divided
- ½ cup orange marmalade spreadable fruit
- 2 tablespoons half-and-half cream
- 2 tablespoons reduced-sodium soy sauce
- 1 tablespoon minced fresh gingerroot
- 4½ teaspoons plus 1 tablespoon reduced-fat butter, divided
- 2 garlic cloves, minced
- 1 tablespoon olive oil
- 1 package (6 ounces) fresh baby spinach

1. Sprinkle salmon with ¼ teaspoon pepper and ⅛ teaspoon salt; set aside.

2. In a small saucepan, combine the marmalade, cream, soy sauce, ginger and 4½ teaspoons butter. Bring to a boil. Reduce heat; simmer, uncovered, until slightly thickened, about 5 minutes; set aside.

3. Moisten a paper towel with cooking oil; using long-handled tongs, lightly coat the grill rack. Place salmon skin side down on grill rack. Grill, covered, over medium heat or broil 4 in. from the heat for 10-12 minutes or until fish flakes easily with a fork.

4. In a large skillet, saute garlic in oil and remaining butter for 1 minute. Add spinach and remaining salt and pepper; cook for 4-5 minutes or until spinach is wilted. Divide spinach among four plates; top each with salmon. Drizzle with marmalade sauce.

CHEESE RAVIOLI WITH PUMPKIN ALFREDO SAUCE

When I first made this recipe, everyone said, "Pumpkin on pasta? Really?" But once they tasted it, they really couldn't believe how much they liked it.

—CHERI NEUSTIFTER STURTEVANT, WI

START TO FINISH: 30 MIN. • **MAKES:** 6 SERVINGS

- 1 package (25 ounces) frozen cheese ravioli
- 3 tablespoons all-purpose flour
- 2 cups fat-free milk
- 1 can (14½ ounces) reduced-sodium chicken broth
- 3 garlic cloves, minced
- 2 tablespoons butter
- ½ cup shredded Parmesan cheese
- ½ cup canned pumpkin
- ¼ cup minced fresh parsley
- 1½ teaspoons minced fresh sage
   Dash ground nutmeg
- ¼ cup pine nuts, toasted
- ¼ cup chopped walnuts, toasted

1. Cook ravioli according to package directions. Meanwhile, in a large bowl, whisk the flour, milk and broth.

2. In a large skillet, saute garlic in butter until tender. Stir in the milk mixture, cheese, pumpkin, parsley, sage and nutmeg. Cook, uncovered, over medium heat for 10-15 minutes or until thickened, stirring occasionally.

3. Drain ravioli and stir into sauce. Sprinkle with nuts.

PECAN TURKEY CUTLETS WITH DILLED CARROTS

The recipe may look a bit long, but don't let it fool you. It's actually very simple because it uses the same everyday ingredients in multiple ways.

—*TASTE OF HOME* TEST KITCHEN

START TO FINISH: 30 MIN. • **MAKES:** 4 SERVINGS

- ¾ cup chopped pecans
- ½ cup grated Romano cheese
- ½ teaspoon seasoned salt
- ½ teaspoon dill weed
- 1 package (17.6 ounces) turkey breast cutlets
- 3 tablespoons butter, divided
- 2 garlic cloves, minced
- 1 teaspoon cornstarch
- ½ cup chicken broth
- 2 tablespoons lime juice
- ½ teaspoon grated lime peel

CARROTS

- 1½ pounds sliced fresh carrots
- 1½ teaspoons butter
- ¾ teaspoon grated lime peel
- ½ teaspoon dill weed
- ¼ teaspoon seasoned salt

1. Place pecans in a food processor; cover and process until ground. Combine the pecans, cheese, seasoned salt and dill in a shallow bowl. Coat turkey with pecan mixture.

2. Cook turkey in batches in 1 tablespoon butter in a large skillet over medium heat for 3-4 minutes on each side or until no longer pink; remove and keep warm. Cook garlic in remaining butter in the same pan.

3. Combine the cornstarch, broth and lime juice until blended; gradually add to the skillet, stirring to loosen browned bits. Bring to a boil; cook and stir for 2 minutes or until thickened. Stir in lime peel. Remove from the heat; keep warm.

4. Meanwhile, place 1 in. of water in a saucepan; add carrots. Bring to a boil. Reduce heat; cover and simmer 7-9 minutes or until crisp-tender. Drain. Stir in the butter, lime peel, dill and seasoned salt. Serve with turkey and sauce.

BBQ HOT DOG & POTATO PACKS

For these nifty foil packs, small hands make quick work of topping potato wedges with a hot dog, onions and cheese.

—**KELLY WESTPHAL** WIND LAKE, WI

START TO FINISH: 20 MIN. • **MAKES:** 4 SERVINGS

- 1 package (20 ounces) refrigerated red potato wedges
- 4 hot dogs
- 1 small onion, cut into wedges
- ¼ cup shredded cheddar cheese
- ½ cup barbecue sauce

1. Divide potato wedges among four pieces of heavy-duty foil (about 18 in. square). Top each with a hot dog, onion wedges and cheese. Drizzle with barbecue sauce. Fold foil around mixture, sealing tightly.

2. Grill, covered, over medium heat 10-15 minutes or until heated through. Open foil carefully to allow steam to escape.

BROCCOLI RABE & GARLIC PASTA

I created this when I needed a quick entree with few ingredients. The garlic-infused oil makes the broccoli rabe less bitter, and with toasted garlic, it's a great dish.
—**MARY ANN LEE** CLIFTON PARK, NY

START TO FINISH: 30 MIN. • **MAKES:** 4 SERVINGS

- 12 **ounces uncooked linguine**
- 1 **pound broccoli rabe**
- 3 **garlic cloves, minced**
- 2 **tablespoons olive oil**
- ¼ **teaspoon salt**
- ¼ **teaspoon pepper**
- ¼ **teaspoon crushed red pepper flakes**
- 1 **cup chicken broth, divided**
- ¼ **cup minced fresh parsley**
- ¼ **cup shredded Parmesan cheese**

1. Cook linguine according to package directions. Meanwhile, trim ½ in. from broccoli rabe stems; discard any coarse or damaged leaves. Rinse broccoli rabe in cold water and cut into 2-in. pieces; set aside.
2. In a large skillet, saute garlic in oil for 1 minute. Add the broccoli rabe, salt, pepper, pepper flakes and ½ cup broth. Bring to a boil.
3. Reduce heat; cover and cook for 3-5 minutes or until broccoli rabe is tender. Drain linguine; add to the pan. Stir in parsley and enough remaining broth to moisten the linguine. Sprinkle with cheese.

CAJUN PECAN CATFISH

I like to serve this favorite recipe with a side salad and biscuits to round out the meal.
—**JAN WILKINS** BLYTHEVILLE, AR

START TO FINISH: 25 MIN. • **MAKES:** 4 SERVINGS

- 2 **tablespoons olive oil**
- 2 **teaspoons lemon juice**
- 1 **teaspoon Cajun seasoning**
- ½ **teaspoon dried thyme**
- ⅓ **cup finely chopped pecans**
- 2 **tablespoons grated Parmesan cheese**
- 1 **tablespoon dry bread crumbs**
- 1 **tablespoon dried parsley flakes**
- 4 **catfish fillets (6 ounces each)**

1. Preheat the oven to 425°. In a small bowl, combine oil, lemon juice, Cajun seasoning and thyme. In another bowl, combine pecans, cheese, bread crumbs, parsley and 1 tablespoon of the oil mixture.
2. Place the catfish on a greased 15x10x1-in. baking pan. Brush with remaining oil mixture. Spread pecan mixture over fillets. Bake 10-15 minutes or until fish flakes easily with a fork.

PORK AND WAFFLES WITH MAPLE-PEAR TOPPING

Maple syrup and Dijon mustard come through beautifully in these upscale, crowd-pleasing waffles.

—TASTE OF HOME TEST KITCHEN

START TO FINISH: 25 MIN. • **MAKES:** 4 SERVINGS

- ½ **cup seasoned bread crumbs**
- 1 **teaspoon dried thyme**
- 1 **pork tenderloin (1 pound), cut into 12 slices**
- 2 **tablespoons olive oil**
- 2 **medium pears, thinly sliced**
- ½ **cup maple syrup**
- 2 **tablespoons Dijon mustard**
- ½ **teaspoon salt**
- 8 **frozen waffles, toasted**
- 2 **tablespoons minced chives**

1. In a large resealable plastic bag, combine bread crumbs and thyme. Add pork, a few pieces at a time, and shake to coat. In a large skillet, cook pork in oil in batches over medium heat for 2-4 minutes on each side or until tender. Remove from the pan and keep warm.

2. Add the pears, syrup, mustard and salt to the skillet; cook and stir for 1-2 minutes or until pears are tender. Serve pork slices and pear mixture over waffles. Sprinkle with chives.

3 bacon strips, finely chopped
¾ cup honey barbecue sauce
¼ cup packed brown sugar
1 tablespoon prepared horseradish
2 teaspoons water
2 teaspoons minced garlic
½ teaspoon crushed red pepper flakes
   Hot cooked rice

In a Dutch oven, saute the kielbasa, onion and bacon until onion is tender; drain. Add the barbecue sauce, brown sugar, horseradish, water, garlic and pepper flakes. Bring to a boil; cook and stir for 2-3 minutes or until sauce is thickened. Serve with rice.

FREEZE OPTION *Place cooled individual portions in freezer containers without rice. Freeze up to 3 months. To use, thaw in the refrigerator overnight. Place in a saucepan; heat through, gently stirring and adding a water if necessary. Serve with rice.*

GARLIC CHICKEN & BACON PIZZA

Garlic cooking creme is the secret to adding a lot of flavor without a lot of fuss. This is our go-to pizza for game night.
—**JOSEE LANZI** NEW PORT RICHEY, FL

START TO FINISH: 20 MIN. • **MAKES:** 6 SERVINGS

1 prebaked 12-inch pizza crust
½ cup Philadelphia savory garlic cooking creme
1 package (6 ounces) ready-to-use grilled chicken breast strips
4 strips ready-to-serve fully cooked bacon, chopped
1 cup (4 ounces) shredded part-skim mozzarella cheese

1. Place pizza crust on a greased 14-in. pizza pan. Spread with cooking creme. Top with the chicken and bacon; sprinkle with cheese.
2. Bake at 425° for 10-15 minutes or until cheese is melted.

SMOKED KIELBASA WITH RICE

With a little bit of zip and just the right amount of smokiness, this sausage-and-rice medley will please a crowd. For an appetizer, omit the rice and serve the sausage pieces with toothpicks.
—**NICOLE JACKSON** EL PASO, TX

START TO FINISH: 25 MIN. • **MAKES:** 6 SERVINGS

2 pounds smoked kielbasa or Polish sausage, halved lengthwise and cut into ¼-inch slices
¼ cup finely chopped onion

25-MINUTE TURKEY CHILI

This is a nice change of pace from traditional beef chili. I like to serve cheddar cheese bread on the side for dipping.

—**TRACI WYNNE** DENVER, PA

START TO FINISH: 25 MIN. • **MAKES:** 8 SERVINGS (2 QUARTS)

- 1¼ pounds ground turkey
- 1 can (16 ounces) kidney beans, rinsed and drained
- 1 can (15 ounces) black beans, rinsed and drained
- 1 can (14½ ounces) Mexican stewed tomatoes, undrained
- 1 can (8 ounces) tomato sauce
- 1 small sweet red pepper, finely chopped
- 1 small onion, chopped
- ½ cup beef broth
- 1 jalapeno pepper, seeded and minced
- 2 tablespoons chili powder
- ½ teaspoon salt
- ¼ teaspoon pepper
  Optional garnish: shredded cheese of your choice

1. Crumble turkey into a pressure cooker. Add remaining ingredients; stir to combine.
2. Close cover securely according to manufacturer's directions. Bring cooker to full pressure over high heat. Reduce heat to medium-high and cook for 5 minutes. (Pressure regulator should maintain a slow steady rocking motion or release of steam; adjust heat if needed.)
3. Immediately cool according to manufacturer's directions until pressure is completely reduced. Stir chili; if desired, top with shredded cheese.
NOTE *Wear disposable gloves when cutting hot peppers; the oils can burn skin. Avoid touching your face.*

MUFFULETTA PASTA

A friend gave me this recipe when she learned that I love muffuletta sandwiches. Very rich and filling, this easy skillet supper goes together quickly when it hits the table.

—**JAN HOLLINGSWORTH** HOUSTON, MS

START TO FINISH: 25 MIN. • **MAKES:** 8 SERVINGS

- 1 package (16 ounces) bow tie pasta
- 1 bunch green onions, chopped
- 2 teaspoons plus ¼ cup butter, divided
- 1 tablespoon minced garlic
- 1 package (16 ounces) cubed fully cooked ham
- 1 jar (12.36 ounces) tapenade or ripe olive bruschetta topping, drained
- 1 package (3½ ounces) sliced pepperoni
- 1 cup heavy whipping cream
- 2 cups (8 ounces) shredded Italian cheese blend

1. Cook pasta according to package directions. Meanwhile, in a large skillet, saute onions in 2 teaspoons butter until tender. Add garlic; cook 1 minute longer. Add the ham, tapenade and pepperoni; saute 2 minutes longer.
2. Cube remaining butter; stir butter and cream into skillet. Bring to a boil over medium heat. Reduce heat; simmer, uncovered, for 3 minutes.
3. Drain the pasta; toss with ham mixture. Sprinkle with cheese.

FETTUCCINE CARBONARA

When a man at church found out how much my family likes fettuccine carbonara, he shared his Italian grandmother's recipe with us. I've made it my own over the last 25 years. Grated Parmesan cheese works just as well as Romano.

—**KRISTINE CHAYES** SMITHTOWN, NY

START TO FINISH: 30 MIN. • **MAKES:** 6 SERVINGS

- ½ pound bacon strips, chopped
- 1 package (16 ounces) fettuccine
- 1 small onion, finely chopped
- 2 garlic cloves, minced
- 1 cup half-and-half cream
- 4 eggs, lightly beaten
- ½ cup grated Romano cheese
- ½ teaspoon salt
- ¼ teaspoon pepper
- 1 tablespoon minced fresh parsley
  Additional grated Romano cheese, optional

1. In a large skillet, cook bacon over medium heat until crisp, stirring occasionally. Remove with a slotted spoon; drain on paper towels. Discard drippings, reserving 1 tablespoon in pan.

2. Meanwhile, in a Dutch oven, cook fettuccine according to package directions. Drain; return to pan.

3. Add onion to drippings in skillet; cook and stir over medium heat 2-3 minutes or until tender. Add garlic; cook 1 minute longer. Reduce heat to medium-low. Stir in cream. In a small bowl, whisk a small amount of warm cream into eggs; return all to pan, whisking constantly. Cook 8-10 minutes or until a thermometer reads 160°, stirring constantly.

4. Stir cheese, salt, pepper and bacon into sauce. Add to fettuccine and toss to combine. Sprinkle with parsley and, if desired, additional cheese. Serve immediately.

PESTO CHICKEN TURNOVERS

When it comes to food, I'm all about anything in a pocket—pita bread, bierocks, empanadas and more. These Italian-inspired handhelds are great for dinner and even better the next day. For smaller turnovers, use a single crescent roll with a level tablespoon of filling.

—**GREG MUNOZ** SACRAMENTO, CA

START TO FINISH: 30 MIN. • **MAKES:** 4 SERVINGS

- 2 tubes (8 ounces each) refrigerated seamless crescent dough sheets
- 1 package (10 ounces) frozen chopped spinach, thawed and squeezed dry
- 1 package (9 ounces) ready-to-use grilled Italian chicken strips
- 1 cup (4 ounces) shredded part-skim mozzarella cheese
- 3 tablespoons prepared pesto

1. Preheat the oven to 375°. Unroll both tubes of crescent dough and cut each into four rectangles.

2. In a large bowl, combine spinach, chicken, cheese and pesto; spoon ¾ cup in the center of each of four rectangles. Top with remaining rectangles; pinch seams to seal. Place on greased baking sheets; cut three slits in top of each turnover. Bake 18-22 minutes or until golden brown.

FREEZE OPTION *Freeze cooled turnovers in a resealable plastic freezer bag. To use, reheat turnovers on a greased baking sheet in a preheated 375° oven until heated through.*

ZUCCHINI EGG SKILLET

My neighbor shared more zucchini with me from his garden than I knew what to do with. He loved this recipe, and it's great for brunch or a special breakfast.

—DARCY KENNEDY NEW WINDSOR, NY

START TO FINISH: 30 MIN. • **MAKES:** 4 SERVINGS

- 2 **tablespoons olive oil**
- 2 **medium red potatoes (about 8 ounces), cut into ¼-inch cubes**
- 1 **medium onion, chopped**
- 2 **small zucchini, shredded (about 3 cups)**
- 4 **frozen fully cooked breakfast sausage links, thawed and cut into ½-inch slices**
- ½ **cup chopped roasted sweet red peppers**
- 6 **cherry tomatoes, quartered**
- ¼ **teaspoon salt**
- ⅛ **teaspoon pepper**
- ½ **cup shredded cheddar cheese**
- 4 **eggs**

1. In a large skillet, heat oil over medium-high heat. Add potatoes and onion; cook and stir 4-6 minutes or until potatoes are crisp-tender. Stir in zucchini and sausage; cook 4-6 minutes longer or until vegetables are tender.
2. Gently stir in red peppers, tomatoes, salt and pepper; sprinkle with cheese. With back of spoon, make four wells in potato mixture; break an egg into each well. Reduce heat to medium. Cook, covered, 4-6 minutes or until egg whites are completely set and yolks begin to thicken but are not hard.

SALSA VERDE CHICKEN CASSEROLE

This is a rich and surprisingly tasty rendition of all the Tex-Mex dishes molded into one packed, beautiful casserole. Best of all, it's ready in no time!

—JANET MCCORMICK PROCTORVILLE, OH

START TO FINISH: 30 MIN. • **MAKES:** 6 SERVINGS

- 2 **cups shredded rotisserie chicken**
- 1 **cup (8 ounces) sour cream**
- 1½ **cups salsa verde, divided**
- 8 **corn tortillas (6 inches)**
- 2 **cups chopped tomatoes**
- ¼ **cup minced fresh cilantro**
- 2 **cups (8 ounces) shredded Monterey Jack cheese**
  Optional toppings: avocado slices, thinly sliced green onions or fresh cilantro leaves

1. Combine the chicken, sour cream and ¾ cup salsa in a small bowl. Spread ¼ cup salsa on the bottom of a greased 8-in.-square baking dish.
2. Layer with half of the tortillas and chicken mixture; sprinkle with the tomatoes, minced cilantro and half of the cheese. Repeat layers with remaining tortillas, chicken mixture and cheese.
3. Bake, uncovered, at 400° for 20-25 minutes or until bubbly. Serve with the remaining salsa and, if desired, optional toppings.

Cooking for Two

Put away that calculator! You won't need to do any division for these recipes— they're ready to serve a duo. Instead of going out, stay in and enjoy a cozy home-cooked meal with your special someone.

SAVORY ONION MUFFINS

I've made these muffins more times than I can count, and my family and friends still really enjoy them.
—**NORMA SAUNDERS** LOS ANGELES, CA

PREP: 20 MIN. • **BAKE:** 20 MIN. • **MAKES:** 2 MUFFINS

- ⅓ cup chopped onion
- 1½ teaspoons butter
- ½ cup biscuit/baking mix
- 1½ teaspoons poppy seeds
- 3 tablespoons 2% milk
- 2 tablespoons beaten egg, divided
- 3 tablespoons sour cream
  Dash pepper
  Dash paprika

1. In a small skillet, saute onion in butter until tender; set aside. In a small bowl, combine biscuit mix and poppy seeds. In another bowl, combine milk and 1 tablespoon egg. Stir into dry ingredients just until moistened.

2. Coat muffin cups with cooking spray; fill three-fourths full with batter. Combine the sour cream, pepper and remaining egg. Spoon onion over muffin batter; spread with sour cream mixture. Sprinkle with paprika.

3. Bake at 400° for 18-20 minutes or until a toothpick comes out clean. Cool for 5 minutes before removing from pan to a wire rack. Serve warm.

BROCCOLI CHEESE SOUP

When my husband and I visit fresh food stands, we often come home with an abundance of veggies. We like to use up extra broccoli in this hearty soup.
—**MARGE HILL** GLENSIDE, PA

PREP: 15 MIN. • **COOK:** 30 MIN. • **MAKES:** 2 SERVINGS

- ¼ cup chopped sweet onion
- 1 garlic clove, minced
- 1 tablespoon all-purpose flour
- 1 cup chicken broth
- 2 cups fresh broccoli florets
- ⅛ to ¼ teaspoon dried tarragon
- ⅛ teaspoon dried thyme
  Dash pepper
- ¾ cup 2% milk
- ⅔ cup shredded cheddar cheese

1. In a large nonstick saucepan coated with cooking spray, saute onion and garlic until tender. Stir in the flour until blended; cook for 1 minute. Gradually whisk in broth. Bring to a boil; cook and stir for 1-2 minutes or until slightly thickened.

2. Add the broccoli, tarragon, thyme and pepper; return to a boil. Reduce heat; cover and simmer for 10 minutes or until broccoli is tender. Add milk; cook, uncovered, 5 minutes longer. Remove from the heat; cool slightly.

3. In a blender, process soup until smooth. Return to pan and heat through (do not boil). Stir in ½ cup of cheese until melted. Sprinkle servings with remaining cheese.

BLT-AND-MORE SALAD FOR TWO

I created this recipe when my husband and I were looking for something quick, yet different. Plus, you really can't go wrong with a BLT salad.
—**PAULA MARCHESI** LENHARTSVILLE, PA

START TO FINISH: 15 MIN. • **MAKES:** 2 SERVINGS

- ¾ cup yellow cherry tomatoes, halved
- ¾ cup cherry tomatoes, halved
- 2 tablespoons cubed avocado
- 1 bacon strip, cooked and crumbled
- 1 tablespoon fat-free sour cream
- 1 tablespoon fat-free mayonnaise
- 1 tablespoon fat-free milk
- 1 garlic clove, minced
- ¼ teaspoon dill weed
  Dash each salt and pepper
- 2 tablespoons crumbled goat cheese
- 1 tablespoon pine nuts
- 2 Bibb lettuce leaves

In a small bowl, combine the tomatoes, avocado and bacon. In another small bowl, whisk the sour cream, mayonnaise, milk, garlic, dill, salt and pepper; pour over salad. Gently toss to coat. Sprinkle with cheese and pine nuts. Serve immediately in lettuce leaves.

PINEAPPLE UPSIDE-DOWN CAKE FOR TWO

Tender, moist and sweet, these two luscious but lighter cakes are extra special.

—TASTE OF HOME TEST KITCHEN

PREP: 15 MIN. • **BAKE:** 20 MIN. • **MAKES:** 2 SERVINGS

- 4 teaspoons butter, melted, divided
- 4 teaspoons brown sugar
- 2 canned unsweetened pineapple slices
- 2 maraschino cherries
- ⅓ cup all-purpose flour
- 3 tablespoons sugar
- ½ teaspoon baking powder
- ⅛ teaspoon salt
  Dash ground nutmeg
- 3 tablespoons fat-free milk
- ¼ teaspoon vanilla extract

1. Pour ½ teaspoon butter into each of two 10-oz. ramekins coated with cooking spray. Sprinkle with brown sugar. Top with a pineapple slice. Place a cherry in the center of each pineapple slice; set aside.

2. In a small bowl, combine the flour, sugar, baking powder, salt and nutmeg. Beat in the milk, vanilla and remaining butter just until combined. Spoon over pineapple.

3. Bake at 350° for 20-25 minutes or until a toothpick inserted near the center comes out clean. Cool for 5 minutes. Run a knife around edges of ramekins; invert onto dessert plates. Serve warm.

FRUIT SALAD WITH LEMON DRESSING

The vibrant colors make this dish a pretty first course or light dessert. You'll simply love the citrusy dressing.

—PATRICIA HARMON BADEN, PA

START TO FINISH: 20 MIN. • **MAKES:** 2 SERVINGS

- 1 can (8 ounces) unsweetened pineapple chunks, drained
- 1 medium nectarine, chopped
- 1 medium kiwifruit, peeled and chopped
- ½ cup halved fresh strawberries
- 2 tablespoons fresh blueberries
- 1 tablespoon lime juice
- 2 teaspoons honey
- ⅛ teaspoon ground nutmeg

DRESSING

- 2 tablespoons mayonnaise
- 2 tablespoons lemon yogurt
- 1 tablespoon honey
- 1 teaspoon lemon juice
- 1 teaspoon orange juice
- ½ teaspoon grated lemon peel
- ½ teaspoon grated orange peel

1. In a small bowl, combine the first five ingredients. Whisk the lime juice, honey and nutmeg; pour over the fruit. Toss to coat.

2. In another bowl, whisk the dressing ingredients; drizzle over salad.

AMBER'S SOURDOUGH STUFFING

All my kids and grandkids absolutely love this stuffing, especially my daughter-in-law, Amber, so I named the recipe for her. I usually have to make a big batch at Thanksgiving.

—**KATHY KATZ** OCALA, FL

PREP: 20 MIN. • **BAKE:** 20 MIN. • **MAKES:** 2 SERVINGS

- 1 tablespoon olive oil
- ⅓ cup sliced fresh mushrooms
- ⅓ cup chopped celery
- ⅓ cup finely chopped carrot
- ⅓ cup finely chopped onion
- 2½ cups cubed sourdough bread
- ½ teaspoon poultry seasoning
- ¼ teaspoon salt
- ⅛ teaspoon pepper
- 2 tablespoons beaten egg
- ½ to ¾ cup chicken broth

1. Preheat oven to 350°. In a large skillet, heat oil over medium-high heat. Add mushrooms, celery, carrot and onion; cook and stir until tender.
2. Transfer to a large bowl. Add the bread cubes and seasonings; toss to combine. Stir in the egg and enough broth to reach desired moistness.
3. Transfer to two greased 10-oz. ramekins or a 1-qt. baking dish. Bake 20-25 minutes or until top is lightly browned and a thermometer reads 160°.

SWISS CHICKEN ROLLS

A simple-to-fix wine sauce complements this impressive entree. When my husband asks me to make it, I always say yes!

—**TONYA DAUGHERTY** MANSFIELD, TX

PREP: 20 MIN. • **BAKE:** 20 MIN. • **MAKES:** 2 SERVINGS

- 2 boneless skinless chicken breast halves (5 ounces each)
- 2 slices Swiss cheese (¾ ounce each)
- 2 thin slices prosciutto or deli ham
- 1 tablespoon butter
- 1 tablespoon olive oil
- ¼ cup chopped onion
- 1 small garlic clove, minced
- 1 teaspoon all-purpose flour
- ⅓ cup Marsala wine or chicken broth
- 2 teaspoons minced fresh parsley
- 1 teaspoon minced fresh rosemary or ¼ teaspoon dried rosemary, crushed
- 1 teaspoon minced fresh thyme or ¼ teaspoon dried thyme
  Dash salt
  Dash pepper

1. Flatten chicken to ¼-in. thickness; place one cheese and prosciutto slice down the center of each. Roll up jelly-roll style, starting with a short side; secure with toothpicks.
2. In a small skillet, brown chicken in butter and oil on all sides; transfer to an 8-in. square baking dish coated with cooking spray. Cover and bake at 350° for 20-25 minutes or until a thermometer reads 170°.
3. In the same skillet, saute onion and garlic until tender. Stir in flour until blended; gradually add wine. Bring to a boil; cook and stir for 2 minutes or until thickened. Stir in the remaining ingredients. Discard toothpicks from chicken rolls; serve with sauce.

EASY SWEET SLAW FOR TWO

I found this recipe in a church cookbook and tweaked it slightly. It's so unique that it's now the only slaw recipe I use.

—**AGNES WARD** STRATFORD, ON

START TO FINISH: 15 MIN. • **MAKES:** 2 SERVINGS

- 2 cups coleslaw mix
- ¼ cup finely chopped onion
- 2 tablespoons finely chopped celery
- 2 tablespoons finely chopped green pepper

DRESSING
- ¼ cup mayonnaise
- 2 tablespoons canned unsweetened crushed pineapple
- 1 tablespoon unsweetened pineapple juice
- 1 tablespoon cider vinegar
- 1 to 2 teaspoons sugar
- ¼ teaspoon salt
- ⅛ teaspoon pepper

In a serving bowl, combine the coleslaw mix, onion, celery and green pepper. Combine the dressing ingredients; pour over cabbage mixture and toss to coat. Chill until serving.

WATERMELON COOLER FOR TWO

Warm weather outside means cooling off with a slice of watermelon and a glass of cold lemonade. This combines two favorites in one.

—**DARLENE BRENDEN** SALEM, OR

START TO FINISH: 10 MIN. • **MAKES:** 2 SERVINGS

- 1 cup lemonade
- 1½ cups seedless watermelon, coarsely chopped
- ½ cup crushed ice

In a blender, combine all ingredients; cover and process until smooth. Pour into chilled glasses; serve immediately.

MUD PIES FOR TWO

After being inspired by recipes that use premade individual pie crusts and ice cream, I created this dessert. I love that it doesn't require any baking.

—**CASSANDRA GOURLEY** WILLIAMS, AZ

START TO FINISH: 10 MIN. • **MAKES:** 2 SERVINGS

- ⅓ cup Nutella
- 2 individual graham cracker tart shells
- 1 cup coffee ice cream
  Whipped cream and chocolate-covered coffee beans

Spoon Nutella into tart shells. Top each with ice cream; garnish with whipped cream and coffee beans.

SNOW PEA & CARROT SAUTE FOR TWO

With bright carrot strips and green snow peas, this eye-popping side goes well with any entree. Short on time? You can buy matchstick carrots to toss in.

—**TASTE OF HOME** TEST KITCHEN

START TO FINISH: 20 MIN. • **MAKES:** 2 SERVINGS

- 6 ounces fresh snow peas
- 1 teaspoon butter
- 1 small carrot, julienned
- 1 small garlic clove, minced
- 4 teaspoons honey
- ⅛ teaspoon salt
  Dash pepper

In a small skillet, saute snow peas in butter for 3 minutes. Add carrots and garlic; saute 1-2 minutes longer or until vegetables are crisp-tender. Add remaining ingredients; heat through.

Apples-a-Plenty!

Enjoy a harvest of sweet, rich flavors when you bite into these appealing recipes. These apple-packed selections will earn you a bushel of compliments.

BAKED APPLE SURPRISE

Sometimes I'll use brie cheese instead of blue cheese in this recipe. I recommend baking the apples in a muffin tin so they don't roll around.
—**JESSICA LEVINSON** NYACK, NY

PREP: 10 MIN. • **BAKE:** 35 MIN. • **MAKES:** 2 SERVINGS

- 2 **medium apples**
- 2 **tablespoons crumbled blue cheese, divided**
- 2 **tablespoons quick-cooking oats**
- 2 **tablespoons bran flakes**
- 1 **tablespoon golden raisins**
- 1 **tablespoon raisins**
- 1 **tablespoon brown sugar**

1. Cut apples in half lengthwise; remove cores. Place in an ungreased 8-in. square baking dish. Fill each half with 1 teaspoon blue cheese.

2. In a small bowl, combine the oats, bran flakes, golden raisins, raisins and brown sugar; spoon into apples. Top with remaining cheese. Bake, uncovered, at 350° for 35-40 minutes or until tender.

APPLE-BEEF PANINI

Horseradish sauce, roast beef and apple slices combined make a surprisingly addictive sandwich. I don't have a panini press, so I use my countertop grill instead.
—**DONNA MARIE RYAN** TOPSFIELD, MA

START TO FINISH: 10 MIN. • **MAKES:** 2 SERVINGS

- 4 **slices multigrain bread**
- 2 **slices reduced-fat cheddar cheese**
- 2 **teaspoons horseradish sauce**
- ½ **medium apple, thinly sliced**
- 4 **ounces sliced deli roast beef**
   Cooking spray

1. Layer two bread slices with cheese, horseradish sauce, apple and beef. Top with remaining bread. Spritz outsides of sandwiches with cooking spray.

2. Cook on a panini maker or indoor grill for 3-4 minutes or until bread is browned and cheese is melted.

WALDORF LENTIL SALAD

This salad includes something I discovered years ago: a touch of ground cloves. It does amazing things for lentils.

—**LILY JULOW** LAWRENCEVILLE, GA

PREP: 30 MIN. + CHILLING • **MAKES:** 2 SERVINGS

- ½ cup dried lentils, rinsed
- 1½ cups water
- ¼ cup mayonnaise
- 4½ teaspoons lemon juice
- ¼ teaspoon sugar
- ⅛ teaspoon salt
- ⅛ teaspoon ground allspice
  Dash ground cloves
  Dash pepper
- 1 medium apple, chopped
- ¼ cup sliced celery
- 2 Bibb lettuce leaves
- ¼ cup coarsely chopped walnuts, toasted

1. In a small saucepan, bring lentils and water to a boil. Reduce heat; cover and simmer for 15-20 minutes or until lentils are tender. Meanwhile, in a small bowl, whisk the mayonnaise, lemon juice, sugar, salt, allspice, cloves and pepper until blended. Stir in apple and celery.
2. Drain and rinse lentils in cold water. Gently stir into apple mixture. Cover and refrigerate for at least 1 hour. Serve on lettuce leaves; sprinkle with walnuts.

CARAMEL APPLE CIDER FLOAT

Who doesn't love caramel, apples and vanilla ice cream together? If I'm feeling fancy, I drizzle caramel syrup around the inside of my glass before adding the apple cider and ginger ale.

—**CINDY REAMS** PHILIPSBURG, PA

START TO FINISH: 10 MIN. • **MAKES:** 2 SERVINGS

- 1 cup chilled apple cider or unsweetened apple juice
- 1 cup chilled ginger ale or lemon-lime soda
- 1 cup vanilla ice cream
- 2 tablespoons caramel sundae syrup

Divide cider and ginger ale between two glasses. Top with ice cream; drizzle with caramel syrup.

TWICE-BAKED BREAKFAST POTATOES FOR TWO

Leftover baked potatoes were the inspiration for this main dish. The bacon and sausage combo makes for a hearty breakfast, but it can become a filling lunch or dinner as well.

—WILLIAM BROCK AMELIA, OH

PREP: 30 MIN. • **BAKE:** 15 MIN. • **MAKES:** 2 SERVINGS

- 1 large baking potato
- ¾ teaspoon butter
- 1 egg, beaten
- 3 ounces bulk pork sausage
- 1 tablespoon sour cream
- 2 bacon strips, cooked and crumbled
- 3 tablespoons shredded cheddar cheese, divided
- 2 tablespoons minced chives, divided
- ¾ teaspoon minced fresh parsley
- ⅛ teaspoon salt
- ⅛ teaspoon pepper
  Additional sour cream, optional

1. Scrub and pierce potato; place on a microwave-safe plate. Microwave, uncovered, on high for 15-17 minutes or until tender, turning once.

2. Meanwhile, in a large skillet, melt butter over medium-high heat. Add the egg; cook and stir until set. Remove and set aside. In the same skillet, cook sausage over medium heat until no longer pink; drain and set aside.

3. When potato is cool enough to handle, cut in half lengthwise. Scoop out pulp, leaving thin shells. In a large bowl, mash the pulp with sour cream. Stir in the bacon, 2 tablespoons cheese, 1 tablespoon chives, parsley, salt, pepper, egg and sausage. Spoon into potato shells.

4. Place on a baking sheet. Bake, uncovered, at 375° for 12-15 minutes or until heated through. Sprinkle with remaining cheese and chives. Serve with additional sour cream if desired.

PEPPERONI BITES

Expecting guests? No problem! Just double or triple the ingredients for these pizza-flavored snacks.

—YVONNE ROCHE LEBANON, MO

START TO FINISH: 20 MIN. • **MAKES:** 2 SERVINGS

- 3 tablespoons tomato sauce
- ¾ teaspoon olive oil
- ¼ teaspoon onion powder
- ¼ teaspoon dried oregano
- ⅛ teaspoon garlic powder
- 1 tube (6 ounces) refrigerated flaky buttermilk biscuits
- 10 slices pepperoni
- 2 tablespoons grated Parmesan cheese

1. In a small bowl, combine the tomato sauce, oil and seasonings. Cut each biscuit in half. Place one pepperoni slice on each half; fold dough over pepperoni and pinch edges to seal. Dip in tomato mixture.

2. Place in a shallow baking pan coated with cooking spray. Sprinkle with Parmesan cheese. Bake in a toaster oven at 450° for 10-12 minutes or until golden brown.

ROASTED BUTTERNUT LINGUINE FOR TWO

Squash is one of our favorite vegetables, and this is my husband's preferred fall dish. It's the perfect amount for just the two of us.

—**KIM CAPUTO** CANNON FALLS, MN

PREP: 10 MIN. • **BAKE:** 45 MIN. • **MAKES:** 2 SERVINGS

- 2 cups cubed peeled butternut squash
- 1 small red onion, chopped
- 4 teaspoons olive oil
- ⅛ teaspoon crushed red pepper flakes
- ¼ pound linguine
- 1 cup shredded Swiss chard
- 1½ teaspoons minced fresh sage
- ¼ teaspoon salt
- ⅛ teaspoon pepper

1. Place the squash and onion in a 15x10x1-in. baking pan coated with cooking spray. Combine the oil and pepper flakes; drizzle over vegetables and toss to coat.
2. Bake, uncovered, at 350° for 45-50 minutes or until tender, stirring occasionally.
3. Meanwhile, cook pasta according to package directions; drain and place in a large bowl. Add the squash mixture, Swiss chard, sage, salt and pepper; toss to combine.

BUFFALO SLOPPY JOES FOR TWO

Think you know sloppy joes? Think again! A hefty splash of hot sauce and optional blue cheese provide an authentic Buffalo-style flavor for this take on the popular sandwich.

—**MARIA REGAKIS** SAUGUS, MA

START TO FINISH: 30 MIN. • **MAKES:** 2 SERVINGS

- ½ pound extra-lean ground turkey
- ¼ cup chopped celery
- 3 tablespoons chopped onion
- 2 tablespoons grated carrots
- 1 garlic clove, minced
- 3 tablespoons tomato sauce
- 2 tablespoons reduced-sodium chicken broth
- 1 tablespoon Louisiana-style hot sauce
- 1½ teaspoons brown sugar
- 1½ teaspoons red wine vinegar
- ¾ teaspoon Worcestershire sauce
  Dash pepper
- 2 hamburger buns, split
- ¼ cup crumbled blue cheese, optional

1. In a Dutch oven, cook the first five ingredients over medium heat until turkey is no longer pink. Stir in the tomato sauce, chicken broth, hot sauce, brown sugar, vinegar, Worcestershire sauce and pepper; heat through.
2. Serve on buns; sprinkle with cheese if desired.

CHERRY BOMBS

After a special dinner, your guests will love breaking open the outer shell of this dessert to get to the chocolate-covered cherry center. It's like an inside-out sundae.

—**LINDA TRIPLETT** RENTON, WA

PREP: 15 MIN. + FREEZING • **MAKES:** 2 SERVINGS

- 1 **cup vanilla ice cream, softened if necessary**
- 2 **chocolate-covered cherries**
- 2 **tablespoons seedless raspberry jam**
- ⅓ **cup chocolate hard-shell ice cream topping**
- ¼ **cup whipped cream**
- 2 **tablespoons chocolate syrup**

1. Line two muffin cups with plastic wrap. Divide ice cream between cups. Press a chocolate-covered cherry into each; smooth ice cream over the cherries. Freeze overnight or until firm.

2. Invert ice cream onto a waxed paper-lined plate; remove and discard plastic wrap. Spread jam over ice cream; freeze until firm.

3. Place a wire rack over a sheet of waxed paper. Using a fork, transfer ice cream to rack. Pour ice cream topping over each to coat. Transfer to dessert plates; freeze until serving. Serve with whipped cream and chocolate syrup.

MANDARIN PORK SALAD

Try something different for dinner tonight. This entree tosses together pork, mandarin oranges, beets and goat cheese. It'll be an explosion for your taste buds.

—**NANCI JENKINS** ANN ARBOR, MI

PREP: 15 MIN. • **GRILL:** 20 MIN. • **MAKES:** 2 SERVINGS

- 1 **pork tenderloin (½ pound)**
- 3 **cups torn mixed salad greens**
- 1 **snack-size cup (4 ounces) mandarin oranges, drained**
- ½ **small red onion, thinly sliced**
- ¼ **cup crumbled goat cheese**
- ¼ **cup canned sliced beets, julienned**
- 2 **tablespoons minced fresh cilantro**
- 1 **teaspoon finely chopped seeded jalapeno pepper**
- 2 **tablespoons balsamic vinegar**
- 2 **teaspoons olive oil**
- ½ **teaspoon salt**

1. Grill pork, covered, over medium heat or broil 4 in. from heat for 8-10 minutes on each side or until a thermometer reaches 160°.

2. Meanwhile, in a large bowl, combine the salad greens, oranges, onion, cheese, beets, cilantro and jalapeno. Transfer to a serving platter. Whisk the vinegar, oil and salt. Thinly slice pork; arrange over salad. Drizzle with dressing.

NOTE *Wear disposable gloves when cutting hot peppers; the oils can burn skin. Avoid touching your face.*

2. Combine the mayonnaise, pesto, basil and oregano; set aside. Brush both sides of tortillas with remaining oil. Grill tortillas, uncovered, over medium heat for 2-3 minutes or until puffed.

3. Remove from the grill. Spread grilled sides with sauce; top with vegetable mixture. Sprinkle with cheese. Grill, covered, for 2-3 minutes or until cheese is melted.

OVEN PARMESAN CHIPS

Potatoes are almost always a daily staple in my home. These delectable sliced potatoes make homemade chips simple!
—**MARY LOU KELLY** SCOTTDALE, PA

START TO FINISH: 25 MIN. • **MAKES:** 2 SERVINGS

- 2 **medium potatoes**
- ¼ **cup butter, melted**
- 1 **tablespoon finely chopped onion**
- ½ **teaspoon salt**
- ⅛ **teaspoon pepper**
  Dash paprika
- 2 **tablespoons grated Parmesan cheese**

1. Preheat oven to 425°. Cut potatoes into ¼-in. slices; arrange in a single layer on two greased baking sheets. In a small bowl, mix butter, onion, salt, pepper and paprika; brush over both sides of potatoes.

2. Roast 15-20 minutes or until potatoes are tender and golden, turning occasionally. Sprinkle with cheese.

GRILLED VEGGIE TORTILLAS FOR TWO

Your garden's bounty will be put to good use in this delightful entree, which resembles a pizza.
—**SHARON DELANEY-CHRONIS** SOUTH MILWAUKEE, WI

START TO FINISH: 25 MIN. • **MAKES:** 2 SERVINGS

- 1 **small zucchini, cut lengthwise into ½-inch slices**
- 1 **small yellow summer squash, cut lengthwise into ½-inch slices**
- ½ **small sweet red pepper, cut in half**
- 1 **tablespoon olive oil, divided**
- ¼ **teaspoon salt**
- 1 **small tomato, chopped**
- 2 **tablespoons reduced-fat mayonnaise**
- 1 **tablespoon prepared pesto**
- 1½ **teaspoons minced fresh basil**
- 1½ **teaspoons minced fresh oregano**
- 2 **whole wheat tortillas (8 inches)**
- ½ **cup shredded part-skim mozzarella cheese**

1. Brush the zucchini, summer squash and red pepper with 1½ teaspoon oil. Sprinkle with salt. Grill vegetables over medium heat for 4-5 minutes on each side or until tender. Cut into ½-in. cubes and place in a small bowl; stir in tomato.

SEARED SCALLOPS WITH CITRUS HERB SAUCE

Be sure to pat the scallops with a paper towel to remove any excess moisture. This helps create perfectly browned and delectable scallops.

—**APRIL LANE** GREENEVILLE, TN

START TO FINISH: 20 MIN. • **MAKES:** 2 SERVINGS

- ¾ **pound sea scallops**
- ¼ **teaspoon salt**
- ¼ **teaspoon pepper**
- ⅛ **teaspoon paprika**
- 3 **tablespoons butter, divided**
- 1 **garlic clove, minced**
- 2 **tablespoons dry sherry or chicken broth**
- 1 **tablespoon lemon juice**
- ⅛ **teaspoon minced fresh oregano**
- ⅛ **teaspoon minced fresh tarragon**

1. Pat scallops dry with paper towels; sprinkle with salt, pepper and paprika. In a large skillet, heat 2 tablespoons butter over medium-high heat. Add scallops; sear for 1-2 minutes on each side or until golden brown and firm. Remove from the skillet; keep warm.
2. Wipe skillet clean if necessary. Saute garlic in remaining butter until tender; stir in sherry. Cook until the liquid is almost evaporated; stir in the remaining ingredients. Serve with the scallops.

ROASTED TOMATO SOUP WITH FRESH BASIL FOR TWO

Use up an abundance of fresh garden tomatoes here. The thyme and basil give the soup a fresher taste than making it from a can.

—**MARIE FORTE** RARITAN, NJ

PREP: 40 MIN. • **COOK:** 5 MIN. • **MAKES:** 2 SERVINGS

- 1¼ **pounds tomatoes (about 4 medium), halved**
- 1 **small onion, quartered**
- 1 **garlic clove, peeled and halved**
- 1 **tablespoon olive oil**
- 1 **tablespoon minced fresh thyme**
- ½ **teaspoon salt**
- ⅛ **teaspoon pepper**
- 4 **fresh basil leaves**
  Salad croutons and additional fresh basil leaves, optional

1. Place the tomatoes, onion and garlic in a greased 15x10x1-in. baking pan; drizzle with oil. Sprinkle with thyme, salt and pepper; toss to coat. Bake at 400° for 25-30 minutes or until tender, stirring once. Cool slightly.
2. In a blender, process tomato mixture and basil leaves until blended. Transfer to a large saucepan and heat through. Garnish each serving with croutons and additional basil if desired.

HOMEMADE TOMATO JUICE

To use extra garden tomatoes, I wash and core them, then puree in a blender with lemon juice, onion and celery to taste for a great vegetable juice.

—**MARION W.** GREENFIELD, WI

PORTOBELLO-GOUDA GRILLED CHEESE

Take a simple grilled cheese sandwich to the next level of deliciousness with portobello mushrooms and Gouda cheese. Served with a side of tomato soup, this just might be the best combination on earth.

—SHERYL BERGMAN SHADY SIDE, MD

START TO FINISH: 20 MIN. • **MAKES:** 2 SERVINGS

- 1 cup sliced baby portobello mushrooms
- 1 tablespoon plus 4 teaspoons butter, divided
- 4 ounces smoked Gouda cheese, sliced
- 4 slices rye bread
- 1 plum tomato, sliced

1. In a large skillet, saute the mushrooms in 1 tablespoon butter until tender. Place cheese on two bread slices; top with mushrooms, tomato and remaining bread. Spread outsides of sandwiches with remaining butter.
2. In a small skillet over medium heat, toast sandwiches for 2-3 minutes on each side or until cheese is melted.

LANDMARK HOT CHOCOLATE

With or without a nip of rum, my hot chocolate recipe has been a Wisconsin winter warmer for years. When the toboggan hills are calling, I skip the whipped cream and take a thermos to go.
—MARK PHILLIPS BAYFIELD, WI

START TO FINISH: 15 MIN. • **MAKES:** 1 SERVING

- ⅓ cup heavy whipping cream
- ¼ cup 2% milk
- 2 ounces dark chocolate candy bar, chopped
- 4½ teaspoons sugar
- 1 cinnamon stick (3 inches)
  Vanilla rum, optional
  Heavy whipping cream, whipped
  Additional cinnamon stick, optional

Heat the first five ingredients over medium heat in a small saucepan just until mixture comes to a simmer, stirring constantly. Remove from heat; stir until smooth. Add rum if desired. Pour into a mug; top with whipped cream. Garnish with cinnamon stick if desired.

FRESH 'N' FRUITY SALMON SALAD

You can customize this light salad with a berry-flavored goat cheese. It's delicious no matter what.

—SHELISA TERRY HENDERSON, NV

START TO FINISH: 20 MIN. • **MAKES:** 2 SERVINGS

- 2 **salmon fillets (6 ounces each)**
- 2 **tablespoons reduced-fat raspberry vinaigrette**
- 3 **cups fresh baby spinach**
- ¾ **cup sliced fresh strawberries**
- 2 **slices red onion, separated into rings**
- 2 **tablespoons crumbled goat cheese**
- 2 **tablespoons chopped pecans, toasted**
  Additional reduced-fat raspberry vinaigrette

1. Place salmon on a broiler pan coated with cooking spray; drizzle with vinaigrette. Broil 3-4 in. from the heat for 10-15 minutes or until fish flakes easily with a fork.

2. Divide spinach between two serving plates. Top with strawberries, onion, cheese and pecans. Flake the salmon; sprinkle over salads. Drizzle with additional vinaigrette.

CROUTON-TOPPED GARLIC SOUP FOR TWO

Pan roasting the garlic gives this soup extra flavor, while a touch of cream lends body. The herbed croutons enhance the soup's taste and add texture, but it's the freshly grated cheese that make this dish taste like heaven!

—CAROLYN KUMPE EL DORADO, CA

PREP: 20 MIN. • **COOK:** 40 MIN. • **MAKES:** 2 SERVINGS

- 10 **garlic cloves, peeled**
- 1½ **teaspoons olive oil**

- 1 **large onion, halved and sliced**
- 1 **tablespoon butter**
- 1¼ **cups reduced-sodium chicken broth**
- 1½ **teaspoons minced fresh thyme or ½ teaspoon dried thyme**
- 1 **bay leaf**
- ½ **cup heavy whipping cream**

CROUTONS
- 1 **cup cubed sourdough bread, crusts removed**
- 1 **tablespoon olive oil**
- ½ **teaspoon minced fresh rosemary or ⅛ teaspoon dried rosemary, crushed**
- ⅛ **teaspoon salt**
- ⅛ **teaspoon pepper**

TOPPINGS
- ¼ **cup Gruyere cheese or shredded Swiss cheese**
- 1 **tablespoon minced fresh parsley**

1. In a small skillet, cook garlic in oil over low heat for 3-5 minutes or until golden brown. Remove from the heat; set aside.

2. In a large saucepan over medium-high heat, cook onions in butter until softened. Reduce heat to medium-low; cook, stirring occasionally, for 30 minutes or until deep golden brown. Add the broth, thyme, bay leaf and reserved garlic. Bring to a boil. Reduce heat; cover and simmer for 20 minutes to allow flavors to blend. Stir in cream; heat through. Discard bay leaf.

3. For croutons, place bread in a small bowl. Combine the oil, rosemary, salt and pepper; drizzle over bread and toss to coat. Place in an ungreased 15x10x1-in. baking pan. Bake at 400° for 15-20 minutes or until golden brown, stirring occasionally.

4. Divide soup among four bowls. Top with croutons, cheese and parsley.

FRIED GREEN TOMATO BLTS

I think of this as Southern-inspired sandwich comfort food with a twist. The chipotle mayonnaise adds a nice kick, while the peppered bacon really punches it up.

—NEILLA ROE KINGSTON, WA

START TO FINISH: 20 MIN. • **MAKES:** 8 SERVINGS

- 1 package thick-sliced peppered bacon strips (24 ounces)
- 1 cup all-purpose flour
- 1 cup cornmeal
- 4½ teaspoons seafood seasoning
- 1 teaspoon pepper
- ⅛ teaspoon salt
- 1 cup buttermilk
- 8 medium green tomatoes, cut into ¼-inch slices
  Oil for deep-fat frying
- 16 slices Texas toast
- ½ cup reduced-fat chipotle mayonnaise
- 8 Boston lettuce leaves

1. In a large skillet, cook bacon over medium heat until crisp. Remove to paper towels to drain. In a small shallow bowl, combine the flour, cornmeal, seafood seasoning, pepper and salt. Place buttermilk and flour mixture in shallow bowl. Dip tomatoes in buttermilk, then coat with flour mixture.

2. In an electric skillet or deep fryer, heat oil to 375°. Fry tomatoes, a few slices at a time, for 1 minute on each side or until golden brown. Drain on paper towels.

3. Serve tomatoes on Texas toast with mayonnaise, bacon and lettuce.

HAM AND SWISS OMELET

Whether you make this easy omelet for breakfast or dinner, this will be a winner.

—AGNES WARD STRATFORD, ON

START TO FINISH: 20 MIN. • **MAKES:** 1 SERVING

- 1 tablespoon butter
- 3 eggs
- 3 tablespoons water
- ⅛ teaspoon salt
- ⅛ teaspoon pepper
- ½ cup cubed fully cooked ham
- ¼ cup shredded Swiss cheese

1. In a small nonstick skillet, melt butter over medium-high heat. Whisk the eggs, water, salt and pepper. Add egg mixture to skillet (mixture should set immediately at edges).

2. As eggs set, push cooked edges toward the center, letting uncooked portion flow underneath. When the eggs are set, place ham on one side and sprinkle with cheese; fold other side over filling. Slide omelet onto a plate.

STRAWBERRY WHITE CHOCOLATE TARTS

Pairing white chocolate with sweet strawberries? Now that's a match made in heaven. The shortbread cookies make a wonderful buttery crust.

—CYNTHIA WIKE CHARLOTTE, NC

PREP: 15 MIN. • **BAKE:** 10 MIN. + CHILLING • **MAKES:** 2 SERVINGS

- 1 cup crushed shortbread cookies
- 5 teaspoons butter, melted
- 3 tablespoons heavy whipping cream
- 3 ounces white baking chocolate, chopped
- ¾ cup sliced fresh strawberries
- 2 tablespoons semisweet chocolate chips

1. Combine cookie crumbs and butter. Press onto the bottoms and up the sides of two greased 4-in. fluted tart pans with removable bottoms. Place on a baking sheet. Bake at 350° for 8-10 minutes or until golden brown. Cool on a wire rack.

2. Place cream in a small microwave-safe bowl. Microwave, uncovered, on high for 15-20 seconds or until cream comes to a boil. Add white chocolate; whisk until smooth. Cool, stirring occasionally, to room temperature.

3. Pour filling into crusts; arrange strawberries over top. In a microwave, melt chocolate chips; stir until smooth. Drizzle over tarts. Refrigerate for at least 1 hour.

Cookies, Bars & Candies

Share joy by the dozen! Invite loved ones over and they'll want to stay awhile when you have these goodies sitting out for them. What says "Come in and relax" better than a plate of warm cookies and a glass of milk?

SUGAR-CONE CHOCOLATE CHIP COOKIES

If I could make a batch of cookies a day, I'd be in baking heaven. I made these for my boys when they were growing up, and now I treat my grandkids, too.

—PAULA MARCHESI LENHARTSVILLE, PA

PREP: 25 MIN. • **BAKE:** 10 MIN./BATCH • **MAKES:** 6 DOZEN

- 1 cup butter, softened
- ¾ cup sugar
- ¾ cup packed brown sugar
- 2 eggs
- 3 teaspoons vanilla extract
- 2¼ cups all-purpose flour
- 1 teaspoon baking soda
- ½ teaspoon salt
- 2 cups milk chocolate chips
- 2 cups coarsely crushed ice cream sugar cones (about 16)
- 1 cup sprinkles

1. Preheat the oven to 375°. In a large bowl, cream butter and sugars until light and fluffy. Beat in eggs and vanilla. In another bowl, whisk flour, baking soda and salt; gradually beat into creamed mixture. Stir in chocolate chips, crushed sugar cones and sprinkles.

2. Drop by tablespoonfuls 2 in. apart onto ungreased baking sheets. Bake 8-10 minutes or until golden brown. Remove from pans to wire racks to cool.

CLASSIC CHERRY PIE COOKIES

These cute cookies will be the hit of any cookie tray. The cocoa-based buttercream frosting is piped over the filling to mimic a lattice crust.

—LORRI REINHARDT BIG BEND, WI

PREP: 1½ HOURS + CHILLING • **BAKE:** 10 MIN./BATCH + COOLING
MAKES: 5 DOZEN

- ½ cup butter, softened
- 1 cup sugar
- 1 egg
- ½ teaspoon vanilla extract
- 1¾ cups all-purpose flour
- ½ teaspoon baking soda
- ¼ teaspoon salt

FROSTING
- ⅔ cup butter, softened
- 5 cups confectioners' sugar
- 1¼ teaspoons vanilla extract
- 5 to 10 teaspoons 2% milk
- ¾ teaspoon baking cocoa
- 2 drops yellow food coloring
- 1 jar (12 ounces) cherry preserves

1. In a large bowl, cream butter and sugar until light and fluffy. Beat in egg and vanilla. Combine the flour, baking soda and salt; gradually add to creamed mixture and mix well. On a lightly floured surface, shape dough into two 6-in. rolls; wrap each in plastic wrap. Refrigerate for 1 hour or until firm.

2. Unwrap and cut into ⅜-in. slices. Place 2 in. apart on greased baking sheets. Bake at 375° for 8-10 minutes or until lightly browned. Remove to wire racks to cool completely.

3. For frosting, in a large bowl, cream butter until light and fluffy. Beat in the confectioners' sugar, vanilla and enough milk to achieve piping consistency. Tint frosting with cocoa and food coloring. Cut a small hole in the corner of a pastry or plastic bag; fill with frosting.

4. Spread preserves over cookies to within ¼ in. of edges. Pipe lines across the top of each cookie, forming a lattice. Pipe a fluted edge around the tops of cookies.

BLUEBERRY PIE COOKIES *Substitute blueberry jam for the cherry preserves.*

LIME & GIN COCONUT MACAROONS

I took these lime and coconut macaroons to our annual cookie exchange, where we name a cookie queen. I won the crown!

—**MILISSA KIRKPATRICK** ANGEL FIRE, NM

PREP: 20 MIN. • **BAKE:** 15 MIN./BATCH + COOLING
MAKES: 2½ DOZEN

- 4 egg whites
- ⅔ cup sugar
- 3 tablespoons gin
- 1½ teaspoons grated lime peel
- ¼ teaspoon salt
- ¼ teaspoon almond extract
- 1 package (14 ounces) flaked coconut
- ½ cup all-purpose flour
- 8 ounces white baking chocolate, melted

1. Preheat oven to 350°. In a small bowl, whisk the first six ingredients until blended. In a large bowl, toss coconut with flour; stir in egg white mixture.

2. Drop by tablespoonfuls 2 in. apart onto greased baking sheets. Bake 15-18 minutes or until tops are light brown. Remove from pans to wire racks to cool completely.

3. Dip bottoms of macaroons into melted chocolate, allowing excess to drip off. Place on waxed paper; let stand until set. Store in an airtight container.

MELTING WHITE CHOCOLATE

Melt white chocolate in a microwave-safe bowl at 70% power for 1 minute; stir. Microwave at additional 10- to 20-second intervals, stirring until smooth. Be sure to not overheat chocolate.

CRANBERRY BARS WITH CREAM CHEESE FROSTING

I often leave a pan of these bars in the teachers' lounge. When I come back after the last bell, the pan is almost always empty. White chocolate chips and cranberries make them impossible to pass by.

—**MIRELLA HACKETT** CHANDLER, AZ

PREP: 30 MIN. • **BAKE:** 25 MIN. + COOLING • **MAKES:** 4 DOZEN

- ¾ cup butter, softened
- 1 cup sugar
- 2 eggs
- ¾ cup sour cream
- ½ teaspoon almond extract
- ½ teaspoon vanilla extract
- 1½ cups all-purpose flour
- 1 teaspoon baking powder
- ⅛ teaspoon salt
- 1 cup white baking chips
- 1 cup dried cranberries
- ½ cup chopped walnuts

FROSTING

- 2 packages (8 ounces each) cream cheese, softened
- ¼ cup butter, softened
- 1 teaspoon vanilla extract
- 2 cups confectioners' sugar
- ½ cup dried cranberries, chopped

1. Preheat oven to 350°. In a large bowl, cream butter and sugar until light and fluffy. Gradually beat in eggs, sour cream and extracts. In a small bowl, whisk flour, baking powder and salt; gradually beat into creamed mixture. Fold in baking chips, cranberries and walnuts. Spread into a greased 15x10x1-in. baking pan.

2. Bake 25-30 minutes or until a toothpick inserted in center comes out clean. Cool completely in the pan on a wire rack.

3. For frosting, in a small bowl, beat cream cheese, butter and vanilla until smooth. Beat in confectioners' sugar; spread over top. Sprinkle with cranberries. Cut into bars or triangles. Refrigerate leftovers.

BLACK FOREST ICEBOX COOKIES

You'll want to keep extra batches of these tasty cookies on hand for when company drops by. The rich chocolate wafers are the perfect complement to the creamy filling's sweet-tart tones.
—*TASTE OF HOME* TEST KITCHEN

PREP: 20 MIN. + CHILLING • **MAKES:** 20 COOKIES

- 3 tablespoons sugar
- 4 teaspoons cornstarch
  Pinch salt
- ¾ cup fresh or frozen pitted tart cherries, thawed and coarsely chopped
- ¾ cup cherry juice blend
- 1½ teaspoons lemon juice
- 1 to 2 drops red food coloring, optional
- ½ cup mascarpone cheese
- 1 tablespoon confectioners' sugar
- 1 teaspoon cherry brandy
- 1 package (9 ounces) chocolate wafers
- ½ cup semisweet chocolate chips
- ¼ cup heavy whipping cream

1. In a small saucepan, combine the sugar, cornstarch and salt. Add the cherries, juice blend and lemon juice. Bring to a boil; cook and stir for 2 minutes or until thickened. Remove from the heat and stir in food coloring if desired. Cool to room temperature.

2. In a small bowl, combine the mascarpone cheese, confectioners' sugar and brandy. Spread about 1 teaspoon cheese mixture onto 20 wafers; top with 2 teaspoons cherry mixture and remaining wafers. Place on a waxed paper-lined baking pan. Place chocolate chips in a small bowl. In a small saucepan, bring cream just to a boil. Pour over chips; whisk until smooth. Drizzle over cookies. Cover and refrigerate cookies for up to 4 hours before serving.

CHOCOLATE-MINT COOKIE CUPS

When chocolate and mint get together with a hint of peppermint, something magical happens. If you don't have mini muffin pans on hand, use disposable foil baking cups instead.
—**PAM CORRELL** BROCKPORT, PA

PREP: 45 MIN. + CHILLING • **BAKE:** 10 MIN./BATCH • **MAKES:** 4 DOZEN

- ½ cup butter, softened
- 1 cup sugar
- 1 egg
- 1 teaspoon peppermint extract
- 1½ cups all-purpose flour
- ½ cup baking cocoa
- ¼ teaspoon baking soda
- ¼ teaspoon baking powder
- ¼ teaspoon salt

TOPPING

- 1 cup (6 ounces) semisweet chocolate chips
- ½ heavy whipping cream
- ¼ cup white baking chips
  Green paste food coloring, optional

1. Preheat oven to 350°. In a large bowl, cream butter and sugar until light and fluffy. Beat in egg and extract. Combine flour, cocoa, baking soda, baking powder and salt; gradually add to creamed mixture and mix well.

2. Shape into 1-in. balls; place in paper-lined miniature muffin cups. Bake 8-10 minutes or until set. Remove to wire racks. Cool completely.

3. Place the chocolate chips in a small bowl. In a small saucepan, bring cream just to a boil. Pour over chocolate; whisk until smooth. Cool to room temperature, stirring occasionally. Refrigerate until ganache reaches a piping consistency, about 20 minutes. Pipe over cookies.

4. In a microwave-safe bowl, melt white baking chips at 50% power 1 minute; stir until smooth. If desired, tint with green food coloring. Pipe over tops.

JOE FROGGERS

Large, soft and chewy, these cookies make a great snack. This classic recipe has a warm blend of spices that are even more obvious the second day.

—TASTE OF HOME TEST KITCHEN

PREP: 15 MIN. + CHILLING • **BAKE:** 15 MIN./BATCH
MAKES: 1½ DOZEN

- ½ cup shortening
- 1 cup packed brown sugar
- 1 cup molasses
- ⅓ cup hot water
- 2 tablespoons rum or 1 teaspoon rum extract
- 3½ cups all-purpose flour
- 1½ teaspoons salt
- 1½ teaspoons ground ginger
- 1 teaspoon baking soda
- ½ teaspoon ground cloves
- ½ teaspoon ground nutmeg
- ¼ teaspoon ground allspice
- Sugar

1. In a large bowl, cream shortening and brown sugar until light and fluffy. In a small bowl, whisk molasses, hot water and rum. In another bowl, whisk the flour, salt and spices; add to creamed mixture alternately with molasses mixture, beating after each addition. Refrigerate, covered, 4 hours or until easy to handle.

2. Preheat oven to 375°. Shape dough into 1½-in. balls and place 3 in. apart on greased baking sheets. Flatten to ½-in. thickness with bottom of a custard cup dipped in sugar.

3. Bake 12-14 minutes or until lightly browned. Cool on pans 2 minutes. Remove to wire racks to cool completely. Store in airtight containers.

MOCHA PECAN BALLS

Dusted in either confectioners' sugar or cocoa, roll up this easy 6-ingredient dough into truffle-like treats. No baking is required!

—LORRAINE DAROCHA MOUNTAIN CITY, TN

START TO FINISH: 25 MIN. • **MAKES:** 4 DOZEN

- 2½ cups crushed vanilla wafers (about 65 wafers)
- 2 cups plus ¼ cup confectioners' sugar, divided
- ⅔ cup finely chopped pecans, toasted
- 2 tablespoons baking cocoa
- ¼ cup reduced-fat evaporated milk
- ¼ cup cold strong brewed coffee
- Additional baking cocoa, optional

1. In a large bowl, combine the wafer crumbs, 2 cups confectioners' sugar, pecans and cocoa. Stir in milk and coffee (mixture will be sticky).

2. With hands dusted in confectioners' sugar, shape dough into ¾-in. balls; roll in remaining confectioners' sugar or additional baking cocoa if desired. Store in an airtight container.

ORANGE SANDWICH COOKIES

Remember those orange Creamsicle treats from your childhood? These cookies taste just like them.
—BENITA VILLINES SPRING HILL, TN

PREP: 30 MIN. • **BAKE:** 10 MIN./BATCH + COOLING
MAKES: 28 COOKIES

- 1 cup butter, softened
- 4 ounces cream cheese, softened
- 1¾ cups confectioners' sugar
- ½ cup thawed orange juice concentrate
- 4 teaspoons grated orange peel
- ½ teaspoon vanilla extract
- 2½ cups all-purpose flour
- ½ teaspoon baking soda
- ¼ teaspoon salt
- 10 drops yellow plus 2 drops red food coloring
  Additional confectioners' sugar

FILLING
- ½ cup butter, softened
- 4 ounces cream cheese, softened
- ¼ teaspoon vanilla extract
- 2 cups confectioners' sugar
- 1 tablespoon orange juice concentrate
- ⅛ teaspoon grated orange peel

1. In a large bowl, cream butter and cream cheese until light and fluffy. Gradually beat in confectioners' sugar. Beat in the orange juice concentrate, peel and vanilla. Combine the flour, baking soda and salt; gradually add to creamed mixture and mix well. Stir in food coloring. (Dough will be soft.)

2. Drop dough by rounded tablespoonfuls 3 in. apart onto ungreased baking sheets. Flatten slightly with a glass dipped in confectioners' sugar.

3. Bake at 400° for 6-9 minutes or until edges begin to brown. Remove to wire racks to cool completely.

4. For filling, in a small bowl, cream the butter, cream cheese and vanilla until light and fluffy. Gradually beat in confectioners' sugar. Add orange juice concentrate and peel.

5. Spread filling on the bottoms of half of the cookies; top with remaining cookies. Store in the refrigerator.

APPLE KUCHEN BARS

This recipe is all about family, comfort and simplicity. My mom made them, and now I bake them in my own kitchen. I make double batches to pass on the love!
—ELIZABETH MONFORT CELINA, OH

PREP: 35 MIN. • **BAKE:** 1 HOUR + COOLING • **MAKES:** 2 DOZEN

- 3 cups all-purpose flour, divided
- ¼ teaspoon salt
- 1½ cups cold butter, divided
- 4 to 5 tablespoons ice water
- 8 cups thinly sliced peeled tart apples (about 8 medium)
- 2 cups sugar, divided
- 2 teaspoons ground cinnamon

1. Preheat oven to 350°. Place 2 cups flour and salt in a food processor; pulse until blended. Add 1 cup butter; pulse until butter is the size of peas. While pulsing, add just enough ice water to form moist crumbs. Press mixture into a greased 13x9-in. baking pan. Bake 20-25 minutes or until edges are lightly browned. Cool on a wire rack.

2. In a large bowl, combine the apples, 1 cup sugar and cinnamon; toss to coat. Spoon over crust. Place remaining flour, butter and sugar in food processor; pulse until coarse crumbs form. Sprinkle over apples. Bake 60-70 minutes or until golden brown and apples are tender. Cool completely on a wire rack. Cut into bars.

PUMPKIN BARS WITH BROWNED BUTTER FROSTING

I based this recipe on one my grandmother used to make, which means sweet memories are baked into every bite. When making the frosting, carefully watch the butter and remove it from the heat as soon as it starts to brown. Do not use margarine in place of butter.

—**MARY WILHELM** SPARTA, WI

PREP: 30 MIN. • **BAKE:** 20 MIN. + COOLING • **MAKES:** 2 DOZEN

- 1½ **cups sugar**
- 1 **cup canned pumpkin**
- ½ **cup orange juice**
- ½ **cup canola oil**
- 2 **eggs**
- 2 **teaspoons grated orange peel**
- 2 **cups all-purpose flour**
- 2 **teaspoons baking powder**
- 2 **teaspoons pumpkin pie spice**
- 1 **teaspoon baking soda**
- ¼ **teaspoon salt**

FROSTING
- ⅔ **cup butter, cubed**
- 4 **cups confectioners' sugar**
- 1 **teaspoon vanilla extract**
- 4 **to 6 tablespoons 2% milk**

1. Preheat oven to 350°. Grease a 15x10x1-in. baking pan. In a large bowl, beat the first six ingredients until well blended. In another bowl, whisk flour, baking powder, pie spice, baking soda and salt; gradually beat into pumpkin mixture.
2. Transfer to prepared pan. Bake 18-22 minutes or until a toothpick inserted in center comes out clean. Cool completely in pan on a wire rack.
3. In a small heavy saucepan, melt butter over medium heat. Heat 5-7 minutes or until golden brown, stirring constantly. Transfer to a large bowl. Gradually beat in confectioners' sugar, vanilla and enough milk to reach desired consistency. Spread over bars; let stand until set.

Enjoy a Little Nibble

When your sweet tooth has a hankering, turn to this section for bite-sized delights. Easy to prepare and present, you'll surprise and delight family and friends with your own homemade treats.

HONEY CARAMELS

I love surprising my family and friends with a batch of homemade honey-sweetened caramels. Sometimes I replace the walnuts with pecans, filberts or almonds.

—ARLINE HOFLAND DEER LODGE, MT

PREP: 25 MIN. • **COOK:** 30 MIN. + STANDING
MAKES: ABOUT 1½ POUNDS

- 1 teaspoon plus ¼ cup butter, divided
- 1 cup heavy whipping cream
- 1 cup honey
- ½ cup sugar
- 1 cup chopped walnuts
- 1 teaspoon vanilla extract

1. Line an 8-in. square pan with foil; grease the foil with 1 teaspoon butter and set aside.
2. In a large heavy saucepan, combine the cream, honey, sugar and remaining butter. Cook and stir over medium-low heat until a candy thermometer reads 238°.
3. Using a pastry brush dipped in cold water, wash down the sides of the pan to eliminate sugar crystals. Cook, stirring constantly, until a candy thermometer reads 255° (hard-ball stage). Stir in walnuts and vanilla; return mixture to 255°.
4. Remove from the heat. Pour into prepared pan (do not scrape saucepan). Let stand until firm, about 5 hours or overnight.
5. Using foil, lift candy out of pan; discard foil. Cut candy into 1-in. squares. Wrap candies individually in waxed paper; twist ends.

NANA'S ROCKY ROAD FUDGE

We make this fudge every Christmas. All the credit goes to my mother-in-law, who gave us this wonderful recipe.

—ASHLEY BERRY MONTGOMERY VILLAGE, MD

PREP: 15 MIN. • **COOK:** 5 MIN. + CHILLING
MAKES: ABOUT 2½ POUNDS

- 1½ teaspoons plus 1 tablespoon butter, divided
- 2 cups (12 ounces) semisweet chocolate chips
- 1 can (14 ounces) sweetened condensed milk
- 2 cups salted peanuts
- 1 package (10½ ounces) miniature marshmallows

1. Line a 13x9-in. baking pan with foil and grease the foil with 1½ teaspoons butter; set aside.
2. In a large saucepan, combine the chocolate chips, milk and remaining butter. Cook and stir over medium heat until mixture is smooth. Remove from heat; stir in the peanuts. Place marshmallows in a large bowl; add chocolate mixture and stir well. Spread into prepared pan. Refrigerate until firm.
3. Using foil, lift fudge out of pan. Cut into 1½-in. squares.

SPICED ALMOND BUTTER CANDY

Roasted almonds and almond butter take center stage in this delectable candy, but the cinnamon, nutmeg and allspice really take it over the top. Every batch I make disappears in a flash.
—**LAURA MCDOWELL** LAKE VILLA, IL

PREP: 10 MIN. • **COOK:** 30 MIN. + COOLING • **MAKES:** 3½ POUNDS

- 1½ teaspoons butter
- 2½ cups almond butter
- 2 cups salted roasted almonds, coarsely chopped
- 2 teaspoons ground cinnamon
- ½ teaspoon ground nutmeg
- ½ teaspoon vanilla extract
- ¼ teaspoon ground allspice
- 2 cups sugar
- 1½ cups light corn syrup
- ¼ cup water
- 1½ teaspoons baking soda
- 1 cup (6 ounces) semisweet chocolate chips or 60% cacao bittersweet chocolate baking chips, melted

1. Line a 15x10x 1-in. pan with foil and grease the foil with butter. In a large bowl, combine the almond butter, almonds, cinnamon, nutmeg, vanilla and allspice; set aside.
2. In a large heavy saucepan, combine the sugar, corn syrup and water; cook and stir over medium heat until sugar is dissolved. Bring to a boil. Using a pastry brush dipped in water, wash down the sides of the pan to eliminate sugar crystals. Cook, without stirring, until a candy thermometer reads 300° (hard-crack stage).
3. Remove from the heat. Immediately stir in almond butter mixture and baking soda. Spread into prepared pan. Cool completely. Break candy into pieces. Drizzle with chocolate. Let stand at room temperature until set. Store in airtight containers.
NOTE *We recommend that you test your candy thermometer before each use by bringing water to a boil; the thermometer should read 212°. Adjust your recipe temperature up or down based on your test.*

MARVELOUS MAPLE FUDGE

Use this deliciously simple recipe for potlucks, large family gatherings or bake sales. Line your pan with foil to make removing the fudge a breeze.
—**JEANNIE GALLANT** CHARLOTTETOWN, PE

PREP: 10 MIN. • **COOK:** 20 MIN. + COOLING
MAKES: 1¾ POUNDS (64 PIECES)

- 1 teaspoon plus 1 cup butter, divided
- 2 cups packed brown sugar
- 1 can (5 ounces) evaporated milk
- 1 teaspoon maple flavoring
- ½ teaspoon vanilla extract
- ⅛ teaspoon salt
- 2 cups confectioners' sugar

1. Line an 8-in.-square pan with foil; grease foil with 1 teaspoon butter.
2. Cube remaining butter. In a large saucepan, combine cubed butter, brown sugar and milk. Bring to a full boil over medium heat, stirring constantly. Cook 10 minutes, stirring frequently. Remove from heat.
3. Stir in the maple flavoring, vanilla and salt. Add the confectioners' sugar; beat on medium speed 2 minutes or until smooth. Immediately spread into prepared pan. Cool completely.
4. Using foil, lift fudge out of pan. Remove foil; cut into 1-in. squares. Store in an airtight container.

CHERRY OAT BARS

Adding dried cherries and cherry preserves makes these granola bars a hit. Each bar provides both a sweet pick-me-up and a boost of energy.

—**KEVIN JOHNSON** GLENDORA, CA

PREP: 30 MIN. • **BAKE:** 25 MIN. + COOLING • **MAKES:** 2 DOZEN

- 2 cups all-purpose flour
- 2 cups old-fashioned oats
- 1 cup chopped pecans
- ½ cup toasted wheat germ
- ½ cup packed brown sugar
- 1 teaspoon salt
- 1 teaspoon baking soda
- 1 teaspoon ground cinnamon
- ½ teaspoon ground allspice
- 1 cup butter, melted
- ½ cup honey
- 2 eggs, beaten
- 1 teaspoon vanilla extract
- 1 jar (12 ounces) cherry preserves
- ⅓ cup dried cherries, chopped
- ½ cup flaked coconut

1. In a large bowl, combine the first nine ingredients. In another bowl, combine the butter, honey, eggs and vanilla. Stir into oat mixture until combined. Set aside 1⅓ cups for the topping.

2. Press remaining oat mixture into a greased 13x9-in. baking pan. Combine preserves and dried cherries; spread over crust. Sprinkle with coconut and reserved oat mixture; press down lightly.

3. Bake at 350° for 25-30 minutes or until golden brown. Cool on a wire rack. Cut into bars.

CHOCOLATE CHAI SNICKERDOODLES

I used to think snickerdoodles could never be improved. But then I added some chocolate! While they're baking, the aromas of chocolate mixed with warming spices reminds me of a cup of hot chai tea.

—**KATIE WOLLGAST** FLORISSANT, MO

PREP: 30 MIN. • **BAKE:** 10 MIN./BATCH • **MAKES:** ABOUT 3 DOZEN

- 2¼ cups sugar
- 1 teaspoon ground ginger
- 1 teaspoon ground cardamom
- 1 teaspoon ground cinnamon
- ½ teaspoon ground allspice
- ¼ teaspoon white pepper
- 1 cup butter, softened
- 2 eggs
- 2 teaspoons vanilla extract
- 2¼ cups all-purpose flour
- ½ cup baking cocoa
- 2 teaspoons cream of tartar
- 1½ teaspoons baking powder
- ½ teaspoon salt

1. Preheat the oven to 350°. In a large bowl, combine the first six ingredients. Remove ½ cup sugar mixture to a shallow dish.

2. Add butter to remaining sugar mixture; beat until light and fluffy. Beat in eggs and vanilla. In another bowl, whisk flour, baking cocoa, cream of tartar, baking powder and salt; gradually beat into creamed mixture.

3. Shape dough into 1½-in. balls. Roll in reserved sugar mixture; place 2 in. apart on ungreased baking sheets. Flatten slightly with bottom of a glass. Bake 10-12 minutes or until edges are firm. Remove to wire racks to cool.

PEANUT BUTTER & BACON BLONDIES

The most unusual bar cookie recipe I have is also my most popular one. Use store-bought bacon bits to help save time.
—**JANIE COLLE** HUTCHINSON, KS

PREP: 20 MIN. • **BAKE:** 25 MIN. + COOLING • **MAKES:** 2 DOZEN

- 2 **cups packed brown sugar**
- 1 **cup butter, melted**
- 2 **eggs**
- 2 **teaspoons vanilla extract**
- 2 **cups all-purpose flour**
- 1 **teaspoon baking powder**
- ¼ **teaspoon baking soda**
  Dash salt
- 8 **bacon strips, cooked and crumbled**

FROSTING
- 1 **cup creamy peanut butter**
- ½ **cup butter, softened**
- 2 **cups confectioners' sugar**
- 1 **teaspoon vanilla extract**
- 3 **to 4 tablespoons 2% milk**
- 6 **bacon strips, cooked and crumbled**

1. Preheat the oven to 350°. Line a 13x9-in. pan with parchment paper, letting ends extend up sides; grease paper.
2. In a large bowl, beat brown sugar and butter until blended. Beat in eggs and vanilla. In another bowl, whisk flour, baking powder, baking soda and salt; gradually beat into sugar mixture. Fold in bacon.
3. Spread into the prepared pan. Bake 25-30 minutes or until a toothpick inserted in center comes out clean (do not overbake). Cool completely in pan on a wire rack. Lifting with parchment paper, remove from pan.
4. For frosting, in a large bowl, beat the peanut butter and butter until blended. Gradually beat in confectioners' sugar, vanilla and enough milk to reach desired consistency. Frost blondies; sprinkle with bacon. Cut into bars. Refrigerate leftovers.

LEMON CORNMEAL COOKIES

Anything lemon makes my day brighter (and more yummy). These tender cookies have a fabulous lemon aroma and a subtle citrus taste I can't resist.
—**THERESA MILLER** SAULT SAINTE MARIE, MI

PREP: 30 MIN. • **BAKE:** 15 MIN./BATCH • **MAKES:** 3 DOZEN

- ¾ **cup butter, softened**
- 1 **package (8 ounces) cream cheese, softened**
- 1 **cup sugar**
- 1 **cup packed brown sugar**
- 1 **egg**
- 3 **tablespoons lemon juice**
- 4 **teaspoons grated lemon peel**
- 1 **tablespoon poppy seeds**
- 3⅓ **cups all-purpose flour**
- ¾ **cup cornmeal**
- 1 **teaspoon baking soda**
- 1 **teaspoon ground ginger**
- ¾ **teaspoon salt**
- 1 **package (10 to 12 ounces) white baking chips**

1. In a large bowl, cream the butter, cream cheese and sugars until light and fluffy. Beat in the egg, lemon juice, peel and poppy seeds. Combine the flour, cornmeal, baking soda, ginger and salt; gradually add to creamed mixture and mix well. Stir in chips.
2. Drop dough by heaping tablespoonfuls 2 in. apart onto parchment paper-lined baking sheets; flatten slightly with a glass. Bake at 350° for 12-15 minutes or until golden brown. Remove to wire racks. Store in an airtight container.

Dazzling Desserts

If you decide to skip straight to dessert after flipping through these enticing recipes, we'll understand! You won't be able to resist making (and digging into) these sweet treats and sharing the goodness. Go ahead and indulge!

ELEGANT ORANGE BLOSSOM CHEESECAKE

The aroma of orange blossoms and zest hints at how heavenly this delicate cheesecake tastes. Gingersnap cookie crumbs make a great crust while glazed orange slices become a lovely topping.
—**SHARON DELANEY-CHRONIS** SOUTH MILWAUKEE, WI

PREP: 40 MIN. • **BAKE:** 70 MIN. + CHILLING • **MAKES:** 12 SERVINGS

- 3 cups crushed gingersnap cookies (about 60 cookies)
- 2 teaspoons plus 2 tablespoons grated orange peel, divided
- ⅓ cup butter, melted
- 1½ cups orange juice
- ⅓ cup sliced fresh gingerroot
- 4 packages (8 ounces each) cream cheese, softened
- ⅔ cup sugar
- 6 ounces white baking chocolate, melted
- 1 tablespoon vanilla extract
- 4 eggs, lightly beaten

CANDIED ORANGE SLICES

- 3 cups water
- 1½ cups sugar
- 2 small navel oranges, thinly sliced

1. Place a greased 9-in. springform pan on a double thickness of heavy-duty foil (about 18 in. square). Securely wrap foil around pan.

2. In a large bowl, combine crumbs, 2 teaspoons orange peel and butter. Press onto bottom and 2-in. up sides of prepared pan.

3. In a large saucepan, combine orange juice and ginger; bring to a boil. Reduce heat and simmer, stirring occasionally, until syrupy and reduced to about 3 tablespoons. Strain and discard ginger.

4. In a large bowl, beat cream cheese and sugar until smooth. Beat in ginger syrup, melted chocolate, vanilla and remaining orange peel. Add eggs; beat on low speed just until combined. Pour into crust. Place springform pan in a large baking pan; add 1 in. of hot water to larger pan.

5. Bake at 325° for 70-80 minutes or until center is just set and top appears dull. Remove springform pan from water bath; remove foil. Cool on a wire rack for 10 minutes. Carefully run a knife around edge of pan to loosen; cool 1 hour longer. Refrigerate overnight.

6. For candied orange slices, in a large skillet, combine water and sugar. Cook and stir over medium heat until sugar is completely dissolved. Add orange slices. Bring to a boil. Reduce heat; simmer for 45 minutes or until translucent. Drain oranges on a wire rack; arrange in a single layer on waxed paper to dry.

7. Remove sides of pan. Top cheesecake with candied orange slices. Refrigerate leftovers.

MANGO SORBET DESSERT

Not only is this tempting recipe easy to put together, it's also packed with fruit so you can feel good while having dessert!
—**KATIE ROSE** PEWAUKEE, WI

START TO FINISH: 10 MIN. • **MAKES:** 4 SERVINGS

- ½ cup seedless raspberry preserves
- 1 tablespoon orange juice
- ¼ teaspoon almond extract
- 4 slices angel food cake
- 4 scoops mango sorbet
- 1 cup fresh raspberries
- ¼ cup sliced almonds

1. In a small microwave-safe bowl, combine preserves and orange juice. Microwave, uncovered, on high for 30 seconds or until heated through. Stir in extract.

2. Divide cake slices among four dessert plates. Top each with sorbet, preserve mixture, raspberries and almonds.

LAVENDER PEACH GELATO

My daughter loves this icy treat, which was the first gelato recipe I ever created. The lavender adds a bit of sophistication.

—**CHRISTINE WENDLAND** BROWNS MILLS, NJ

PREP: 40 MIN. + FREEZING • **MAKES:** 3 CUPS

- 2 **cups 2% milk**
- 2 **tablespoons cardamom pods, crushed**
- 1 **tablespoon dried lavender flowers**
- 1 **vanilla bean**
- ¾ **cup sugar**
- 5 **egg yolks, beaten**
- 2 **medium peaches, peeled and finely chopped**

1. In a large heavy saucepan, combine the milk, cardamom pods and lavender. Split vanilla bean and scrape seeds; add bean and seeds to milk mixture. Heat until bubbles form around sides of pan. Remove from the heat; cover and let steep for 10 minutes. Strain, discarding flowers and spices.
2. Return milk to the heat; stir in sugar. Cook until bubbles form around sides of pan. Whisk a small amount of hot mixture into the egg yolks. Return all to the pan, whisking constantly.
3. Cook and stir over low heat until mixture is thickened and coats the back of a spoon. Quickly transfer to a bowl; place in ice water and stir for 2 minutes. Press waxed paper onto surface of custard. Refrigerate for several hours or overnight.
4. Fill cylinder of ice cream freezer two-thirds full; freeze according to the manufacturer's directions. When gelato is frozen, stir in peaches. Transfer to a freezer container; freeze for 2-4 hours before serving.
NOTE *Look for dried lavender flowers in spice shops. If using lavender from the garden, make sure it hasn't been treated with chemicals.*

RHUBARB-BLUEBERRY CRUMBLE

Rhubarb and strawberry are a well-known pairing, but blueberries and rhubarb together are just as good.

—**MIKE SCHULZ** TAWAS CITY, MI

PREP: 15 MIN. • **BAKE:** 40 MIN. • **MAKES:** 8 SERVINGS

- ⅔ **cup sugar**
- 2 **tablespoons cornstarch**
- ¼ **teaspoon salt**
- 3 **cups fresh blueberries**
- 3 **cups sliced fresh or frozen rhubarb, thawed**

TOPPING

- ¾ **cup biscuit/baking mix**
- ⅓ **cup sugar**
- ⅛ **teaspoon salt**
- ⅓ **cup cold unsalted butter, cubed**
- ½ **cup old-fashioned oats**
- ½ **cup chopped almonds**

1. Preheat the oven to 375°. In a large bowl, mix sugar, cornstarch and salt. Add blueberries and rhubarb; toss to coat. Transfer to a greased 8-in.-square baking dish.
2. For topping, in a small bowl, mix baking mix, sugar and salt. Cut in butter until crumbly; stir in oats and almonds. Sprinkle over filling. Bake 40-45 minutes or until filling is bubbly and topping is golden brown.
NOTE *If using frozen rhubarb, measure rhubarb while still frozen, then thaw completely. Drain in a colander, but do not press liquid out.*

HONEYED PEARS IN PUFF PASTRY

A honey of a salute to late-summer pear season, this cozy dessert has plenty of the wow factor. Wrapped in puffed pastry, it resembles a beehive.
—**HEATHER BAIRD** KNOXVILLE, TN

PREP: 25 MIN. • **BAKE:** 25 MIN. • **MAKES:** 4 SERVINGS

- 4 **small pears**
- 4 **cups water**
- 2 **cups sugar**
- 1 **cup honey**
- 1 **small lemon, halved**
- 3 **cinnamon sticks (3 inches)**
- 6 **to 8 whole cloves**
- 1 **vanilla bean**
- 1 **sheet frozen puff pastry, thawed**

1. Core pears from bottom, leaving stems intact. Peel pears; cut ¼ in. from the bottom of each to level if necessary.
2. In a large saucepan, combine the water, sugar, honey, lemon halves, cinnamon and cloves. Split vanilla bean and scrape seeds; add bean and seeds to sugar mixture. Bring to a boil. Reduce heat; place pears on their sides in saucepan and poach, uncovered, for 18-22 minutes or until pears are almost tender, basting occasionally with poaching liquid.
3. Remove pears with a slotted spoon; cool slightly. Strain and reserve 1½ cups poaching liquid; set aside.
4. Unfold puff pastry on a lightly floured surface. Cut into ½-in.-wide strips. Starting at the bottom of a pear, wrap a pastry strip around pear, adding additional strips until pear is completely wrapped in pastry. Repeat with remaining pears and puff pastry.

5. Transfer to a parchment paper-lined 15x10x1-in. baking pan. Bake at 400° for 20-25 minutes or until golden brown.
6. Meanwhile, bring reserved poaching liquid to a boil; cook until liquid is thick and syrupy, about 10-15 minutes. Place pears on dessert plates and drizzle with syrup. Serve warm.

BERRIES & CREAM BRUSCHETTA

Watch out, Mr. Bagel, because there's more than one way to spread cream cheese. The topping here is delicious on morning toast, too, if you can keep it around that long.
—**DEBBIE LIMAS** NORTH ANDOVER, MA

START TO FINISH: 25 MIN. • **MAKES:** 6 SERVINGS

- 1 **package (8 ounces) cream cheese, softened**
- 6 **tablespoons orange juice**
- 1 **teaspoon grated orange peel**
- 2 **cups sliced fresh strawberries**
- 1 **cup each fresh blueberries, blackberries and raspberries**
- 6 **slices pound cake**
  Whipped cream in a can, optional

In a small bowl, beat the cream cheese, orange juice and peel until blended. In a large bowl, combine the berries. Place a cake slice on each of six dessert plates; top with cream cheese mixture and berries. Garnish with whipped cream, if desired.

PUMPKIN MOUSSE PIE WITH GINGERSNAP CRUST

The gingersnap cookies and pumpkin taste so good together in this pie. It's always a must-have dessert for our parties.

—**BERNICE JANOWSKI** STEVENS POINT, WI

PREP: 45 MIN. + CHILLING • **MAKES:** 8 SERVINGS

- 1½ cups finely crushed gingersnap cookies (about 30 cookies)
- 1 cup finely chopped pecans, toasted
- ⅓ cup butter, melted
- 1 envelope unflavored gelatin
- ¼ cup cold water
- ½ cup packed brown sugar
- ½ cup half-and-half cream
- 3 egg yolks
- 1 can (15 ounces) solid-pack pumpkin
- 2 teaspoons pumpkin pie spice
- 2 cups whipped topping
- ¼ cup butterscotch-caramel ice cream topping
- ½ cup chopped pecans, toasted

1. Preheat oven to 350°. In a small bowl, mix crushed cookies and chopped pecans; stir in butter. Press onto bottom and up sides of an ungreased 9-in. deep-dish pie plate. Bake 10-12 minutes or until lightly browned. Cool on a wire rack.

2. In a microwave-safe bowl, sprinkle gelatin over cold water; let stand 1 minute. Microwave on high for 30-40 seconds. Stir and let stand 1 minute or until gelatin is completely dissolved.

3. In a large saucepan, whisk brown sugar, cream and egg yolks until blended. Cook over low heat until a thermometer reads at least 160°, stirring constantly. (Do not allow to boil.) Remove from heat; stir in pumpkin, pie spice and gelatin mixture. Cool completely.

4. Fold in whipped topping. Pour into crust; refrigerate until set. Drizzle with ice cream topping; sprinkle with the pecans.

NOTE *To toast nuts, spread in a 15x10x1-in. baking pan. Bake at 350° for 5-10 minutes or until lightly browned, stirring occasionally. Or, spread in a dry nonstick skillet and heat over low heat until lightly browned, stirring occasionally.*

COCONUT-STREUSEL PEAR PIE

I remember my mom making this pie when I was young. Now I make several while I have fresh pears from the family tree, then freeze them for later.

—**PAULA HOFFMAN** PLAINVIEW, NE

PREP: 20 MIN. • **BAKE:** 20 MIN. + COOLING • **MAKES:** 8 SERVINGS

    Pastry for single-crust pie (9 inches)
- ⅓ cup sugar
- ¼ cup all-purpose flour
- ¼ teaspoon salt
- 6 cups sliced peeled fresh pears
- 1 tablespoon lemon juice

TOPPING
- 3 tablespoons sugar
- 3 tablespoons all-purpose flour
- 4½ teaspoons cold butter
- ⅓ cup flaked coconut

1. Line a 9-in. pie plate with pastry; trim and flute edges. In a large saucepan, combine the sugar, flour and salt. Add pears and lemon juice. Cook and stir over medium heat for 4-5 minutes or until thickened. Pour into pastry.

2. For topping, in a small bowl, combine sugar and flour. Cut in butter until crumbly. Stir in coconut; sprinkle over top. Bake at 400° for 20-25 minutes or until filling is bubbly and topping is lightly browned. Cool on a wire rack.

Cupcakes Galore!

Whether you need the perfect party starter or an end-of-the-meal treat, cupcakes are the way to go. No two cupcake recipes are quite the same, especially since the topping possibilities are endless!

JALAPENO POPPER CORN CUPCAKES

Sweet cornmeal cupcakes and jalapenos may seem like an unusual dessert, but we guarantee these treats will please.
—*TASTE OF HOME* TEST KITCHEN

PREP: 40 MIN. • **BAKE:** 25 MIN. + COOLING • **MAKES:** 1 DOZEN

- 1¼ cups all-purpose flour
- 1 cup sugar
- ½ cup cornmeal
- 2 teaspoons baking powder
- ¼ teaspoon salt
- 2 eggs
- ½ cup 2% milk
- ½ cup olive oil
- ½ teaspoon vanilla extract
- ¾ cup frozen corn, thawed
- 2 tablespoons finely chopped seeded jalapeno pepper

FROSTING
- ¼ cup panko (Japanese) bread crumbs
- 4 ounces cream cheese, softened
- ¼ cup butter, softened
- 1¾ cups confectioners' sugar
- 1 teaspoon vanilla extract
  Sliced jalapeno peppers

1. In a large bowl, combine the flour, sugar, cornmeal, baking powder and salt. In another bowl, combine the eggs, milk, oil and vanilla. Stir into dry ingredients just until moistened. Fold in corn and jalapeno.

2. Fill greased or paper-lined muffin cups three-fourths full. Bake at 350° for 24-28 minutes or until a toothpick inserted in a cupcake comes out clean. Cool for 5 minutes before removing from pan to a wire rack to cool completely.

3. Place bread crumbs on an ungreased baking sheet. Bake at 400° for 2-3 minutes or until toasted. Cool. In a large bowl, beat cream cheese and butter until fluffy. Add the confectioners' sugar and vanilla; beat until smooth. Frost cupcakes. Garnish with toasted bread crumbs and jalapeno slices. Store in the refrigerator.

NOTE *Wear disposable gloves when cutting hot peppers; the oils can burn skin. Avoid touching your face.*

STRAWBERRY SURPRISE CUPCAKES

Kids love the fruity surprise tucked inside these cupcakes. They really wow at parties, bake sales and snacktime.
—**MARGARET WILSON** SUN CITY, CA

PREP: 25 MIN. • **BAKE:** 25 MIN. + COOLING • **MAKES:** 2 DOZEN

- 1 package strawberry cake mix (regular size)
- 2 cups (16 ounces) sour cream
- 2 eggs
- ¼ cup strawberry preserves
- 1 can (16 ounces) vanilla frosting
  Halved fresh strawberries

1. Preheat oven to 350°. Line 24 muffin cups with paper liners. In a large bowl, combine the cake mix, sour cream and eggs. Beat on low speed 30 seconds. Beat on medium for 2 minutes.

2. Fill prepared cups half full. Drop ½ teaspoon preserves into center of each cupcake; cover with remaining batter.

3. Bake 22-27 minutes or until a toothpick inserted in the cake portion comes out clean. Cool in pans 10 minutes before removing to wire racks to cool completely.

4. Pipe frosting over cupcakes and top each with a strawberry half.

VERY VANILLA CUPCAKES

My recipe is a vanilla lover's dream—it's a vanilla cupcake topped with vanilla buttercream. For the best taste, I suggest using pure vanilla extract.

—**MICHELLE DORSEY** WILMINGTON, DE

PREP: 15 MIN. • **BAKE:** 20 MIN. + COOLING • **MAKES:** 2 DOZEN

- ¾ cup unsalted butter, softened
- 1½ cups sugar
- 3 eggs
- 1½ teaspoons vanilla extract
- 2⅓ cups cake flour
- 2½ teaspoons baking powder
- ½ teaspoon salt
- ¾ cup whole milk

FROSTING

- 1 cup unsalted butter, softened
- 3 teaspoons clear vanilla extract
- 2½ cups confectioners' sugar
  Paste food coloring, optional
  Colored sprinkles and nonpareils

1. In a large bowl, cream butter and sugar until light and fluffy. Add eggs, one at a time, beating well after each addition. Beat in vanilla. In another bowl, mix the flour, baking powder and salt; add to creamed mixture alternately with milk, beating well after each addition.

2. Fill paper-lined muffin cups two-thirds full. Bake at 350° for 18-22 minutes or until a toothpick inserted in center comes out clean. Cool in pans for 10 minutes. Remove to wire racks to cool completely.

3. For frosting, in a small bowl, beat butter and vanilla until blended. Gradually beat in confectioners' sugar until smooth. If desired, tint with food coloring. Frost cupcakes. Decorate as desired.

FRENCH TOAST CUPCAKES

Whenever I feel down or stressed, I know I can go into the kitchen and whip up a batch of these delicious cupcakes. They're a taste of Sunday brunch.

—**JENNY WEAVER** GLENDALE, AZ

PREP: 25 MIN. • **BAKE:** 20 MIN. + COOLING • **MAKES:** 1½ DOZEN

- ½ cup butter, softened
- 1½ cups sugar
- 2 eggs
- 2 teaspoons vanilla extract
- 2 cups all-purpose flour
- 2 teaspoons ground cinnamon
- ½ teaspoon baking powder
- ½ teaspoon baking soda
- ¼ teaspoon salt
- ¼ teaspoon ground nutmeg
- 1⅓ cups buttermilk

MAPLE BUTTERCREAM FROSTING

- ½ cup butter, softened
- ¼ cup shortening
- ½ cup maple syrup
  Dash salt
- 2½ cups confectioners' sugar
- 6 bacon strips, cooked and crumbled, optional

1. In a large bowl, cream butter and sugar until light and fluffy. Add eggs, one at a time, beating well after each addition. Beat in vanilla. Combine the flour, cinnamon, baking powder, baking soda, salt and nutmeg; add to the creamed mixture alternately with buttermilk, beating well after each addition.

2. Fill paper-lined muffin cups two-thirds full. Bake at 350° for 17-22 minutes or until a toothpick inserted near the center comes out clean. Cool for 10 minutes before removing from pans to wire racks to cool completely.

3. For frosting, in a small bowl, beat butter and shortening until fluffy. Beat in maple syrup and salt. Add confectioners' sugar; beat until smooth. Frost cupcakes. Sprinkle with bacon if desired.

HOT COCOA SOUFFLE

A friend invited me to go to a cooking demo at her church years ago, and one of the recipes prepared was this luscious souffle. It's decadently good.

—JOAN HALLFORD FORT WORTH, TX

PREP: 20 MIN. • **BAKE:** 40 MIN. • **MAKES:** 6 SERVINGS

- 5 eggs
- 4 teaspoons plus ¾ cup sugar, divided
- ½ cup baking cocoa
- 6 tablespoons all-purpose flour
- ¼ teaspoon salt
- 1½ cups fat-free milk
- 2 tablespoons butter
- 1½ teaspoons vanilla extract

1. Separate the eggs; let stand at room temperature for 30 minutes. Coat a 2-qt. souffle dish with cooking spray and lightly sprinkle with 4 teaspoons sugar; set aside.

2. In a small saucepan, combine the cocoa, flour, salt and remaining sugar. Gradually whisk in milk. Bring to a boil, stirring constantly. Cook and stir 1-2 minutes longer or until thickened. Stir in butter. Transfer to a large bowl.

3. Stir a small amount of hot mixture into egg yolks; return all to the bowl, stirring constantly. Add vanilla; cool slightly.

4. In another large bowl with clean beaters, beat egg whites until stiff peaks form. With a spatula, stir a fourth of the egg whites into chocolate mixture until no white streaks remain. Fold in remaining egg whites until combined.

5. Transfer to the prepared dish. Bake at 350° for 40-45 minutes or until the top is puffed and center appears set. Serve immediately.

CHOCOLATE-STRAWBERRY CREAM CHEESE TART

Bound to impress, this dessert features velvety cream cheese, lovely red strawberries and a drizzle of fudge atop a crunchy chocolate almond crust. It's too gorgeous to resist.

—PRISCILLA YEE CONCORD, CA

PREP: 20 MIN. • **BAKE:** 15 MIN. + CHILLING • **MAKES:** 12 SERVINGS

- ¾ cup all-purpose flour
- ½ cup finely chopped almonds, toasted
- 6 tablespoons butter, melted
- ⅓ cup baking cocoa
- ¼ cup packed brown sugar

FILLING

- 2 packages (8 ounces each) cream cheese, softened
- 1 cup confectioners' sugar
- 1 teaspoon vanilla extract
- 3 cups halved fresh strawberries
- 3 tablespoons hot fudge ice cream topping

1. Preheat oven to 375°. In a small bowl, combine the first five ingredients; press onto the bottom and up the sides of an ungreased 9-in. fluted tart pan with removable bottom. Bake 12-15 minutes or until crust is set. Cool on a wire rack.

2. In another small bowl, beat cream cheese, confectioners' sugar and vanilla until smooth. Spread over bottom of prepared crust. Arrange strawberry halves, cut side down, over filling. Cover and refrigerate at least 1 hour.

3. Just before serving, drizzle fudge topping over tart. Refrigerate leftovers.

MINT PATTY CAKE

Each slice of this dreamy layer cake contains cool peppermint. The chopped peppermint patties in the frosting are also a refreshing surprise.

—TASTE OF HOME TEST KITCHEN

PREP: 35 MIN. + CHILLING • **BAKE:** 20 MIN. + COOLING
MAKES: 16 SERVINGS

- 1 package devil's food cake mix (regular size)
- 1⅓ cups water
- 3 eggs
- ½ cup canola oil
- 1 teaspoon mint extract

FROSTING
- 4 cups white baking chips
- 1 cup heavy whipping cream
- 2 tablespoons butter
- 9 miniature chocolate-covered peppermint patties, finely chopped
- Additional miniature chocolate-covered peppermint patties

1. In a large bowl, combine the cake mix, water, eggs, oil and extract; beat on low speed for 30 seconds. Beat on medium for 2 minutes.

2. Pour into three greased and floured 9-in. round baking pans. Bake at 350° for 18-22 minutes or until a toothpick inserted near the center comes out clean. Cool for 10 minutes before removing from pans to wire racks to cool completely.

3. Place white chips in a large bowl. In a small saucepan, bring cream just to a boil. Pour over chips; whisk until smooth. Stir in butter. Chill for 30 minutes, stirring once.

4. Beat on high for 2-3 minutes or until soft peaks form and frosting is light and fluffy. Set aside 2½ cups for frosting cake. Stir patties into remaining frosting.

5. Place one cake layer on a serving plate; spread with half of the peppermint patty filling. Repeat layers. Top with remaining cake layer. Frost top and sides of cake with reserved frosting. Store in the refrigerator. Garnish with additional patties.

FAMILY-FAVORITE PEANUT BUTTER CAKE

My grandmother and aunts would make this for family gatherings to go along with fresh homemade ice cream. I now share it during special events.

—KEITH GABLE GODDARD, KS

PREP: 20 MIN. • **BAKE:** 15 MIN. + COOLING • **MAKES:** 24 SERVINGS

- ½ cup creamy peanut butter
- 6 tablespoons butter, cubed
- 1 cup water
- 2 cups all-purpose flour
- 1½ cups sugar
- ½ cup buttermilk
- ¼ cup unsweetened applesauce
- 2 eggs, lightly beaten
- 1¼ teaspoons baking powder
- 1 teaspoon vanilla extract
- ½ teaspoon salt
- ¼ teaspoon baking soda

FROSTING
- ¼ cup butter, cubed
- ¼ cup creamy peanut butter
- 2 tablespoons fat-free milk
- 1¾ cups confectioners' sugar
- 1 teaspoon vanilla extract

1. In a large saucepan, bring peanut butter, butter and water just to a boil. Immediately remove from the heat; stir in the flour, sugar, buttermilk, applesauce, eggs, baking powder, vanilla, salt and baking soda until smooth.

2. Pour into a 15x10x1-in. baking pan coated with cooking spray. Bake at 375° for 15-20 minutes or until golden brown and a toothpick inserted near the center comes out clean. Cool on a wire rack for 20 minutes.

3. In a small saucepan, melt butter and peanut butter over medium heat; add milk. Bring to a boil. Remove from the heat. Gradually whisk in confectioners' sugar and vanilla until smooth. Spread over warm cake. Cool completely on a wire rack. Refrigerate leftovers.

MAGNIFICENT CARROT CAKE

You really can't beat a fresh carrot cake covered in rich cream cheese frosting. A touch of rum extract adds a little something wonderful to every bite of this baked-from-scratch indulgence.

—MELANIE MADEIRA DALLAS, PA

PREP: 40 MIN. • **BAKE:** 30 MIN. + COOLING • **MAKES:** 16 SERVINGS

- 2 cups sugar
- ¾ cup buttermilk
- ¾ cup canola oil
- 3 eggs
- 3 teaspoons rum extract
- 2 cups all-purpose flour
- 2 teaspoons baking soda
- 2 teaspoons ground cinnamon
- ½ teaspoon salt
- ½ teaspoon ground allspice
- 2 cups shredded carrots
- 1 can (8 ounces) crushed pineapple, drained
- ¾ cup chopped walnuts
- ¾ cup dried currants

GLAZE

- ½ cup sugar
- ¼ cup buttermilk
- ¼ cup butter, cubed
- ½ teaspoon corn syrup
- ¼ teaspoon baking soda
- ½ teaspoon vanilla extract

FROSTING

- 2 packages (8 ounces each) cream cheese, softened
- ⅔ cup butter, softened
- 4 cups confectioners' sugar
- 4 teaspoons rum extract

1. Preheat the oven to 350°. In a large bowl, beat sugar, buttermilk, oil, eggs and extract until well blended. In another bowl, combine flour, baking soda, cinnamon, salt and allspice; gradually beat into sugar mixture until blended. Stir in carrots, pineapple, walnuts and currants.

2. Transfer to two greased and floured 9-in. round baking pans. Bake 30-35 minutes or until a toothpick inserted in center comes out clean.

3. Meanwhile, for glaze, combine the sugar, buttermilk, butter, corn syrup and baking soda in a small saucepan. Bring to a boil; cook and stir 4 minutes. Remove from heat; stir in vanilla.

4. Pour glaze over hot cakes; cool 10 minutes before removing from pans to wire racks to cool completely.

5. For frosting, in a large bowl, beat cream cheese and butter until fluffy. Add confectioners' sugar and extract; beat until smooth.

6. Place one cake layer on a serving plate; spread with 1 cup frosting. Top with remaining cake layer. Frost top and sides of cake. Store in the refrigerator.

CARAMEL CUSTARD PIE

Here's a traditional custard pie recipe that's been in our family for more than a century. A fun layer of caramel jazzes up the creamy old-fashioned flavor.

—ROGER CLAPPER DELAVAN, WI

PREP: 15 MIN. • **BAKE:** 55 MIN. + CHILLING • **MAKES:** 8 SERVINGS

- Pastry for single-crust pie (9 inches)
- ⅔ cup packed brown sugar
- 4 teaspoons all-purpose flour
- 3 eggs
- 2 cups 2% milk
- ¼ cup sugar
- 1 teaspoon vanilla extract
- ⅛ teaspoon salt
- ⅛ teaspoon ground nutmeg

1. Line a 9-in. pie plate with pastry; trim and flute edges. Combine the brown sugar and flour; press into pastry.

2. In a large bowl, combine the eggs, milk, sugar, vanilla and salt; pour over brown sugar mixture.

3. Bake at 350° for 55-60 minutes or until a knife inserted near the center comes out clean. Cover edges with foil during the last 15 minutes to prevent overbrowning if necessary. Cool on a wire rack; sprinkle with nutmeg. Refrigerate for at least 2 hours before serving.

STORE PIES THE RIGHT WAY

Allow custard pies to cool on a wire rack for 1 hour after baking. Custard or cream pies can be kept in the refrigerator for up to 3 days, while fruit pies should be kept at room temperature for only 1 day.

BERRY MINI CHEESECAKES

There's always room for dessert when it's just a bite! Serve these delights at a special occasion or just for a pick-me-up at home after a long day.
—*TASTE OF HOME* TEST KITCHEN

PREP: 20 MIN. • **BAKE:** 15 MIN. + CHILLING • **MAKES:** 1½ DOZEN

- 1 **cup graham cracker crumbs**
- 3 **tablespoons butter, melted**
- 1 **package (8 ounces) cream cheese, softened**
- ⅓ **cup sugar**
- 1 **teaspoon vanilla extract**
- 1 **egg, lightly beaten**
- 18 **fresh raspberries**

1. Preheat oven to 350°. In a small bowl, combine graham cracker crumbs and butter. Press gently onto the bottom of 18 paper-lined miniature muffin cups. In another small bowl, beat cream cheese, sugar and vanilla until smooth. Add egg; beat on low speed just until combined. Spoon over the crusts.

2. Bake 12-14 minutes or until the centers are set. Cool 10 minutes before removing from pan to a wire rack to cool completely. Refrigerate at least 1 hour.

3. To serve, remove paper liners from cheesecakes; top cheesecakes with raspberries.

S'MORES-DIPPED APPLES

I don't think you can beat marshmallows, graham crackers and apples together in a snack. Whenever I take these to a bake sale, they sell out in a flash.
—**MARIA REGAKIS** SAUGUS, MA

PREP: 20 MIN. • **COOK:** 10 MIN. + CHILLING • **MAKES:** 8 SERVINGS

- 8 **large Granny Smith apples**
- 8 **wooden pop sticks**
- 2 **tablespoons butter**
- 2 **packages (16 ounces each) large marshmallows**
- 2 **cups coarsely crushed graham crackers**
- 1 **package (11½ ounces) milk chocolate chips**

1. Line a baking sheet with waxed paper; generously coat waxed paper with cooking spray. Wash and dry apples; remove stems. Insert pop sticks into apples.

2. In a large heavy saucepan, melt butter over medium heat. Add marshmallows; stir until melted. Dip apples, one at a time, into warm marshmallow mixture, allowing excess to drip off. Place on prepared baking sheet and refrigerate until set, about 15 minutes.

3. Place graham cracker crumbs in a shallow dish. In top of a double boiler or a metal bowl over barely simmering water, melt chocolate chips; stir until smooth. Dip bottom half of apples in chocolate; dip bottoms in cracker crumbs. Place on baking sheet. Refrigerate until set.

HOMEMADE BUTTERSCOTCH PUDDING

There's something special about homemade pudding because it's extra rich and amazing. The essence of butterscotch here adds a caramel-sweet touch.

—**TERESA WILKES** PEMBROKE, GA

PREP: 10 MIN. • **COOK:** 10 MIN. + CHILLING • **MAKES:** 6 SERVINGS

- ½ cup sugar
- ½ cup packed dark brown sugar
- 3 tablespoons cornstarch
- ¼ teaspoon salt
- ⅛ teaspoon ground nutmeg
- 3 cups 2% milk
- 3 egg yolks
- 2 tablespoons butter, cubed
- 2 teaspoons vanilla extract
  Whipped cream, optional

1. In a large heavy saucepan, combine sugars, cornstarch, salt and nutmeg. Stir in milk until smooth. Cook and stir over medium-high heat until thickened and bubbly. Reduce heat to low; cook and stir 2 minutes longer. Remove from the heat.

2. Stir a small amount of hot mixture into the egg yolks; return all to the pan. Bring to a gentle boil, stirring constantly; cook 2 minutes or until mixture is thickened and coats the back of a spoon. Remove from the heat.

3. Stir in the butter and vanilla. Cool for 15 minutes, stirring occasionally. Transfer to six dessert dishes. Cover and refrigerate until chilled. Garnish with whipped cream if desired.

CARAMEL CASHEW CAKE POPS

Nothing beats the pairing of buttery caramel and crunchy cashews; add it to a chocolaty cake pop and you have one irresistible little snack.

—**TASTE OF HOME** TEST KITCHEN

PREP: 1½ HOURS + CHILLING • **MAKES:** 4 DOZEN

- 1 package chocolate cake mix (regular size)
- ¾ cup dulce de leche
- 48 lollipop sticks
- 2½ pounds milk chocolate candy coating, coarsely chopped
  Chopped cashews

1. Prepare and bake cake mix according to package directions, using a greased 13x9-in. baking pan. Cool completely on a wire rack.

2. Crumble cake into a large bowl. Add dulce de leche and mix well. Shape into 1-in. balls. Place on baking sheets; insert sticks. Freeze for at least 2 hours or refrigerate for at least 3 hours or until cake balls are firm.

3. In a microwave, melt the candy coating. Dip each cake ball in coating; allow excess to drip off. Coat with cashews. Insert cake pops into a styrofoam block to stand. Let stand until set.

NOTE *This recipe was tested with Nestle La Lechera dulce de leche; look for it in the international foods section. If using Eagle Brand dulce de leche (caramel flavored sauce), thicken according to package directions before using.*

FRENCH LEMON-APRICOT TART

If you like the tang of citrus, you'll love this lemon tart. The apricot preserves on top add a nice bit of sweetness.

—**PEGGY LUNDE** COSTA MESA, CA

PREP: 40 MIN. + CHILLING • **BAKE:** 10 MIN + COOLING
MAKES: 12 SERVINGS

- ¾ cup plus 2 tablespoons all-purpose flour
- ½ cup confectioners' sugar
- ¼ cup cold butter, cubed
- ⅛ teaspoon salt
- 1 egg yolk

FILLING

- 3 eggs
- ¾ cup lemon juice
- ½ cup plus 2 tablespoons sugar
- 2 tablespoons grated lemon peel
- 3 tablespoons butter
- ⅓ cup apricot preserves, warmed
- Lemon peel curls or fresh mint leaves, optional

1. Place the flour, confectioners' sugar, butter and salt in a food processor. Cover and pulse until mixture resembles coarse crumbs. Add egg yolk, processing just until mixture forms a soft dough. Shape into a ball, then flatten into a disk. Wrap in plastic wrap and refrigerate for at least 1 hour.

2. Press dough onto the bottom and up the sides of an ungreased 9-in. fluted tart pan with a removable bottom. Bake at 400° for 10-12 min. or until golden brown. Cool on a wire rack. Reduce heat to 325°.

3. In a small heavy saucepan over medium heat, whisk the eggs, lemon juice, sugar and lemon peel until blended. Add butter; cook, whisking constantly, until mixture is thickened and coats the back of a spoon. Pour into crust. Bake for 8-10 minutes or until set. Cool on a wire rack.

4. Spread preserves over tart. Garnish with lemon peel curls or mint if desired. Refrigerate leftovers.

3. Bake at 325° on lowest oven rack 40-50 minutes or until top springs back when lightly touched. Immediately invert pan; cool completely, about 1½ hours. Run a knife around sides and center tube of pan; remove cake.

4. For filling, in a double boiler or a metal bowl over simmering water, combine the sugar, flour and salt. Add the orange juice, egg and orange peel. Constantly whisk until mixture reaches 160° or is thick enough to coat the back of a spoon. Remove from heat and cool completely. Fold in whipped topping.

5. Cut cake horizontally into three layers. Place bottom layer on a serving plate; top with one-third of the filling. Repeat layers twice. Serve immediately or refrigerate.

GRILLED PINEAPPLE & MAPLE SUNDAES

This is one of our all-time favorite summer desserts. Give it a try at your next barbecue.

—SHERALYN FRIESEN WINNIPEG, MB

PREP: 10 MIN. + MARINATING • **GRILL:** 10 MIN. • **MAKES:** 8 SERVINGS

- ¾ **cup maple syrup**
- 2 **tablespoons brown sugar**
- ¾ **teaspoon ground cinnamon**
- 1 **fresh pineapple, peeled, cut into 8 wedges**
- 8 **scoops vanilla ice cream**

1. In a large resealable bag, combine the syrup, brown sugar and cinnamon; add pineapple. Seal bag and turn to coat. Refrigerate for 10-20 minutes. Drain, reserving syrup mixture.

2. Moisten a paper towel with cooking oil; using long-handled tongs, lightly coat the grill rack. Grill pineapple, covered, over medium heat or broil 4 in. from the heat for 8-10 minutes or until lightly browned, turning once.

3. Serve pineapple with ice cream and drizzle with reserved syrup mixture.

CEREAL & MILK ICE CREAM SANDWICHES

Adults and kids alike will enjoy this sweet treat. Experiment with different cereal combos—who knows what clever creation will become your new warm weather go-to!

—TASTE OF HOME TEST KITCHEN

PREP: 10 MIN. + FREEZING • **MAKES:** 4 SERVINGS

- 2 **tablespoons Cap'n Crunch cereal**
- 2 **tablespoons Froot Loops cereal**
- 2 **tablespoons Fruity Pebbles cereal**
- ¾ **cup dulce de leche ice cream, softened**
- 4 **Rice Krispies treat (2.2 ounces each), halved lengthwise**
- 1 **tablespoon hot caramel ice cream topping, warmed**

In a shallow bowl, combine cereals. Spread ice cream onto the bottom half of each Rice Krispies treat. Drizzle with ice cream topping. Replace top half of Rice Krispies treat. Rolls sides in cereal mixture. Place on a baking sheet; freeze for at least 1 hour.

 **ORANGE CREAM CHIFFON CAKE**

The perfect light dessert to serve after a filling meal, this divine cake will be impossible to pass up.

—FAITH SOMMERS BANGOR, CA

PREP: 1 HOUR • **BAKE:** 40 MIN. + COOLING • **MAKES:** 12 SERVINGS

- 9 **eggs, separated**
- 1 **cup sugar, divided**
- ¼ **cup orange juice**
- 4 **teaspoons grated orange peel**
- 1 **cup plus 2 tablespoons all-purpose flour**
- 1 **teaspoon cream of tartar**
- ½ **teaspoon salt**

FILLING

- 1 **cup sugar**
- ¼ **cup all-purpose flour**
- ¼ **teaspoon salt**
- ½ **cup orange juice**
- 1 **egg, lightly beaten**
- 4 **teaspoons grated orange peel**
- 1 **carton (12 ounces) frozen whipped topping, thawed**

1. Place egg whites in a large bowl; let stand at room temperature for 30 minutes. In another large bowl, beat egg yolks until slightly thickened. Gradually add ⅓ cup sugar, beating until thick and lemon-colored. Blend in orange juice and peel. Add flour and remaining sugar to yolk mixture; mix well.

2. Add cream of tartar and salt to egg whites; beat with clean beaters until stiff peaks form. Fold into batter. Gently spoon into an ungreased 10-in. tube pan. Cut through batter with a knife to remove air pockets.

MAPLE PEANUT BUTTER PIE

Maple nut goodies have been a favorite candy of mine since I was a child, and I think the flavors taste just as great in a pie! This pie freezes well, too. Just remember to take it out to thaw 30 minutes before serving.
—**CRYSTAL SCHLUETER** NORTHGLENN, CO

PREP: 25 MIN. + CHILLING • **MAKES:** 8 SERVINGS

- 1½ cups crushed cream-filled maple sandwich cookies (about 12 cookies)
- 3 tablespoons butter, melted
- ⅓ cup hot fudge ice cream topping
- 1 package (8 ounces) cream cheese, softened
- 1 cup creamy peanut butter
- 1 teaspoon maple flavoring
- 1¼ cups confectioners' sugar
- 1 carton (8 ounces) frozen whipped topping, thawed
- 1 cup heavy whipping cream
- 2 tablespoons maple syrup
- ¼ cup chocolate-covered peanuts, coarsely chopped

1. In a small bowl, mix crushed cookies and butter. Press onto bottom and up sides of an ungreased 9-in. pie plate. Freeze 5 minutes.

2. In a microwave, warm fudge topping 5-10 seconds or until spreadable; spread over bottom and up sides of crust. In a large bowl, beat cream cheese, peanut butter and flavoring until blended. Gradually beat in confectioners' sugar; fold in whipped topping. Spoon into crust, spreading evenly. Refrigerate 4 hours or until set.

3. In a small bowl, beat cream until it begins to thicken. Add syrup; beat until stiff peaks form. Serve with pie; top with peanuts.

PISTACHIO CAKE WITH WALNUTS

It didn't take long for this dessert to become the favorite birthday cake of my husband, Joe.
—**PATTY LANOUE STEARNS** TRAVERSE CITY, MI

PREP: 20 MIN. • **BAKE:** 40 MIN + COOLING • **MAKES:** 12 SERVINGS

- 1 package white cake mix (regular size)
- 1 package (3.4 ounces) instant pistachio pudding mix
- 3 eggs
- 1 cup club soda
- ¾ cup canola oil
- 1 cup chopped walnuts

FROSTING

- 1 package (3.4 ounces) instant pistachio pudding mix
- 1 cup 2% milk
- 1 carton (8 ounces) frozen whipped topping, thawed

1. Preheat oven to 350°. Grease and flour a 10-in. fluted tube pan.

2. In a large bowl, combine the first five ingredients; beat on low speed 30 seconds. Beat on medium 2 minutes. Fold in walnuts. Transfer to the prepared pan. Bake 40-45 minutes or until a toothpick inserted in center comes out clean. Cool in pan 10 minutes before removing to a wire rack to cool completely.

3. For frosting, in a large bowl, combine pudding mix and milk; beat on low speed 1 minute. Fold in whipped topping. Spread over cake. Refrigerate leftovers.

NOTE *For easier removal of cakes, use solid shortening to grease plain and fluted tube pans.*

PEACHES & CREAM JELLY ROLL

Cake rolls make a lovely presentation for a party, and they are simple to cut into even slices. My father was the one to teach me how to make them, and sometimes we get together to create them for family and friends.
—**MALENA COLEMAN** ROCKVILLE, IN

PREP: 20 MIN. • **BAKE:** 10 MIN. + CHILLING • **MAKES:** 12 SERVINGS

- 3 eggs
- ¼ teaspoon vanilla extract
- ⅛ teaspoon salt
- ¾ cup sugar
- ¾ cup biscuit/baking mix
- 1 cup heavy whipping cream
- ¼ cup confectioners' sugar, divided
- 3 cups chopped peeled fresh peaches

1. Line a greased 15x10x1-in. baking pan with waxed paper and grease the paper; sprinkle with flour and set aside.

2. In a large bowl, beat eggs on high speed for 3 minutes. Beat in vanilla and salt. Gradually add sugar, beating until mixture becomes thick and lemon-colored. Fold in biscuit mix. Spread in prepared pan.

3. Bake at 375° for 8-10 minutes or until cake springs back when lightly touched. Cool for 5 minutes. Invert onto a kitchen towel dusted with confectioners' sugar. Gently peel off waxed paper. Roll up cake in the towel jelly-roll style, starting with a short side. Cool completely on a wire rack.

4. For filling, in a small bowl, beat cream until it begins to thicken. Add 3 tablespoons confectioners' sugar; beat until stiff peaks form.

5. Unroll cake; spread half of whipped cream over cake to within ½ in. of edges. Top with peaches and remaining whipped cream. Roll up again. Place seam side down on a serving platter. Dust with remaining confectioners' sugar. Refrigerate for 2 hours.

CRUMB-TOPPED APPLE PIE

This pie is absolutely scrumptious. Feel free to use a store-bought pie crust to get a head start. You'll get a bushel of compliments either way.
—**VIRGINIA OLSON** WEST DES MOINES, IA

PREP: 45 MIN. + CHILLING • **BAKE:** 1 HOUR • **MAKES:** 8 SERVINGS

- 1¼ cups all-purpose flour
- ½ teaspoon salt
- ½ cup shortening
- ¼ cup cold water

FILLING
- 5 large tart apples, peeled and thinly sliced
- ⅔ cup sugar
- 5 teaspoons all-purpose flour
- 1¼ teaspoons ground cinnamon

TOPPING
- ⅔ cup all-purpose flour
- ½ cup sugar
- ¼ cup cold butter

1. In a large bowl, combine flour and salt; cut in shortening until crumbly. Gradually add water, tossing with a fork until dough forms a ball. Wrap in plastic wrap. Refrigerate for 1 to 1½ hours or until easy to handle.

2. Preheat oven to 450°. Roll out pastry to fit a 9-in. pie plate. Transfer pastry to pie plate. Trim pastry to ½ in. beyond edge of plate; flute edges.

3. For filling, place apples in crust. Combine the sugar, flour and cinnamon; sprinkle over apples.

4. For topping, combine the flour and sugar in a small bowl; cut in butter until crumbly. Sprinkle over the filling. Bake 10 minutes. Reduce heat to 350°; bake 50-60 minutes or until topping is golden brown and filling is bubbly. Cool on a wire rack.

RASPBERRY & WHITE CHOCOLATE CHEESECAKE

My mom makes this cheesecake a lot. And you'll see why!

—PEGGY ROOS MINNEAPOLIS, MN

PREP: 40 MIN. • **BAKE:** 1¾ HOURS + CHILLING • **MAKES:** 16 SERVINGS

- 1 package (10 ounces) frozen sweetened raspberries, thawed
- 1 tablespoon cornstarch

CRUST
- 1 cup all-purpose flour
- 2 tablespoons sugar
- ½ cup cold butter

FILLING
- 4 packages (8 ounces each) cream cheese, softened
- 1½ cups sugar
- 1¼ cups heavy whipping cream
- 2 teaspoons vanilla extract
- 2 eggs, lightly beaten
- 12 ounces white baking chocolate, melted and cooled

1. In a small saucepan, mix raspberries and cornstarch until blended. Bring to a boil; cook and stir 1-2 minutes or until thickened. Press through a fine-mesh strainer into a bowl; discard seeds. Cool completely.

2. Preheat oven to 350°. Place a greased 9x3-in. deep springform pan on a double thickness of heavy-duty foil (about 18 in. square). Wrap foil securely around pan.

3. For crust, in a small bowl, mix flour and sugar. Cut in butter until crumbly. Press onto bottom of the prepared pan. Place pan on a baking sheet. Bake 20-25 minutes or until golden brown. Cool on a wire rack. Reduce oven setting to 325°.

4. For filling, in a large bowl, beat cream cheese and sugar until smooth. Beat in cream and vanilla. Add eggs; beat on low speed just until blended. Stir in cooled chocolate. Pour half of the mixture over crust. Spread with half of the raspberry puree. Top with remaining batter. Drop the remaining puree by tablespoonfuls over top. Cut through batter with a knife to swirl.

5. Place springform pan in a larger baking pan; add 1 in. of hot water to larger pan. Bake 1¾ to 2 hours or until edge of cheesecake is set and golden. (Center of cheesecake will jiggle when moved.) Remove springform pan from water bath. Cool cheesecake on a wire rack for 10 minutes. Loosen cheesecake from pan with a knife; remove foil. Cool 1 hour longer. Refrigerate overnight. Remove rim from pan.

BANANA CHIP CAKE

This is my version of Ben & Jerry's Chunky Monkey Ice Cream (my favorite!) in a cake. The hardest part is waiting for it to cool.

—BARBARA PRYOR MILFORD, MA

PREP: 25 MIN. • **BAKE:** 40 MIN. + COOLING • **MAKES:** 16 SERVINGS

- 1 package yellow cake mix (regular size)
- 1¼ cups water
- 3 eggs
- ½ cup unsweetened applesauce
- 2 medium bananas, mashed
- 1 cup miniature semisweet chocolate chips
- ½ cup chopped walnuts

1. In a large bowl, combine the cake mix, water, eggs and applesauce; beat on low speed for 30 seconds. Beat on medium for 2 minutes. Stir in the bananas, chips and walnuts.

2. Transfer to a 10-in. fluted tube pan coated with cooking spray and sprinkled with flour. Bake at 350° for 40-50 minutes or until a toothpick inserted near the center comes out clean. Cool for 10 minutes before removing from pan to a wire rack to cool completely.

Substitutions & Equivalents

EQUIVALENT MEASURES

3 teaspoons	= 1 tablespoon	16 tablespoons	= 1 cup
4 tablespoons	= ¼ cup	2 cups	= 1 pint
5⅓ tablespoons	= ⅓ cup	4 cups	= 1 quart
8 tablespoons	= ½ cup	4 quarts	= 1 gallon

FOOD EQUIVALENTS

GRAINS

Macaroni	1 cup (3½ ounces) uncooked	= 2½ cups cooked
Noodles, Medium	3 cups (4 ounces) uncooked	= 4 cups cooked
Popcorn	⅓ to ½ cup unpopped	= 8 cups popped
Rice, Long Grain	1 cup uncooked	= 3 cups cooked
Rice, Quick-Cooking	1 cup uncooked	= 2 cups cooked
Spaghetti	8 ounces uncooked	= 4 cups cooked

CRUMBS

Bread	1 slice	= ¾ cup soft crumbs, ¼ cup fine dry crumbs
Graham Crackers	7 squares	= ½ cup finely crushed
Buttery Round Crackers	12 crackers	= ½ cup finely crushed
Saltine Crackers	14 crackers	= ½ cup finely crushed

FRUITS

Bananas	1 medium	= ⅓ cup mashed
Lemons	1 medium	= 3 tablespoons juice, 2 teaspoons grated peel
Limes	1 medium	= 2 tablespoons juice, 1½ teaspoons grated peel
Oranges	1 medium	= ¼ to ⅓ cup juice, 4 teaspoons grated peel

VEGETABLES

Cabbage	1 head	= 5 cups shredded	Green Pepper	1 large	= 1 cup chopped
Carrots	1 pound	= 3 cups shredded	Mushrooms	½ pound	= 3 cups sliced
Celery	1 rib	= ½ cup chopped	Onions	1 medium	= ½ cup chopped
Corn	1 ear fresh	= ⅔ cup kernels	Potatoes	3 medium	= 2 cups cubed

NUTS

Almonds	1 pound	= 3 cups chopped	Pecan Halves	1 pound	= 4½ cups chopped
Ground Nuts	3¾ ounces	= 1 cup	Walnuts	1 pound	= 3¾ cups chopped

EASY SUBSTITUTIONS

When you need...		Use...
Baking Powder	1 teaspoon	½ teaspoon cream of tartar + ¼ teaspoon baking soda
Buttermilk	1 cup	1 tablespoon lemon juice or vinegar + enough milk to measure 1 cup (let stand 5 minutes before using)
Cornstarch	1 tablespoon	2 tablespoons all-purpose flour
Honey	1 cup	1¼ cups sugar + ¼ cup water
Half-and-Half Cream	1 cup	1 tablespoon melted butter + enough whole milk to measure 1 cup
Onion	1 small, chopped (⅓ cup)	1 teaspoon onion powder or 1 tablespoon dried minced onion
Tomato Juice	1 cup	½ cup tomato sauce + ½ cup water
Tomato Sauce	2 cups	¾ cup tomato paste + 1 cup water
Unsweetened Chocolate	1 square (1 ounce)	3 tablespoons baking cocoa + 1 tablespoon shortening or oil
Whole Milk	1 cup	½ cup evaporated milk + ½ cup water

COOKING TERMS

Here's a quick reference for some of the most common cooking terms used in recipes:

BASTE To moisten food with melted butter, pan drippings, marinades or other liquid to add more flavor and juiciness.

BEAT A rapid movement to combine ingredients using a fork, spoon, wire whisk or electric mixer.

BLEND To combine ingredients until *just* mixed.

BOIL To heat liquids until bubbles form that cannot be "stirred down." In the case of water, the temperature will reach 212°.

BONE To remove all meat from the bone before cooking.

CREAM To beat ingredients together to a smooth consistency, usually in the case of butter and sugar for baking.

DASH A small amount of seasoning, less than ⅛ teaspoon. If using a shaker, a dash would comprise a quick flip of the container.

DREDGE To coat foods with flour or other dry ingredients. Most often done with pot roasts and stew meat before browning.

FOLD To incorporate several ingredients by careful and gentle turning with a spatula. Used generally with beaten egg whites or whipped cream when mixing into the rest of the ingredients to keep the batter light.

JULIENNE To cut foods into long thin strips much like matchsticks. Used most often for salads and stir-fry dishes.

MINCE To cut into very fine pieces. Used often for garlic or fresh herbs.

PARBOIL To cook partially, usually used in the case of chicken, sausages and vegetables.

PARTIALLY SET Describes the consistency of gelatin after it has been chilled for a short amount of time. Mixture should resemble the consistency of egg whites.

PUREE To process foods to a smooth mixture. Can be prepared in an electric blender, food processor, food mill or sieve.

SAUTE To fry quickly in a small amount of fat, stirring almost constantly. Most often done with onions, mushrooms and other chopped vegetables.

SCORE To cut slits partway through the outer surface of foods. Often used with ham or flank steak.

STIR-FRY To cook meats and/or vegetables with a constant stirring motion in a small amount of oil in a wok or skillet over high heat.

GENERAL RECIPE INDEX

ALPHABETICAL RECIPE INDEX